THE EXTERNAL DIMENSION OF EU PRIVATE INTERNATIONAL LAW AFTER OPINION 1/13

THE EXTERNAL DIMENSION OF EU PRIVATE INTERNATIONAL LAW AFTER OPINION 1/13

Edited by

Pietro FRANZINA

intersentia
Cambridge – Antwerp – Portland

Intersentia Ltd
Sheraton House | Castle Park
Cambridge | CB3 0AX | United Kingdom
Tel.: +44 1223 370 170 | Fax: +44 1223 370 169
Email: mail@intersentia.co.uk
www.intersentia.com | www.intersentia.co.uk

Distribution for the UK and Ireland:
NBN International
Airport Business Centre, 10 Thornbury Road
Plymouth, PL6 7 PP
United Kingdom
Tel.: +44 1752 202 301 | Fax: +44 1752 202 331
Email: orders@nbninternational.com

Distribution for Europe and all other countries:
Intersentia Publishing nv
Groenstraat 31
2640 Mortsel
Belgium
Tel.: +32 3 680 15 50 | Fax: +32 3 658 71 21
Email: mail@intersentia.be

Distribution for the USA and Canada:
International Specialized Book Services
920 NE 58th Ave. Suite 300
Portland, OR 97213
USA
Tel.: +1 800 944 6190 (toll free) | Fax: +1 503 280 8832
Email: info@isbs.com

The External Dimension of EU Private International Law after Opinion 1/13

Cover image: © Assadour, Untitled – Hand-coloured engraving (ca 2000) – Private collection

ISBN 978-1-78068-437-6
D/2016/7849/165
NUR 828

British Library Cataloguing in Publication Data. A catalogue record for this book is available from the British Library.

PREFACE

The scope of the external competence of the EU as regards judicial cooperation in civil matters, the conditions upon which this competence is to be regarded as exclusive and the principles that should govern its exercise are among the most controversial issues that arise in connection with the emergence of a regional system of private international law in Europe.

The external dimension of EU private international law provoked discussions even before the European legislature adopted its first measures in this area.[1] The matter has since been one of keen interest for Member States and in the relationship between the political institutions of the Union.

The Court of Justice, for its part, has had various opportunities, over the years, to consider the legal problems involved in the international projection of judicial cooperation in civil matters. Its key decisions in this regard, Opinion 1/03 of 7 February 2006 on the competence of the Community (as it was then) to conclude the revised Lugano Convention on jurisdiction and the recognition of judgments in civil and commercial matters,[2] and Opinion 1/13 of 14 October 2014 on the Union's competence regarding the acceptance of third States' accessions to the Hague Convention of 1980 on the civil aspects of international child abduction, provided a significant contribution to the understanding of the topic.[3]

The debate, however, has not ended with the Court's interventions. The views expressed by the Court, heavily criticised by some commentators, have been triggering further discussions, and several questions are awaiting answers.

The statements made by Germany and the United Kingdom upon the adoption of a Council Decision authorising Austria and Malta to ratify or accede to the Hague Convention of 1965 on the service of documents abroad in the interest of the Union[4] provide the most recent illustration of the uncertainties

---

1 See, in particular, doc. No 6683/99 and doc. No 7871/00, available through the Public Register of Council Documents at <http://register.consilium.europa.eu>.

2 EU:C:2006:81.

3 EU:C:2014:2303.

4 Decision (EU) 2016/414 of 10 March 2016 [2016] OJ L 75/1. For the statements of Germany and the United Kingdom see, respectively, doc. No 13240/15 ADD 1 and ADD 2, in the Public Register of Council Documents.

that still surround the development of the external relations of the EU in judicial cooperation. Taking into account the characteristics and the content of the Hague Service Convention and of EU legislation on the service of documents from one Member States to another, the two delegations expressed their doubts as to whether the conclusion of the former should be regarded as falling within the exclusive external competence of the Union.

Actually, the participation of the EU in international efforts towards the unification or harmonisation of the rules on jurisdiction, applicable law and the international circulation of judgments and other acts raises a number of complex issues, which lie at the crossroads of public international law, private international law, and EU institutional law.

Furthermore, the development of the external relations of the EU in this area implies some politically sensitive questions. The expansion of the exclusive external competence of the EU obviously limits the ability of individual Member States to pursue their own policies in this field in their relations with third countries and within international organisations. Some Member States seem to regard these limitations as a serious handicap in their international relations, whether with neighbouring third countries, with countries with which the Member States in question entertain special political or historical ties, or globally.

A recent measure adopted by the European Parliament and the Council shows just how difficult it is for the Member States to accept that EU legislation might have such a precluding effect. Reference is made to Regulation (EU) 2016/1191 of 6 July 2016 on the simplification of the requirements for presenting certain public documents in the European Union.[5] Member States have for a long time negotiated and concluded bilateral and multilateral agreements dealing with legalisation and related issues, and seem to be eager to keep these matters, internationally, in their hands. The Regulation, pursuant to Article 12(4), does 'not preclude Member States from negotiating, concluding, acceding to, amending or applying international agreements and arrangements with third countries', insofar as these agreements and arrangements apply to public documents 'to be used in relations between the Member States and the third countries concerned'. For the same reason, the Regulation does not preclude Member States 'from deciding on the acceptance of the accession of new contracting parties to such agreements and arrangements to which one or more Member States is or may decide to become party'. This provision, which only surfaced in the negotiations after the Court of Justice issued Opinion 1/13, may in fact be regarded as a sort of reaction to the principle stated therein: the principle whereby, given the nature and content of the Child Abduction Convention and the relationship between the provisions of the Convention and EU legislation

5 [2016] OJ L 200/1.

dealing with the return of wrongfully removed or retained children, the acceptance of the accession of a third State to the Hague Convention comes with the exclusive external competence of the EU.

The papers collected in this book discuss some of the key aspects of EU external relations law with respect to judicial cooperation in civil matters, in particular as it stands after Opinion 1/13.

The book is divided into four parts. Part I outlines the wider context in which the external dimension of EU private international law is developing, and addresses some of the basic issues that arise in connection with this area of EU law. Marise Cremona examines the implications of Opinion 1/13 and Opinion 2/13, regarding the accession of the EU to the European Convention on Human Rights, for the development of EU external relations law. Serena Forlati further discusses the relationship between the legal order of the EU and the European Convention on Human Rights, focusing on the impact of such a relationship on private international law.

Part II is specifically concerned with Opinion 1/13. Paul Beaumont offers a critical assessment of the judicial activism displayed by the Court of Justice in the Opinion. Karen Vandekerckhove and Giorgio Gaja analyse some of the implications of the Court's decision, as regards, *inter alia*, the immediate consequences of the Opinion as to the treatment of third States' accessions to the Hague Child Abduction Convention and the competence of the Union concerning acts related to the Convention other than the acceptance of accessions. Chiara Tuo further unfolds the reasoning of the Court to inquire into the standards to be used to assess the Union's external competence in matters not already covered by EU legislative measures.

The evolving features of the external dimension of EU private international law are examined in Part III. Alex Mills discusses the general approaches that the EU, based on its external powers, might pursue through an 'outward facing' private international law. The contribution of Alessandra Zanobetti is concerned with the dialogue that the EU entertains with the international organisations involved in the unification of private international law, namely the Hague Conference on Private International and Unidroit. Chris Thomale critically examines the prospects of the particular legal framework provided by the Lugano Convention to govern cross-border situations involving the EU, on the one hand, and some of its neighbours, on the other. Jan-Jaap Kuipers looks at the instruments elaborated by the European institutions to allow individual Member States to negotiate and conclude agreements with third countries in respect of particular matters that come with the exclusive external competence of the Union.

Finally, Part IV looks at EU legislation in the field of private international law and considers its relationship to international developments and situations connected with one or more third countries. The opening contribution, by the editor of this book, gives an account of the different ways in which EU legislative measures may relate to international agreements that do not bind the EU, and discusses the political significance of each pattern. Focusing on the Regulation (EC) No 650/2012 on successions upon death, Fabrizio Marongiu Buonaiuti provides an in-depth analysis of some of the ways in which EU legislation may address situations connected with a non-Member State, in particular as regards jurisdiction and the treatment of parallel proceedings.

Most of the contributions in this book are based on papers that were presented at a seminar that took place on 13 February 2015 at the Department of Law of the University of Ferrara. The editor wishes to thank Giorgio Gaja and Alfonso-Luis Calvo Caravaca for chairing the two sessions of the seminar, as well as the various scholars – among whom Cristina Mariottini, Emmanuel Guinchard, Marta Pertegás and Francesco Salerno – who joined in the discussion or otherwise contributed to the initiative.

The editor is also indebted to Ilaria Aquironi, Pietro Alessandro Barcellona, Ester di Napoli, Irene Maccagnani and Omar Vanin for their help in the organisation of the seminar, and to Adrienne Lester-Fitje and Martina Mantovani for their precious assistance in the editing of the book.

Pietro Franzina
Ferrara, 20 August 2016

CONTENTS

Preface v

PART I.
THE INTERNATIONAL PROJECTION OF EU PRIVATE INTERNATIONAL LAW – SOME BASIC ISSUES 1

Opinions 1/13 and 2/13 and EU External Relations Law
Marise CREMONA 3

1. Introduction: Two Significant Opinions 3
2. Private International Law and EU External Powers........ 5
3. The Role of the Court of Justice 14
4. Conclusion: the Specificity of the EU as an International Actor 19

Between Mutual Trust and Respect for Fundamental Rights – Judicial Cooperation in Civil Matters and the European Convention on Human Rights After Opinion 2/13
Serena FORLATI 21

1. Introduction 21
2. The ECHR and European Judicial Cooperation in Civil Matters..... 24
3. The Treatment of EU Law by the European Court of Human Rights 27
4. Conclusions........ 38

PART II.
OPINION 1/13 AND ITS IMPLICATIONS 41

A Critical Analysis of the Judicial Activism of the Court of Justice of the European Union in Opinion 1/13
Paul BEAUMONT 43

1. Introduction 43
2. Background to Opinion 1/13........ 44
3. Background to Judicial Activism 45
4. Opinion 1/13 – Admissibility........ 48
5. Opinion 1/13 – Substance........ 50
6. Conclusion........ 60

The Implications of the European Union's Exclusive Competence with Regard to the Child Abduction Convention
Giorgio GAJA 63

1. The Basis and Extent of the Exclusive Competence of the EU Concerning International Child Abduction 63
2. The Scope of the Exclusive Competence of the EU as Regards Actions Relating to the Child Abduction Convention 66
3. The Procedure for Exercising the Competence of the EU as Regards the Child Abduction Convention 66
4. Does the Child Abduction Convention Bind the EU? 67
5. The Role of the Court of Justice in the Interpretation of the Child Abduction Convention 69

Consequences of Opinion 1/13 on the Acceptance in the EU of Accessions to the Hague Child Abduction Convention
Karen VANDEKERCKHOVE 71

1. Introduction 71
2. Acceptance of Accessions to the 1980 Hague Child Abduction Convention – The Way Forward 73
3. Conclusion 75

International Agreements on Private International Law Matters Not Covered by EU Legislation – Which Test Should Be Adopted to Assess the Competence of the EU?
Chiara E. TUO 77

1. The Position of The ECJ on the External Competence of the EU in the Area of Private International Law 77
2. The 'Effect on EU Law Test' as Opposed to the 'Necessity Test' of Opinion 1/76 84
3. The EU Legal Framework on Free Movement Of Citizens as the Yardstick Against Which the Exclusive External Competence in Private International Law Matters Should Be Assessed 88
4. From Theory to Practice: the 'Effect on EU Law Test' Applied to the Intercountry Adoption Convention 91

PART III.
THE CHANGING FEATURES OF EU EXTERNAL RELATIONS IN THE AREA OF PRIVATE INTERNATIONAL LAW 99

EU External Relations and Private International Law: Multilateralism, Plurilateralism, Bilateralism, or Unilateralism?
Alex MILLS 101

1. Introduction 101
2. Multilateralism 104
3. Plurilateralism or Bilateralism 107
4. Unilateralism 110
5. Conclusions 115

EU Cooperation in Civil Matters and Multilevel Unification of Private International Law: Some Remarks
Alessandra ZANOBETTI 117

1. The Multilevel Unification of Private International Law 117
2. The Europeanisation of Private International Law and Its Impact on the Adoption of Uniform Rules at Regional and Universal Level 118
3. The Interaction Between EU Private International Law and Other Private International Law Instruments 123
4. EU Private International Law as a Tool for the Establishment of an Area of Freedom, Security And Justice 124
5. EU and Uniform Instruments in the Field of International Trade ... 127
6. Perspectives on the Unification of Private International Law 129

The Lugano Model – Cooperative Enhancement Over Enhanced Cooperation
Chris THOMALE 131

1. Introduction 131
2. The Lugano Convention: Cooperative Enhancement Towards an Integrated European Economic Area 133
3. Differentiated Integration in Europe: The Lugano Convention as a Multilateral International Treaty with a Qualified Connection to EU Law 139
4. Lugano Outdated: Why Lugano in Its *Status Quo* Is No Viable Model of European or Global Integration 141
5. Lugano Reloaded: Further Potential in Service of Documents and Taking of Evidence 145

Regulations (EC) Nos 662/2009 and 664/2009: Can Exclusivity Be Successfully Reconciled with Flexibility?
Jan-Jaap KUIPERS 149

1. Introduction 149
2. Evolving Union Competences in Private International Law 151

3. The External Dimension of the EU Private International Law Regulations 153
4. The Regulations 167
5. Conclusion 179

PART IV.
EU LEGISLATION ON PRIVATE INTERNATIONAL LAW AND EXTRA-EUROPEAN SITUATIONS 181

The Interplay of EU Legislation and International Developments in Private International Law
Pietro FRANZINA 183

1. The Virtual Global Reach of EU Legislation on Private International Law 183
2. The Articulation of EU Legislation and International Developments: A Matter of Convergence, Combination and Confrontation 190
3. Convergence 192
4. Combination 199
5. Confrontation 204
6. Concluding Remarks 209

Jurisdiction Under the EU Succession Regulation and Relationships with Third Countries
Fabrizio MARONGIU BUONAIUTI 211

1. The Limited *Erga Omnes* Approach Underlying the Succession Regulation's Rules On Jurisdiction 211
2. Rules Addressing Issues of Coordination with Third-Country Courts 220
3. The Unilateral Coordination with the Jurisdiction of Third-Country Courts Pursued by Article 12(1) of the Regulation 225
4. Concluding Remarks 226

PART I

THE INTERNATIONAL PROJECTION OF EU PRIVATE INTERNATIONAL LAW – SOME BASIC ISSUES

OPINIONS 1/13 AND 2/13 AND EU EXTERNAL RELATIONS LAW

Marise Cremona
European University Institute

1. INTRODUCTION: TWO SIGNIFICANT OPINIONS

Towards the end of 2014 two Opinions of the Court of Justice were handed down which have significant implications for EU external relations law: Opinion 1/13 on the 1980 Hague Convention on the civil aspects of international child abduction,[1] and Opinion 2/13 on the accession of the European Union to the European Convention on Human Rights.[2] Opinion 1/13 sheds light on the increasingly important role played by the EU externally in the field of private international law, against a background in which the Member States have historically taken the lead. It also, at a more technical level, is one of a series of judgments in which the Court of Justice is exploring the implications of the Lisbon Treaty for EU external relations. Opinion 2/13 has been regarded as a landmark judgment, one which will have profound implications for the development of the EU's legal order and its relationship with international law, at least as if not more important than the judgment in *Kadi*.[3] This short chapter cannot of course explore all the dimensions of Opinion 2/13; its main aim is to put Opinion 1/13 into the broader context of EU external relations law and to touch upon those aspects of Opinion 2/13 which link to this broader picture.

The two Opinions were delivered by the Court in response to requests under Article 218(11) TFEU, which gives the Court jurisdiction to deliver an opinion as to whether an 'envisaged agreement' is compatible with the EU Treaties.

1 Opinion 1/13, EU:C:2014:2303.

2 Opinion 2/13, EU:C:2014:2454.

3 Joined Cases C-402/05 P and C-415/05 P, *Yassin Abdullah Kadi and Al Barakaat International Foundation v Council and Commission*, EU:C:2008:461. On Opinion 2/13, see among many comments, 'The EU's Accession to the ECHR – a "NO" from the ECJ', Editorial Comment in (2015) 52 *Common Market Law Review* 1; and those in (2015) 16 *German Law Journal*, 'Special Section: Opinion 2/13'.

Despite being called an 'opinion' the Court's ruling under this procedure is certainly not simply advisory;[4] in the case of an adverse opinion then either the envisaged agreement or the Treaties must be amended to remove the incompatibility before the agreement can enter into force for the Union.[5] The objective is to forestall the legal and diplomatic difficulties that would arise if after its conclusion an international treaty were found to conflict with EU law.[6] Opinion 2/13 deals with arguments of substantive (in)compatibility of specific provisions of the envisaged agreement with Union law, a question which rarely arises in practice despite the wording of Article 218(11).[7] Opinion 1/13 deals with the balance of powers between Union and Member States, an issue which has long been accepted as falling within the scope of the Article 218(11) procedure.[8] Both Opinions in fact concern well-established international treaties to which all the Member States, but not (so far) the EU, are parties and the interaction between EU law and external international legal regimes. And in both cases the Court of Justice can be accused, rightly or wrongly, of defending the EU's own system – and perhaps also its own position – at the expense of international law.

The following discussion will look at these issues from two perspectives. The first, in the next section, is the development of EU external powers in the field of private international law against a background of an extensive network of existing Member State treaties. We see the impact of the growing amount of EU legislation on private international law, its aim being 'the creation of a genuine judicial area' with as its cornerstone the principle of mutual recognition of judicial decisions based on mutual trust.[9] An impact which is heightened, not lessened, by the deliberate choice to create links in the Union legislation ('connection clauses')[10] to an existing international regime.

4 Indeed in Opinion 1/91, EU:C:1991:490, para. 61, the non-binding nature of the Court's advisory opinions under the proposed EEA agreement was one of the incompatibilities identified by the Court: 'it is unacceptable that the answers which the Court of Justice gives to the courts and tribunals in the EFTA States are to be purely advisory and without any binding effects. Such a situation would change the nature of the function of the Court of Justice as it is conceived by the EEC Treaty, namely that of a court whose judgments are binding. Even in the very specific case of Article 228 [now Article 218(11) TFEU], the Opinion given by the Court of Justice has the binding effect stipulated in that article'.

5 Article 218(11) TFEU. Article 6(2) TEU on the accession of the EU to the ECHR may be seen as an example of a Treaty amendment responding to the Court's negative opinion in Opinion 2/94, EU:C:1996:140.

6 Opinion 1/75, EU:C:1975:145, [1975] ECR 1355, at 1360-61.

7 For another example see Opinion 1/92, EU:C:1992:189.

8 Opinion 2/00, EU:C:2001:664, para. 3.

9 Regulation (EC) No 2201/2003 concerning jurisdiction and the recognition and enforcement of judgments in matrimonial matters [2003] OJ L 338/1, Recitals 2 and 21.

10 See further M Cremona, 'A Triple Braid – Interactions between international law, EU law and private law', in M Cremona and H-W Micklitz (eds), *Private Law in the External Relations of the EU* (Oxford University Press 2016), 33.

The second perspective is that of the role of the Court of Justice, a key institution of course in managing the relationship between international and EU law. What is the scope of its jurisdiction over Member State agreements, and Member State obligations under mixed agreements? Under what conditions can the Union participate in international regimes which impinge on domestic law, and which may include adjudicatory mechanisms, while protecting the autonomy of the Union's legal order? What are the effects of 'connection clauses' between EU law and an international treaty, whether substantive (as in the case of Opinion 1/13, the Brussels IIa Regulation and the Hague Convention) or procedural (as in the case of Opinion 2/13, and the draft accession agreement to the European Convention on Human Rights with its prior-involvement procedure)? When might a 'disconnection clause' be required? We will thus begin to explore some of the implications in external relations of the EU's increasing activity in the field of private international law.

2. PRIVATE INTERNATIONAL LAW AND EU EXTERNAL POWERS

The systemisation of the provisions dealing with EU external relations in the Lisbon Treaty did not include the express conferral of external powers in each policy field. Instead the Lisbon Treaty inserted a new provision in the TFEU which was intended to reflect the doctrine of implied powers as developed by the case law of the Court of Justice since the famous *AETR* case of 1971.[11] According to Article 216(1) of the TFEU:

> The Union may conclude an agreement with one or more third countries or international organisations where the Treaties so provide or where the conclusion of an agreement is necessary in order to achieve, within the framework of the Union's policies, one of the objectives referred to in the Treaties, or is provided for in a legally binding Union act or is likely to affect common rules or alter their scope.

This provision may be said to express in more specific terms the principle established by the Court of Justice in Opinion 2/94:

> [The] principle of conferred powers must be respected in both the internal action and the international action of the Community. The Community acts ordinarily on the basis of specific powers which, as the Court has held, are not

[11] Case 22/70, *Commission v Council*, EU:C:1971:32.

> necessarily the express consequence of specific provisions of the Treaty but may also be implied from them.[12]

Both express and implied powers are here referred to as 'specific powers': that is, derived from a specific provision of the Treaty, as distinct from the unspecific or residual power contained in what is now Article 352 TFEU.[13] According to Article 216(1) TFEU then, express external powers may be conferred on the EU either by the Treaties themselves or by a secondary act which is legally binding (such as a Regulation or Directive). In addition treaty-making power may be implied either where necessary to achieve a Treaty objective within the framework of a Union policy (such as its policy on civil justice cooperation), or where the common rules which have been established in a field (ie, the existence of secondary legislation) may be affected by the proposed international agreement. These two bases for implied treaty-making power correspond to rationales of *effet utile* and pre-emption respectively, the latter sometimes being referred to as the '*AETR* rationale'.[14] In both cases, logically, there is an emphasis on the link to an internal policy field – either the need to achieve policy objectives or the fact that existing internal measures may be disturbed (affected or altered in scope) by the external action.

It is against this background that we need to consider the EU's external powers in the field of private international law, and the implications of Opinion 1/13. Title V of Part III TFEU, on the Area of Freedom, Security and Justice, contains only two explicit references to external action, both in the chapter on borders, asylum and immigration.[15] The single Article on judicial cooperation in civil matters (Article 81 TFEU) refers to the adoption of measures for the approximation of the laws of the Member States and more generally to judicial cooperation in civil matters having cross-border implications, and sets out a number of specific fields including conflict of laws, jurisdiction, mutual recognition and enforcement of judgments, and family law. There is no express mention of external action, nor are there references to EU treaty-making in

---

12 Opinion 2/94, n 5, paras 24-25.

13 Ibid, para. 29, the Court described this provision as 'designed to fill the gap where no specific provisions of the Treaty confer on the Community institutions express or implied powers to act, if such powers appear none the less to be necessary to enable the Community to carry out its functions with a view to attaining one of the objectives laid down by the Treaty' and was careful to make clear that it could not be used to undermine the principle of conferral (para. 30).

14 See further M Cremona, 'The Union's External Competences and the Principle of Conferral', in R Schütze and T Tridimas (eds), *Oxford Principles of European Union Law* (Oxford University Press, forthcoming).

15 Under Article 78(2)(g) TFEU the common European asylum system will include partnership and cooperation with third countries on managing inflows of people applying for asylum or subsidiary protection; under Article 79(3) TFEU the EU may conclude agreements with third countries on readmission of third-country nationals illegally present in a Member State.

existing internal legislation. The EU's external powers in this policy field are therefore primarily[16] based on implied powers, on *effet utile* and / or the *AETR* rationale derived from the EU's internal powers and legislation on civil justice cooperation. This was in fact the starting point of the Court of Justice in its Opinion 1/03 on the conclusion by the EU of the revised Lugano Convention.[17] Although the main point at issue in this case was not the existence of EU external powers but the question whether the EU's competence was exclusive (on which see the discussion below), the Court started by affirming that the EU's competence was based on the existence of internal legislation, in particular the Brussels I Regulation:[18]

> Suffice it to note in this regard that the Community has already adopted internal rules relating to jurisdiction and the recognition and enforcement of judgments in civil and commercial matters, whether in the form of Regulation No 44/2001, adopted on the basis of Articles 61(c) EC and 67(1) EC, or the specific provisions which appear in sectoral regulations, such as Title X of Regulation No 40/94 or Article 6 of Directive 96/71.[19]

The fact that this landmark decision on EU external competence was handed down in 2004 is an indication that the EU has been a relative 'late starter' as far as private international law is concerned.[20] Historically, the international fora for the development of traditional private international law have been the Hague Conference on private international law (founded in 1893) and the Council of Europe (founded in 1949), not the EU. These are classic intergovernmental organisations working through international conventions and the EU Member States have over the years helped to create a substantial body of international treaty law in the field of private international law. Insofar as the EU entered the picture at this stage, it was not as a treaty-party but as the framework in which the Member States developed specific private international law instruments, in

16 Other possibilities exist where civil justice cooperation forms part of broader policy agendas with their own legal bases; for example Association Agreements concluded with third countries may include provisions in all policy fields covered by the EU Treaties, and more recent Association Agreements will often contain provisions on civil justice cooperation. See for example the Association Agreement with Ukraine [2014] OJ L 161/3, which provides in Article 24(2): 'The Parties agree to facilitate further EU-Ukraine judicial cooperation in civil matters on the basis of the applicable multilateral legal instruments, especially the Conventions of the Hague Conference on Private International Law in the field of international Legal Cooperation and Litigation as well as the Protection of Children.'

17 Opinion 1/03, EU:C:2006:81, para. 114.

18 Regulation (EC) No 44/2001 on jurisdiction and the recognition and enforcement of judgments in civil and commercial matters [2001] OJ L 12/1.

19 Ibid, para. 134.

20 See further M Cremona, 'A Triple Braid – interactions between international law, EU law and private law', n 10.

particular the Brussels Convention on Jurisdiction and Enforcement of Judgments in Civil and Commercial Matters, an intra-EU Convention concluded between the six (at the time) EEC Member States as early as 1968: an international law instrument, but with strong links to the EU.[21] The Brussels Convention itself expanded with the enlargement of the Community, but in addition it developed an external dimension with the extension of the Brussels regime to some third countries (members of EFTA) through the Lugano Convention in 1988.[22]

The new competence in civil justice cooperation (including private international law) introduced by the Treaty of Amsterdam prompted the adoption of a number of EU instruments: the transformation of the Brussels Convention into the Brussels I Regulation; the adoption of the Rome I and Rome II Regulations[23] as well as other regulations on private international law.[24] When the Brussels Convention became the Brussels I Regulation, the Lugano Convention was revised and the question of the EU becoming a party to Lugano II in place of the Member States was raised and considered by the Court in Opinion 1/03, the Court finding in February 2006 that the EU was exclusively competent to do so on the basis of implied external powers. However the inability, prior to 2007, of the EU to participate in Conventions negotiated within the framework of the Hague Conference meant that in many cases the Member States continued to act alone. After Opinion 1/03 and where as a result of that Opinion parts of a proposed international agreement were a matter of exclusive EU competence, the Council would adopt a Decision authorising the Member States to ratify or accede to it.[25] The EC (now EU) acceded to the Hague Conference on 3 April

---

21 1968 Brussels Convention on jurisdiction and the enforcement of judgments in civil and commercial matters [1972] OJ L 299/32. The use of such international conventions between the Member States in fields which were not (then) envisaged as falling within the scope of EEC activity, was foreseen in Article 220 EEC. On the debate concerning the status in EU law of these Article 220 EEC / Article 293 EC conventions, see R Schütze, *Foreign Affairs and the EU Constitution* (Cambridge University Press 2014), 146-150.

22 Lugano Convention on jurisdiction and the enforcement of judgments in civil and commercial matters, concluded between the EU Member States and the then EFTA States Austria, Finland, Iceland, Norway, Sweden and Switzerland [1988] OJ L 319/9.

23 Regulation (EC) No 593/2008 on the law applicable to contractual obligations (Rome I) [2008] OJ L 177/6; Regulation (EC) No 864/2007/EC on the law applicable to non-contractual obligations (Rome II) [2007] OJ L 199/40.

24 For example, Regulation No 2201/2003, n 9; Regulation (EC) No 4/2009 on jurisdiction, applicable law, recognition and enforcement of decisions and cooperation in matters relating to maintenance obligations [2009] OJ L 7/1.

25 Council Decision 2008/431/EC authorising the Member States to ratify / accede to the 1996 Hague Convention on Jurisdiction, Applicable Law, Recognition, Enforcement and Cooperation in respect of Parental Responsibility and Measures for the Protection of Children [2008] OJ L 151/36. As the Preamble to the Decision recognises in recital 6, this agreement falls within shared competence; however the EC could not accede to it since it contains no provision for accession by a regional economic integration organisation (REIO).

2007,[26] and where provision is made for participation by a regional economic integration organisation (REIO), the EU can participate on its own or alongside Member States.

In 2005 the Council adopted a Strategy paper on the global dimension of Justice and Home Affairs,[27] and this was followed up by strategies specifically on civil justice cooperation.[28] These documents do not contain detailed programmes of action but they indicate the EU's priorities. They emphasise, first, the link between external action and the exercise of competence internally: cooperation with third countries in the field of judicial cooperation in civil matters 'should focus on the areas covered by EC legislation';[29] second, the importance of international negotiations at multilateral level, especially in the context of the Hague Conference on Private International Law; and third, that bilateral cooperation should prioritise the candidate and potential candidate states, the Lugano states,[30] and other neighbourhood states.

Thus although the EU is now a member of the Hague Conference, an active participant in international treaties on private international law,[31] and integrates civil justice cooperation into its broader relations with its neighbours,[32] it has inherited and operates within a complex web of prior international conventions – private international law regimes – developed by its Member States. The interaction between these regimes and internal EU legislation, and the implications of that interaction for the Member States – who remain parties to these earlier treaties – are among the issues raised by Opinion 1/13.

The Opinion concerned the 1980 Hague Convention on the civil aspects of international child abduction. Its subject was not EU accession to the Convention (it is open to accession only by States), but concerned rather the acceptance of the accession of third States to the Convention: should this acceptance be a matter for the EU or the Member States? In other words it concerned the ongoing management of a regime established by a private international law Convention to which the Member States are parties but the EU itself is not, in a

---

26 Decision 2006/719 on the accession of the Community to the Hague Conference on Private International Law [2006] OJ L 297/1.

27 A Strategy for the External Dimension of JHA: Global Freedom, Security and Justice, doc. No 5003/1/06 REV 1.

28 Aspects of judicial cooperation in civil matters in the framework of the Strategy for the External Dimension of JHA: Global freedom, Security and Justice, 11 April 2006, doc. No 8140/06. External relations strategy in the field of judicial cooperation in civil matters, 7 May 2008, doc. No 9045/08.

29 Ibid, para. 6.

30 That is, Iceland, Norway, Switzerland.

31 For example the 2007 Convention on the international recovery of child support and other forms of family maintenance [2011] OJ L 192/51; the 2007 Hague Protocol on the law applicable to maintenance obligations [2009] OJ L 331/17; the 2005 Hague Convention on choice of court agreements [2014] OJ L 353/5.

32 See above, n 16.

situation in which the Convention regime was closely connected to internal EU legislation, legislation designed in fact to build upon the Convention regime.[33] It might seem that accession of new parties would be a matter for the Member States, as existing parties. That indeed was the view taken by the Council, which did not act on Commission proposals that the Council should adopt a position on such questions by way of a decision which would be binding on the Member States. However the Commission asked the Court whether the acceptance of new parties to the Hague Convention falls within the EU's exclusive competence, and the Court decided that it does.

The Court in its Opinion separates the issue of the existence of EU powers from the question of their exclusivity, as it did also in Opinion 1/03 on the Lugano Convention.[34] However it deals rather cursorily with the existence of powers. It is noteworthy that although Article 81 coupled with Article 216(1) TFEU forms the basis for the EU's competence, the Court referred to Article 216(1) only incidentally. It preferred to base itself on the existence of a substantive competence (here Article 81 TFEU) and then to refer to its own doctrine of implied powers as set out in Opinion 1/03, simply adding that this basis for external competence is 'also referred to' in Article 216(1) TFEU.[35] The Court holds first that the EU has internal competence in the field covered by the Convention, second that it has exercised that competence by adopting Regulation 2201/2003/EU (the Brussels IIa Regulation) and third that 'in these circumstances' the EU has external powers. The existence of the Regulation (the 'common rules' referred to in Article 216(1) TFEU) meant that the Court did not need to address whether the international commitments in the Convention are 'necessary' to attain the objectives of Article 81.

It is the discussion of exclusivity that forms the core of the Opinion. The Convention does not of course fall within a field that is defined as exclusive to the Union *a priori* (that is, under Article 3(1) TFEU) such as the common commercial policy. But EU competence with respect to an international agreement may nevertheless be exclusive 'when its conclusion is provided for in a legislative act of the Union or is necessary to enable the Union to exercise its internal competence, or in so far as its conclusion may affect common rules or alter their scope' (Article 3(2) TFEU). As with Article 216(1) TFEU (the wording of which is confusingly similar), this provision is intended to reflect earlier case law of the Court, from which the doctrine of exclusive Union powers is derived. The

---

33 Regulation No 2201/2003, n 9; this aspect will be discussed further below.

34 Opinion 1/03, n 17, paras 114-115.

35 Opinion 1/13, n 1, para. 67. This is also the practice of the institutions when concluding an international agreement: the decision of the Council will refer to the substantive legal basis and to the procedural provision (Article 218 TFEU) but not to Article 216(1) TFEU. For a view that Article 216(1) TFEU should be included alongside the substantive legal basis, see Opinion of AG Kokott in Case C-81/13, *UK v Council*, EU:C:2014:2114, para. 104.

Court applies this earlier case law to the interpretation of Article 3(2). This is not surprising and follows the line it had already taken a few months before. In Opinion 1/13 the Court merely refers to that earlier judgment;[36] there, it set out its reasoning a little more fully:

> In that regard, it must be stated that the words used in that last clause [of Article 3(2) TFEU] correspond to those by which the Court, in paragraph 22 of the judgment in *ERTA* (EU:C:1971:32), defined the nature of the international commitments which Member States cannot enter into outside the framework of the EU institutions, where common EU rules have been promulgated for the attainment of the objectives of the Treaty. Those words must therefore be interpreted in the light of the Court's explanation with regard to them in the judgment in *ERTA* (EU:C:1971:32) and in the case-law developed as from that judgment.[37]

As this indicates, it is the third basis for exclusivity mentioned in Article 3(2) that is at issue here: 'namely that the EU has exclusive competence for the conclusion of an international agreement in so far as its conclusion "may affect common rules or alter their scope"'.[38] This is consistent with its approach to the existence of Union competence in this case, which as we have seen was also based on the existence of internal Union rules (that is, the Brussels IIa Regulation). The Court then proceeds in two stages.

First it looks at the degree to which the Convention and the Regulation cover the same matters. It is not necessary for every element of the Convention to be reflected in Union legislation as long as the Convention commitments are covered 'to a large extent' by such common rules.[39] Here the fact that the Regulation refers expressly to the Convention is important. The Regulation provides that in relations between Member States the Regulation shall take precedence over (*inter alia*) the Hague Convention; however in matters not governed by the Regulation, the Hague Convention will continue to apply between the Member States.[40] According to Advocate General Jääskinen, for certain issues '[t]he legislature has therefore chosen to refer to the provisions of an existing instrument of public international law rather than adopt provisions of European Union law concerning the same matters.'[41] The Court holds that – for the Member States – the two instruments form a 'unitary body of rules' on the return of wrongfully removed children that have to be applied together.

---

36 Opinion 1/13, n 1, paras 71-74.

37 Case C-114/12, *Commission v Council*, EU:C:2014:2151, paras 66-67.

38 Opinion 1/13, n 1, para. 70.

39 Ibid, para. 73.

40 Regulation No 2201/2003, n 9, Articles 60 and 62.

41 View of AG Jääskinen in Case C-400/10 PPU, *J. McB.v L.E.*, EU:C:2010:544, para 40.

Second, the Court turns to the specific issue before it. Given that the Convention will only apply between an acceding State and those existing parties that have accepted its adherence to the Convention, would it affect the 'common rules' of the EU system if the Member States were to take individual decisions on the acceptance of new State parties? The Court finds that indeed this would have an effect since cases may arise involving two or more Member States and a third State, and were the EU Member States to have different positions on whether the Convention applies in their relations with the third State, 'there would be a risk of undermining the uniform and consistent application of Regulation No 2201/2003 and, in particular, the rules concerning cooperation between the authorities of the Member States'.[42] This rather lapidary reasoning becomes clearer when one reads the 'View' of Advocate General Jääskinen. The Advocate General points out that although the Brussels IIa Regulation builds upon the Convention, it forms closer ties based on mutual trust between the Member States, which change the balance between the requested State and the State of origin.[43] In his view it is therefore important that the conditions under which a third State accession is accepted are uniform among the EU's Member States:

> It appears to me to be essential that the reliability of any acceding third State, in so far as concerns judicial and administrative cooperation, should be assessed jointly under the coordination of the Council pursuant to a proposal from the Commission. In the absence of such an initiative for concerted action, there is a risk of compromising the uniform and consistent application of the provisions of the Brussels IIa Regulation and the proper functioning of the system which it establishes, which would undermine the full effectiveness of the rules of EU law, according to the criteria for assessment defined by the Court of Justice.[44]

On the one hand, then, the Court is recognising the importance for Union law of the Member States' existing international commitments. As the Court put it, 'the provisions of the Convention may have an effect on the meaning, scope and effectiveness of the rules laid down in Regulation No 2201/2003'.[45] On the other hand, we can see that as a result the Member States' position as State parties to the international Convention is affected by Union law. The Convention, although not as such a formal source of Union law (the EU is not a party) has, as a result of the Regulation's explicit reference, become closely integrated with the EU legal regime and consequently subject to the need for uniform application by the Member States.

---

42 Opinion 1/13, n 1, para. 89.

43 View of AG Jääskinen on Opinion 1/13, EU:C:2014:2292, para. 96.

44 Ibid, para. 98 (footnotes omitted).

45 Opinion 1/13, n 1, para. 85.

This is the dynamic revealed by Opinion 1/13. The Union system operates alongside, and is to a degree integrated with, a regime established by international treaty. This integration or articulation between EU law and the international regime may in itself, as this Opinion shows, form the basis for a finding of exclusive EU competence, and so restrict the freedom of the EU Member States as parties to the Convention. One striking aspect of this case is the fact that, as has already been mentioned, the exclusive competence of the EU operates in a context where the EU itself cannot (at least at present) become a party to the Convention in question, and its competence must be exercised through the Member States. The Member States act on behalf, and in the interests, of the EU.[46] In practical terms, the Member States may act only via common action, with positions being determined in advance through Council decisions.[47]

Two further points may be briefly added. The first is that the duty on the Member States to coordinate their positions on the acceptance of new parties to the 1980 Hague Convention, although based by the Court in Opinion 1/13 on a finding of exclusive EU competence, could also have arisen had competence been shared rather than exclusive. The duty of sincere cooperation, operating in a context of shared competence, may also restrain Member States from acting within the framework of an international treaty regime other than through collective positions.[48]

The second point concerns the possible application of Article 351 TFEU, as regards those Member States that became parties to the 1980 Hague Convention before joining the EU.[49] Article 351(1) TFEU provides that the 'rights and obligations' under such prior agreements with third States 'shall not be affected' by the EU Treaties. This provision may in principle protect a Member State from an accusation of failing to comply with its EU law obligations where this failure derives from the need to comply with a prior treaty obligation towards a third State. However, its scope is limited; it does not operate simply to 'protect' a prior international treaty from the operation of EU law obligations on a Member State. The Court of Justice has interpreted the provision to refer to the 'rights' of third States and the 'obligations' of the Member States. Thus, the purpose of Article 351(1) is to protect the rights of third States by allowing Member States

[46] Case C-45/07, *Commission v Greece*, EU:C:2009:81, paras 30-31; Opinion 2/91, EU: C:1993:106, para. 5. See further M Cremona, 'Member States as Trustees of the Union Interest: participating in international agreements on behalf of the European Union', in A Arnull, C Barnard, M Dougan and E Spaventa (eds), *A Constitutional Order of States: Essays in European Law in Honour of Alan Dashwood* (Hart 2011), 435.

[47] Case C-399/12, *Germany v Council*, EU:C:2014:2258, paras 48-55.

[48] Article 4(3) TFEU. We may note that AG Jääskinen in his View on Opinion 1/3, rightly refers to the duty of sincere cooperation as one of the foundations for exclusive competence (n 43, para 99); however the duty applies also in cases of shared competence: Case C-246/07, *Commission v Sweden*, EU:C:2010:203.

[49] This applies to a number, but not all, EU Member States.

to fulfil their international obligations, not to allow Member States to set aside EU law so as to exercise their rights under a pre-existing treaty regime.[50] In the case at issue in Opinion 1/13, therefore, Article 351(1) would not apply: there is no right under the Hague Convention for newly acceding States to have their accession accepted by existing parties, and no corresponding obligation on the Member State parties.

In fact it might be argued that Article 351(2) TFEU provides an additional ground on which to base the obligation on Member States to act through the EU. Under Article 351(2) the Member States are under an obligation to take steps to eliminate any incompatibilities between the prior agreement and the EU Treaties, assisting each other to this end and where necessary adopting a common attitude. It might be argued that the exclusive EU competence brought about by the Brussels IIa Regulation has created an incompatibility in the sense that the Convention does not provide for EU accession. This incompatibility may be mitigated, if not completely eliminated, by ensuring that the Member States, while remaining parties, act in the interest of the Union by way of common action agreed in the Council under the procedure established by Article 218(9) TFEU.[51]

3. THE ROLE OF THE COURT OF JUSTICE

The EU legal order is open both to the Member States' existing international commitments (Opinion 1/13) and to the possibility of the EU becoming part of another international system and subject to the international adjudication and dispute settlement (Opinion 2/13).[52] These relations may be managed through systems of connection (creating legal links between EU law and an international treaty) and disconnection (designed to preserve the autonomy of EU law). In this respect both Opinions confirm existing positions.[53] But both Opinions also demonstrate clearly that these possibilities are subject to oversight by the Court of Justice by means of the prior control procedure offered by Article 218(11) TFEU, coupled with the doctrines of exclusivity, primacy, autonomy and sincere cooperation. Indeed the Court may exercise control over a Member State's international agreements (not only those of the EU itself) where EU legislation contains explicit references to such an agreement and as a result the Court

---

50 Case C-170/98, *Commission v Belgium*, EU:C:1999:411; Case C-62/98, *Commission v Portugal*, EU:C:2000:358; Case C-84/98, *Commission v Portugal*, EU:C:2000:359.

51 On the use of Article 218(9) TFEU even where the EU is not a party to an international treaty, see C-399/12, *Germany v Council*, n 47.

52 Opinion 1/91, n 4, paras 39-40.

53 See for example Cases 21 to 24/72, *International Fruit Company*, EU:C:1972:115, Opinion 1/92, n 7, and Opinion 1/94, EU:C:1994:384.

holds that the agreement falls within exclusive EU competence. As Opinion 1/13 shows, this applies also to the powers exercised by a Member State as a treaty party.[54]

The Opinions shed light on the scope of the Court's jurisdiction under Article 218(11). The procedure applies to 'envisaged agreements' and from its context we must assume that the provision is intended to apply to agreements between the Union and third countries or international organisations (Article 218(1) TFEU). The Court interprets its jurisdiction relatively broadly. The term 'agreement' covers any international instrument intended to be legally binding. As in other cases,[55] the Court in Opinion 1/13 turns to international treaty law for guidance and is prepared to accept as an 'agreement' two related instruments which between them create legal effects for the parties (here, the instrument of accession of the third State and the declaration of acceptance of accession made by the EU Member State(s)). Referring to Article 2(1)(a) of the 1969 Vienna Convention on the Law of Treaties the Court finds that 'the act of accession and the declaration of acceptance of such an accession, although each is effected by means of a separate instrument, give expression, overall, to the 'convergence of intent' of the States concerned and thus amount to an international agreement'.[56] The Court is then prepared to regard one of those instruments – the declaration of acceptance – as 'encompassed by the concept of agreement' for the purposes of Article 218 TFEU.[57]

But does the Court have jurisdiction under Article 218(11) to consider an agreement to be concluded *by a Member State*? Here the Court takes an EU law perspective; what matters is not who are the parties in international law, but rather the competence to conclude the agreement. As it says,

> the request for an opinion concerns the question of the competence of the EU, judged solely by reference to the rules of EU law ... It does not concern the obstacles which the EU may encounter in the exercise of its competence because of international rules relating to the conclusion of such agreements.[58]

Indeed, as we have already seen, given that the EU has an exclusive competence the Member States in concluding the agreement will act in the Union interest and on behalf of the EU. From that perspective the obstacles that prevent the EU from directly exercising its powers do not limit the Court's jurisdiction.

---

54 See also Case C-399/12, *Germany v Council*, n 47.

55 For example, Cases C-103/12 and C-165/12, *European Parliament / Commission v Council*.

56 Opinion 1/13, n 1, para. 41.

57 Ibid, para. 42.

58 Ibid, para. 43.

What does it mean to say that an agreement is envisaged? Agreements that have already been concluded by the EU are excluded,[59] but otherwise the Court may consider anything from a finalized text even to cases where an agreed text does not yet exist, as long as it has 'sufficient information on the actual content of [the] agreement',[60] although the absence of a final text may mean that the Court cannot give its view on all aspects of compatibility.[61] In Opinion 1/13 a different aspect of the concept of 'envisaged' was raised. It was argued by the Council that the agreement was not envisaged by the Union, since the Commission's proposal to adopt a Union decision had been rejected. As has often been the case in the past the procedure was being used as part of an inter-institutional argument. The Court defended the Commission's right to ask for an Opinion: an agreement is envisaged by the Union, it argued, when it is envisaged by any one of the institutions that plays a part in the procedure under Article 218 TFEU, and the Commission is certainly one of those institutions. Thus the Court does not let the inter-institutional disagreement affect the scope of its own jurisdiction. As it points out, 'the right to submit a request for an opinion is not conditional upon the EU institutions having reached final agreement on whether the exercise of the EU's external competence is possible or appropriate.'[62]

Nevertheless Opinion 2/13 points to limits to the Court's jurisdiction under Article 218(11). While the draft accession instruments allowed an assessment of their compatibility with the Treaties, questions as to the internal implementing rules could not be considered by the Court. Not only is the Article 218(11) procedure limited to international agreements (there is no prior legality control for internal acts), but to consider such hypothetical internal rules before their adoption would encroach on the competence of the legislature.[63]

Thus in both Opinion 1/13 and 2/13 we can see the Court maximizing its jurisdiction over proposed international agreements, while at the same time keeping a balance between its role and that of the legislature. This sense of the proper role of the Court pervades Opinion 2/13, and indeed much of the criticism of the Opinion. Did the Court's Opinion in this instance respect the political judgment of the Union's institutions to accede to the Convention, which in itself was based on a Treaty-mandate? Given that Article 6 TEU provides that the Union 'shall accede' to the Convention, should not the Court have given

---

59 Opinion 3/94, EU:C:1995:436. In such cases it may be possible to challenge before the Court the legality of the Council decision concluding the agreement: see for example Cases C-317/04 and C-318/04, *European Parliament* v *Council*, EU:C:2006:346.

60 Opinion 2/13, n 2, para. 147.

61 Opinion 2/94, n 5.

62 Opinion 1/13, n 1, para. 49.

63 Opinion 2/13, n 2, para. 150.

more weight to this injunction when considering the potentially problematic aspects of the draft accession agreement?

The Court starts the substantive discussion in its Opinion by reaffirming the distinctive character of the EU's legal system. It is not to be seen as simply one among other international treaty regimes but as 'a new kind of legal order, the nature of which is peculiar to the EU, its own constitutional framework and founding principles, a particularly sophisticated institutional structure and a full set of legal rules to ensure its operation'.[64] Part of this structure is the EU's judicial system, and this aspect of the accession agreement with its possibility of external adjudication is the Court's particular concern. An external agreement may grant an external court powers over the enforcement of agreement itself, including the power to determine the compliance of the EU or a Member State with its provisions.[65] However it must not be allowed to compromise the exclusive jurisdiction of the Court of Justice under Article 344 TFEU, and this means that the external court should not rule on questions of EU law, and because the agreement itself, once concluded by the EU, becomes part of EU law and binding on the Member States and the institutions,[66] the external court must not be able to rule on the application of the agreement as between the Member States, or as between the Member States and the EU.

What is striking about the Court's stance is that in its view it is not sufficient for the agreement to be permissive as regards the jurisdiction of the Court of Justice, to allow EU procedures to settle questions of EU law, relying on the EU law obligation under Article 344 TFEU to enforce the exclusive jurisdiction of the Court of Justice.[67] The Court requires the international agreement *itself* to rule out recourse to the external court in all circumstances where Article 344 might be infringed thereby: 'only the express exclusion of the ECtHR's jurisdiction under Article 33 of the ECHR over disputes between Member States or between Member States and the EU in relation to the application of the ECHR within the scope *ratione materiae* of EU law would be compatible with Article 344 TFEU'.[68] The Court is thus requiring a disconnection clause in the agreement that would protect the procedural as well as the substantive autonomy of EU law: as between the EU and Member State parties, it is EU law and EU enforcement procedures that should apply.[69]

64 Ibid, para. 158.

65 Ibid, para. 182.

66 Article 216(2) TFEU; Case 181/73, *Haegeman v Belgian State*, EU:C:1974:41, para 5.

67 As happened in Case C-459/03, *Commission v Ireland*, EU:C:2006:345.

68 Opinion 2/13, n 2, para. 213.

69 On disconnection clauses see further M Cremona, 'Disconnection Clauses in EC Law and Practice', in C Hillion and P Koutrakos (eds), *Mixed Agreements Revisited - The EU and its Member States in the World* (Hart 2010), 160.

Here we can draw a link with the Hague Convention on the Civil Aspects of International Child Abduction which was at issue in Opinion 1/13. This Convention, as we have seen, is closely connected to EU law, despite the fact that the EU is not a party; so closely that the Court has referred to the Convention and the Brussels IIa Regulation as a 'unitary body of rules' and has found the EU to have exclusive competence over the field covered by the Convention.[70] However the Hague Convention has also been the subject of interpretation by the ECtHR. Indeed the approach of the ECtHR to the Hague Convention when dealing with cases of child abduction in the context of Article 8 ECHR has been identified by Rietiker as a notable example of the ECtHR's practice of 'systemic integration', that is, its practice when interpreting the ECHR of taking account of its broader legal environment.[71] He points out that the ECtHR looks so closely at the Hague Convention that 'it is sometimes difficult to tell whether the judges are applying the European Convention on Human Rights or the Hague Convention or both' and that a breach of the Hague Convention can lead 'almost automatically' to a finding of violation of the ECHR.[72] Just as the ECtHR's interpretation of the Hague Convention will influence its interpretation of Article 8 ECHR, so its interpretation of the Convention may in turn affect national courts in their interpretation of the Brussels IIa Regulation. In the light of the EU Court of Justice's view of the Hague Convention, should we then regard a case before the ECtHR involving the ECHR, the Hague Convention and an EU Member State as a matter falling 'within the scope *ratione materiae* of EU law'? The connection between EU law and the Hague Convention affirmed by the Court in Opinion 1/13 would thus trigger the disconnection between EU law and the ECtHR that the Court of Justice in Opinion 2/13 found to be necessary. The procedural connection, or *renvoi* back to the Court of Justice, represented by the prior involvement procedure was found by the Court not to be sufficient.

---

70 Opinion 1/13, n 1, para. 78.

71 D Rietiker, 'The Principle of "Effectiveness" in the Recent Jurisprudence of the European Court of Human Rights: Its Different Dimensions and Its Consistency with Public International Law – No Need for the Concept of Treaty Sui Generis' (2010) 79 *Nordic Journal of International Law* 245, 271-4. Thanks to Magarethe Wewerinke for drawing my attention to this study. The expression 'systemic integration' is taken from M Koskenniemi, *Fragmentation of International Law: difficulties arising from the diversification and expansion of international law*, Report of the Study Group of the International Law Commission, doc. A/CN.4/L.682.

72 D Rietiker, n 71, at 273, citing ECtHR, *Carlson v Switzerland*, ECHR:2008:1106JUD004949206.

4. CONCLUSION: THE SPECIFICITY OF THE EU AS AN INTERNATIONAL ACTOR

What do these Opinions add to our understanding of the EU as an international actor, and specifically as an actor in the field of private international law?

First, nowhere so clearly have the implications of the EU's constitutional framework and its legal structure been spelled out for the EU as a treaty-maker as in Opinion 2/13. The commitment to the ECHR found in Article 6 TEU – and indeed the commitment to international law and an international rule of law more generally – are expressions of the EU's values, but must take effect within the framework of its constitutional structure. As expressed by the Court: 'Fundamental rights, as recognised in particular by the Charter, must therefore be interpreted and applied within the EU in accordance with the [Union's] constitutional framework'.[73] In Opinion 2/13 the Court says clearly that the EU is 'not a State' and its specificity flows from the fact that both the EU and the Member States have the capacity to act internationally, and are often both parties to the same agreements, as well as from the special status that EU law holds within the Member State legal orders. EU law has needed to find ways of handling the large numbers of international treaty commitments of its Member States. It has been creative in devising different mechanisms for connecting and disconnecting the EU regime from other international regimes. It is hardly surprising that these connections and disconnections are made on the EU's own terms; that EU law itself decides on what basis, to what extent and under which conditions it takes account of its own and its Member States' treaty commitments. In this it is behaving like a domestic legal system. But this has consequences for private international law.

Private international law is intended to establish rules (of jurisdiction, applicable law and enforcement) which apply without distinction to all national legal systems. The EU has been successful in crafting a EU-wide system of private international law but in so doing it has inevitably created distinctions between 'inside' and 'outside', between the system which applies between the Member States, with its high level of mutual trust and emphasis on 'free movement of judgments', and the private international law systems of non-EU Member States. It thus challenges one of the foundations of private international law. The EU's own international action, including its participation in the work of the Hague Conference, is one way of mitigating this effect but, as we have seen, in articulating the relationship between EU private international law and international regimes, the Court's priority has been to ensure the integrity and internal functionality of the EU system.

---

73 Opinion 2/13, n 2, para. 177.

Second, in both Opinions we see the impact of EU law on relations between Member States as parties to an international treaty. The Member States are parties as sovereign States, but they are also 'EU Member States' and this affects the way they exercise their powers and implement their obligations under an agreement. They may, as in Opinion 1/13, find themselves compelled under Union law to coordinate their acts through the Union institutions and thus subject to EU decision-making procedures and subject to the control of the Court of Justice. And where the Member States are implementing a treaty, even a human rights treaty, they are bound by their EU law obligations and this includes the mutual trust between Member States underpinned by the EU's own standards of protection.[74] A high level of mutual trust is indeed a hallmark of the EU's own system of private international law as well as its system for the protection of fundamental rights. Opinion 2/13 essentially requires that within the scope of Union law it is EU law that should apply between the Member States (including the presumption of fundamental rights compliance based on mutual trust), not the Convention: 'the Member States have, by reason of their membership of the EU, accepted that relations between them as regards the matters covered by the transfer of powers from the Member States to the EU are governed by EU law to the exclusion, if EU law so requires, of any other law.'[75] This statement by the Court helps us to understand the position it took in Opinion 1/13, in articulating the relationship between the Hague Convention and Union law. Thus the two Opinions, delivered a few months apart and at first sight of rather different import, together offer us important perspectives on the EU's external action in the field of private international law.

---

74 Ibid, paras 191-192; Case C-399/11, *Stefano Melloni v Ministerio Fiscal*, EU:C:2013:107.

75 Opinion 2/13, n 2, para. 193.

BETWEEN MUTUAL TRUST AND RESPECT FOR FUNDAMENTAL RIGHTS – JUDICIAL COOPERATION IN CIVIL MATTERS AND THE EUROPEAN CONVENTION ON HUMAN RIGHTS AFTER OPINION 2/13

Serena FORLATI *
University of Ferrara

1. INTRODUCTION

This chapter discusses the relationship between the EU legal order and a rather peculiar component of its 'external dimension', namely its relationship to the European Convention on Human Rights and Fundamental Freedoms (ECHR).

The possible impact of the Court of Justice's Opinion 2/13[1] on this relationship will be addressed mainly from the perspective of the ECHR and of the European Court of Human Rights (ECtHR), rather than that of the EU. Moreover, the focus will be specifically on the ECHR's influence on EU judicial cooperation in civil matters and, more specifically, on issues of private international law.

At first glance, it may seem that the Opinion issued on 18 December 2014 has no impact at all on this relationship. Differently from what might be expected, the Court of Justice concluded that the accession agreement

> is not compatible with Article 6(2) TEU or with Protocol (No 8) relating to Article 6(2) of the Treaty on European Union.[2]

* I am grateful to Francesco Salerno for helpful discussions.

1 Opinion 2/13, EU:C:2014:2454.

2 Ibid, operative part.

The existence of an express legal basis for accession, enshrined in Article 6(2) TEU,[3] the involvement of the Court of Justice in the negotiation process and the (essentially positive) views of AG Kokott[4] suggested that at a different outcome could be possible. Yet the difficulty for the Court of Justice to accept the direct supervision of the European Court of Human Rights has been apparent ever since Opinion 2/94.[5] The conditions for accession set out in the Treaties, notably in Protocol no. 8 TEU and in the Declaration on Article 6(2), paved the way for the rigid approach to the issue adopted by the Court of Justice in its last opinion.[6] At least for the time being, therefore, the autonomy of the EU legal order, which was one of the main preoccupations of the ECJ in the negotiation phase,[7] has been 'preserved':[8] the European Convention will continue to bind the EU only under EU law, and there will be no direct external control over acts of EU Institutions, including the Court of Justice itself, by the European Court of Human Rights. The situation is of course different for the Member States, which remain bound by the ECHR even in matters falling under the scope of EU law.

With this in mind, it may be tempting to assume that the policy of mutual cooperation and comity, whereby the Court of Justice takes into account the case law of the Strasbourg Court when applying EU law, especially the Charter of Fundamental Rights under Articles 52(3) and 53 thereof, and the ECtHR exercises a measure of self-restraint in cases involving the responsibility of EU member States where the compatibility of EU law with the Convention is at stake, will simply continue: some commentators maintain that this scenario is actually to be preferred to accession.[9] However, Opinion 2/13 will inevitably have some consequences on the rather delicate relationship between the two Courts, which has been shifting over time and is less positive than it would appear at first sight.

The analysis will focus on this relationship, which can be properly understood only by keeping in mind the broader, complex system of protection of fundamental rights in Europe, where national courts and institutions also play a key role. In some respects, the case law of the two Courts reflects a different, potentially clashing, vision of how the European system of human rights pro-

---

3 Consolidated Version of the Treaty on European Union [2010] OJ C 83/13.

4 View on Opinion 2/13, EU:C:2014:2475, para. 280: the Advocate General proposed that the Draft Accession Agreement be declared compatible with EU law subject to some adjustments.

5 EU:C:1996:140.

6 Opinion 2/13 relies on both Protocol No 8 and the Declaration when stressing the need not to affect the specific characteristics of the EU and of the EU legal order (cf paras 161-162).

7 See A Gianelli, 'After the Accession: The Relationship between the EU Legal System and the ECHR', in B Cortese (ed), *Essays in Honour of Laura Picchio Forlati* (Giappichelli 2014), 341.

8 Cf Opinion 2/13, n 1, para 174.

9 B Conforti, 'L'adhésion de l'Union Européenne à la Convention Européenne des Droits de l'Homme', in L Weitzel (ed), *L'Europe des droits fondamentaux: Mélanges en hommage à Albert Weitzel* (Pedone 2013), 21, 27.

tection should be designed. In this regard, it was suggested that Opinion 2/13 'exudes the impression of being strongly influenced by the endeavour of the ECJ to defend its position vis-à-vis the ECtHR rather than by a spirit of cooperation',[10] and that the ECJ rejected the very idea of external control, which is a keystone of the ECHR system.[11] The core of the problem is not so much (or not only) the identification of the appropriate standard of protection of fundamental rights, but rather who is ultimately entitled to strike the right balance between the interest of regional integration and the protection of fundamental human rights and when.[12] In this respect, the Court of Justice seemed to be seeking a 'disconnection clause' whereby the ECHR can be set aside, in the relations between EU member States, insofar as this is required for the full implementation of EU law.[13] Thus, according to the Opinion,

> [i]n so far as the ECHR would, in requiring the EU and the Member States to be considered Contracting Parties not only in their relations with Contracting Parties which are not Member States of the EU but also in their relations with each other, including where such relations are governed by EU law, require a Member State to check that another Member State has observed fundamental rights, even though EU law imposes an obligation of mutual trust between those Member States, accession is liable to upset the underlying balance of the EU and undermine the autonomy of EU law.[14]

These concepts were reiterated where the Court of Justice considered that the draft accession agreement 'is liable adversely to affect the specific characteris-

---

10 Editorial Comments, (2015) 52 *Common Market Law Review* 1, 13. See also LS Rossi, 'Il parere 2/13 della CGUE sull'adesione dell'UE alla CEDU: scontro fra Corti?', *SIDIblog*, 22 December 2014 <http://www.sidi-isil.org/sidiblog/?p=1228>, noting that the Court of Justice transforms a clash between Courts into a clash between legal orders; and S Vezzani, 'L'autonomia ordinatoria dell'ordinamento giuridico dell'Unione europea. Riflessioni all'indomani del parere 2/13 della Corte di Giustizia', (2016) 99 *Rivista di diritto internazionale*, 68, 70, stressing that fundamental rights are at the core of the friction between different legal orders as they shape their identity..

11 LS Rossi, n 10; V Zagrebelsky, 'L'UE e il controllo esterno della protezione dei diritti e delle libertà fondamentali in Europa. La barriera elevata dalla Corte di Giustizia', (2015) 9 *Diritti umani e diritto internazionale*, 1, 6.

12 See V Tzevelekos, 'When Elephants Fight it is the Grass that Suffers: 'Hegemonic Struggle' in Europe and its Side-Effects for International Law', in K Dzehtsiarou, T Konstantinides, T Lock and N O'Meara (eds), *Human Rights Law in Europe: The Influence, Overlaps and Contradictions of the EU and the ECHR* (Routledge 2014), 9, 12.

13 See G Gaja, 'Una mancata disconnessione relativamente alla Convenzione europea dei diritti dell'uomo?', (2015) 98 *Rivista di diritto internazionale*, 148. Cf O De Schutter and F Tulkens, 'Confiance mutuelle et droits de l'homme. La Convention européenne des droits de l'homme et la transformation de l'intégration européenne', in *Liège, Strasbourg, Bruxelles: parcours des droits de l'homme: Liber amicorum Michel Melchior* (Anthémis 2010), 947.

14 Opinion 2/13, n 1, para. 194.

tics and the autonomy of EU law' as it 'does not avert the risk that the principle of Member States' mutual trust under EU law may be undermined'.[15]

As is pointed out elsewhere in this book, the Court of Justice thus emphasised the importance of the principle of mutual trust – together with the principle of autonomy – to the detriment of other key EU constitutional principles.[16] Among the latter is, notably, the requirement to respect fundamental rights as guaranteed by the ECHR:[17] the Opinion stresses that such rights

> constitute general principles of EU law. However, as the EU has not acceded to the ECHR, the latter does not constitute a legal instrument which has been formally incorporated into the legal order of the EU.[18]

This stance is of course correct, but the fact remains that also general principles of EU law are a fully-fledged component of the EU legal order – whereas the ECJ's reasoning seems to set this element aside, or at least to lessen its importance in the overall picture of EU institutional architecture.

Rather than engaging in a detailed discussion of Opinion 2/13, this analysis will focus on the principle of mutual trust, which lies at the core of the 'clash of visions' between Strasbourg and Luxembourg.[19] The ECJ expressly discussed the principle of mutual trust with reference to the 'Dublin' system[20] and to judicial cooperation in criminal matters;[21] however, the principle also plays a key role in EU judicial cooperation in civil matters, which is by now covering many aspects of private international law. A closer look at the impact of the ECHR on this aspect of EU legal integration may help to understand the reasons why it has given rise to difficulties in the relationship between the two Courts.

2. THE ECHR AND EUROPEAN JUDICIAL COOPERATION IN CIVIL MATTERS

The impact of International Human Rights Law on Private International Law has been perceived since the adoption of the Universal Declaration on Human

---

15 Opinion 2/13, n 1, para. 258.

16 See the contribution of M Cremona to this book. Cf also 'Editorial Comments', n 10, 12.

17 Article 6(3) TEU; cf Opinion 2/13, n 1, para. 179.

18 Ibid.

19 M Weller, 'Mutual Trust: In Search of the Future of European Private International Law', (2015) 11 *Journal of Private International Law* 64. In the broader perspective of the Area of Freedom, Security and Justice see V Mitsilegas (C Grandi ed), *Justice and Trust in the European Legal Order – The Copernicus Lectures* (Jovene 2016), 39 ff.

20 Opinion 2/13, n 1, para 191, mentions Cases C-411/10 and C-493/10, *N.S. and others v United Kingdom*, EU:C:2011:865.

21 See again Opinion 2/13, n 1, para 191, where the Court of Justice refers to Case C-399/11, *Melloni*, EU:C:2013:107.

Rights[22] and has been growing in importance and scope.[23] It is therefore not surprising that the case law of the ECtHR in the field of private international law has evolved significantly in the last decade; the Strasbourg Court has by now had the opportunity to address a broad number of private international law issues, mainly under Articles 6 and 8 of the Convention.[24] The ECtHR is confronted with a growing number of cases relating to the exercise of jurisdiction by national courts[25] or closely connected issues, such as return orders in child abduction cases,[26] and recognition and enforcement of foreign judgments[27] and of foreign public acts concerning status and family ties, as in the controversial cases of *Menesson v France* and *Labassee v France*[28] or, more recently, in *Paradiso and Campanelli v Italy*.[29] The latter case, which concerned a surrogate motherhood where no biological ties existed between the child and the persons identified as parents in a Russian birth certificate, confirms that the Strasbourg Court is prepared to supervise the application of national rules identifying the law applicable to a given situation. The Court considered that the decision of Italian Courts to apply Italian law in assessing the existence of a parent-child relation was not arbitrary, in a situation where the biological parents were unknown and the nationality of the child could not be determined. In the ECtHR's words,

> l'application des lois italiennes qui a été faite en l'espèce par le tribunal pour mineurs découle de la règle des conflits des lois selon laquelle la filiation est

22 P Lerebours-Pigeonnière, 'La déclaration universelle des droits de l'homme et le droit international privé français', in *Le droit privé français au milieu du XXe siècle - Études offertes à Georges Ripert* (LGDJ 1950), 255.

23 See P Kinsch, 'Droits de l'homme, droits fondamentaux et droit international privé', (2005) 318 *Recueil des cours de l'Académie de droit international de La Haye* 9; and the contributions of A Davì, P Kinsch, C Campiglio, F Salerno and N Foggetti in R Sapienza (ed), *La tutela dei diritti umani e il diritto internazionale* (Editoriale Scientifica 2012), 209.

24 See J Fawcett, 'The Impact of Article 6 ECHR on Private International Law' (2007) 56 *International and Comparative Law Quarterly* 1; LR Kiestra, *The Impact of the European Convention on Human Rights on Private International Law* (Asser Press 2014).

25 See for instance *Bayrak v Germany*, ECHR:2000:0706DEC002793795; *Naït-Liman v Switzerland*, ECHR:2016:0621JUD005135707. See further P Franzina, 'Seeking Compensation for Torture Suffered Abroad: The Issue of Adjudicatory Jurisdiction from a European Perspective', in L Zagato and S De Vido (eds), *Il divieto di tortura e di altri comportamenti inumani o degradanti nelle migrazioni* (Cedam 2013), 83. Cf further LR Kiestra, n 24, 94 ff. On the relationship between the rules on civil jurisdiction and the right of access to justice see A Bucher, 'La competence universelle civile' (2015) 372 *Recueil des cours de l'Académie de droit international de La Haye* 12.

26 PR Beaumont, 'The Jurisprudence of the European Court of Human Rights and of the European Court of Justice on the Hague Convention on International Child Abduction' (2008) 335 *Recueil des cours* 9.

27 See *Pellegrini v Italy*, ECHR:2001:0720JUD003088296; *Wagner et J.M.W.L. v Luxembourg*, ECHR:2007:0628JUD007624001; *Negrepontis-Giannisis v Greece*, ECHR:2011:0503JUD005675908.

28 Respectively Nos 65192/11 and 65941/11.

29 ECHR:2015:0127JUD002535812. The Chamber judgment is currently under review by the Grand Chamber upon request of the Italian Government: see Press Release ECHR 179 (2015).

> déterminée par la loi nationale de l'enfant au moment de la naissance. En l'espèce, compte tenu de ce que l'enfant est issu de gamète de donneurs inconnus, la nationalité de l'enfant n'était pas établie. Dans cette situation, la Cour estime que l'application du droit italien par les juridictions nationales ayant abouti au constat que l'enfant était en état d'abandon ne saurait passer comme étant arbitraire.[30]

While these judgments do not involve issues of EU law, the number of cases in which the latter is of direct relevance is growing almost by the day. Notably, the Brussels IIa Regulation[31] has been at stake in several cases relating to parental responsibility, including those of the *Povse* saga. In this instance, the Court of Justice ruled that, under the latter Regulation, Austrian courts could not deny the enforcement of a return order issued by the Venice Youth Court out of consideration for the child's best interest;[32] thereafter, a ECtHR decision[33] declared the abducting mother's claim under Article 8 ECHR to be manifestly ill-founded, and a more recent judgment[34] assessed that Austria was in breach of Article 8 in respect of the child's father for not executing the return order. The Brussels I Regulation[35] has come into play in *Avotiņš v Latvia*, a case relating to the recognition and enforcement of a Cypriot judgment in Latvia,[36] whereas several other pronouncements touch upon international agreements that are connected to judicial cooperation in civil matters and fall now under the external competence of the EU. This is the case, notably, of the Hague Conventions on international child abduction[37] and on the service of documents abroad,[38]

30 Para. 77. On the ECtHR's previous case law see P Kinsch, '*Harroudj v. France*: Indications from the European Court of Human Rights on the Nature of Choice of Law Rules and on Their Potentially Discriminatory Effect' (2013/2014) 15 *Yearbook of Private International Law* 39.

31 Regulation (EC) No 2201/2003, concerning jurisdiction and the recognition and enforcement of judgments in matrimonial matters and the matters of parental responsibility [2003] OJ L 338/1. The difficulties in the implementation of the Regulation as regards parental responsibility matters have now led the EU Commission to put forward a new proposal for a Regulation on jurisdiction, the recognition and enforcement of decisions in matrimonial matters and the matters of parental responsibility, and on international child abduction (recast), COM (2016) 411 final.

32 Case C-211/10 PPU, *Doris Povse v Mauro Alpago*, EU:C:2010:400.

33 *Sofia Povse and Doris Povse v Austria*, ECHR:2013:0618DEC000389011.

34 *M.A. v Austria*, ECHR:2015:0115JUD000409713.

35 Regulation (EC) No 44/2001 on jurisdiction and the recognition and enforcement of judgments in civil and commercial matters [2001] OJ L 12/1.

36 ECHR:2016:0523JUD001750207, where the Grand Chamber confirmed the finding of non violation by the Fourth Section (ECHR:2014:0225JUD001750207). See further below, n 48 ff and corresponding text.

37 Convention of 25 October 1980 on the civil aspects of international child abduction, on which see, for instance, *Neulinger and Shuruk v Switzerland*, ECHR:2010:0706JUD004161507; *X v Latvia*, ECHR:2013:1126JUD002785309; *Hoholm v Slovakia*, ECHR:2015:0113JUD003563213. See further P Beaumont, n 26.

38 Convention of 15 November 1965 on the service abroad of judicial and extrajudicial documents in civil or commercial matters, on which see *Kaufmann v Italy*, ECHR:2005:0519JUD001402102.

the Lugano Convention on jurisdiction and the recognition and enforcement of judgments in civil and commercial matters,[39] the New York Convention on recovery abroad of maintenance,[40] and bilateral conventions relating to areas which are now governed by EU acts.[41] It may be interesting to take a closer look at how the Strasbourg Court deals with EU law in such contexts.

3. THE TREATMENT OF EU LAW BY THE EUROPEAN COURT OF HUMAN RIGHTS

3.1. POSITIVE INTERACTIONS: SYSTEMIC INTEGRATION AND THE USE OF EU LAW AS AN EXPRESSION OF 'EUROPEAN CONSENSUS'

In most instances relating to judicial cooperation in civil matters, the ECtHR uses EU law as an important tool of systemic interpretation of the Convention, in order to specify the content of positive obligations stemming from the ECHR – notably, from Articles 6 and 8 thereof. In this significant line of cases, EU law is treated exactly as other international rules not linked to EU integration, such as, for instance, the Hague Convention on international child abduction. A recent example of this is *M.A. v Austria*, mentioned above, where the ECtHR considered that

> the Convention must be applied in accordance with the principles of international law, in particular with those relating to the international protection of human rights. … [I]n the area of international child abduction, the positive obligations that Article 8 of the Convention lays on the Contracting [Parties] must be interpreted in the light of the Hague Convention of 25 October 1980 on the Civil Aspects of International Child Abduction … and the Convention on the Rights of the Child of 20 November 1989 …, which attach paramount importance to the best interests of the child … In addition, the Court notes that the present case concerns the return of a child from one EU member State to another. In relations between EU member States the rules on child abduction contained in the Brussels IIa Regulation supplement those already laid down in the Hague Convention. Both instruments are based on the philosophy that in all decisions concerning children, their best interest must be paramount.[42]

---

39 On the Convention of 16 September 1988 see ECtHR, *Matrakas and others v Poland and Greece*, ECHR:2013:1107JUD004726806.

40 Convention of 20 June 1956, in 268 *United Nations Treaty Series*, 3. See again *Matrakas*, n 39.

41 See, for example, *Agache v Romania*, ECHR:2011:1004JUD003503209, on the Treaty between Romania and Hungary regarding judicial assistance in civil, family and criminal cases.

42 *M.A. v Austria*, n 33, paras 108, 112. See also *Ignaccolo-Zenide v Romania*, ECHR:2000:0125JUD003167996, para. 95; *Cavani v Hungary*, ECHR:2014:1028JUD000549313, para. 53.

This position, which indirectly contributes to ensure respect for international obligations other than those stemming from the ECHR, is not limited to the field of private international law; it is an expression of the more general approach of the Strasbourg Court, according to which the Convention should not be read in a vacuum, but rather be interpreted in the light of other applicable principles of international law.[43] Such an approach is often justified through an explicit reference to Article 31(3)(c) of the Vienna Convention on the law of treaties.[44] However, the ECtHR actually goes beyond the terms of the latter provision, and also refers to teleological interpretation under Article 31(1) of the Vienna Convention, when it relies upon EU law, including the Charter of Fundamental Rights, as an important expression of 'European consensus' also in cases concerning States that are not Members of the EU.[45] As the ECtHR itself put it,

> when [the Court] considers the object and purpose of the Convention provisions, it also takes into account the international law background to the legal question before it. Being made up of a set of rules and principles that are accepted by the vast majority of States, the common international or domestic law standards of European States reflect a reality that the Court cannot disregard when it is called upon to clarify the scope of a Convention provision that more conventional means of interpretation have not enabled it to establish with a sufficient degree of certainty ... [I]n searching for common ground among the norms of international law it has never distinguished between sources of law according to whether or not they have been signed or ratified by the respondent State.[46]

3.2. THE MANAGEMENT OF POSSIBLE CONFLICTS

3.2.1. *Supervision of Contracting States' discretionary choices*

This 'positive' use of EU law (as interpreted by the ECJ) by the Strasbourg Court concerns the vast majority of cases; generally speaking, there seems to be no real conflict between the two Courts as to the appropriate level of protection to

---

43 Cf G Gaja, 'Does the European Court of Human Rights use its Stated Methods of Interpretation?', *Studi in onore di Francesco Capotorti* (Giuffré 1999), I, 213, 223 ff; G Cohen-Jonathan and J-F Flauss, 'Cour européenne des droits de l'homme et droit international général' (2005) 51 *Annuaire français de droit international* 675.

44 1155 *United Nations Treaty Series*, 331. Cf C McLachan, 'The Principle of Systemic Integration and Article 31(3)(c) of the Vienna Convention' (2005) 54 *International and Comparative Law Quarterly*, 279. See, for instance, *Nada v Switzerland*, ECHR:2012:0912JUD001059308, para. 169.

45 A Adinolfi, 'La rilevanza esterna della Carta dei diritti fondamentali', in *Scritti in onore di Giuseppe Tesauro* (Editoriale Scientifica 2014), 27, 58, 62; K Dzehtsiarou, *European Consensus and the Legitimacy of the European Court of Human Rights* (Cambridge University Press 2015).

46 *Demir and Bakyara v Turkey*, ECHR:2008:1112JUD003450397, paras 76 f. Cf already *Ignaccolo-Zenide v Romania*, n 40, para. 95; *Genovese v Malta*, ECHR:2011:1011JUD005312409, para. 44.

be afforded to specific individual rights, also in light of what is now provided in Article 6(3) TEU and Articles 52(3) and 53 of the EU Charter of Fundamental Rights. However, as was mentioned above, there are also situations where a difference in approach arises as to when, and by whom, the protection of fundamental rights enshrined in the ECHR should be ensured in cases involving Member States. Specifically as regards mutual trust, the question at issue is the point up to which the principle should be applied whenever there is a risk of affecting fundamental rights in specific cases. At least from the ECtHR's perspective, a distinction should be drawn, in this regard, between situations where EU law leaves Member States some discretion to take into account considerations relating to respect for fundamental rights in implementing the relevant obligations, and situations where automatic respect for the principle of mutual trust is required at the EU level.

The first situation arises, notably, in cases concerning the system of recognition and enforcement of judgments under the Brussels I Regulation (now superseded by Regulation 1215/2012, Brussels Ia),[47] which was at issue in *Avotiņš v Latvia*, mentioned above. In that case, the applicant invoked Article 6(1) ECHR claiming that Latvian national courts should not have ordered enforcement of a civil judgment issued in Cyprus, as he had not been granted the possibility of arranging for a suitable defence in civil proceedings in Cyprus. After analysing Article 34(2) of the Brussels I Regulation[48] and the Court of Justice's relevant case law,[49] the ECtHR's Chamber judgment interpreted the guarantees enshrined in Article 6 ECHR consistently with those elements and rejected the application on the merits. In doing so, it reiterated that the execution by Member States of obligations stemming from EU law fulfils a 'general interest',[50] stressed that the applicant had not even attempted to challenge the judgment issued in Cyprus although he had an opportunity to do so[51] and concluded that the Supreme Court of Latvia had taken into sufficient account the interests of the applicant.[52]

The case is, in this respect, another example of the positive harmonization between the EU legal order and the ECHR discussed above. Yet, a 'non-viola-

---

47 Regulation (EU) No 1215/2012 on jurisdiction and the recognition and enforcement of judgments in civil and commercial matters [2012] OJ L 351/1.

48 See now Article 45(1)(b) of Regulation 1215/2012.

49 *Avotiņš v Latvia*, n 36 (Chamber), paras 26 ff., 50.

50 Ibid, para. 49. The Grand Chamber also considered 'the creation of an area of freedom, security and justice in Europe, and the adoption of the means necessary to achieve it, to be wholly legitimate in principle from the standpoint of the Convention' (para. 113).

51 Ibid, para. 51: 'The Court observes that, indeed, the applicant did not even attempt any kind of remedy against the Limassol District Court judgment of 24 May 2004. The Court is not convinced by the reasons advanced by the applicant to justify that omission'.

52 Ibid, para. 52. The Grand Chamber judgment, para. 121, adopted a partly different stance on this issue.

tion' outcome could not be taken for granted, also in light of the standards set by previous case law of the ECtHR with regard to the compatibility of recognition and enforcement of foreign judgments with Article 6 ECHR.[53] The Chamber reached its conclusions in *Avotiņš* by relying on the 'specific circumstances of the case';[54] furthermore, it observed that the relationship between Article 6 ECHR and the Brussels I Regulation is 'an issue of importance at both [the] domestic and European level';[55] both the Chamber and the Grand Chamber expressly applied the presumption of 'equivalent protection' that is set out in *Bosphorus*.[56] Moreover, in the Chamber phase, Judges Ziemele, Bianku and De Gaetano considered, contrary to the majority, that the treatment by Latvian courts of the applicant's contention that he had not been properly notified of the Cypriot judgment was not compatible with Article 6 ECHR:

> The answer that the applicant's arguments, which go to the very essence of the issue before the Latvian courts, have no importance is clearly contrary to Article 6 guarantees. It should have been for the domestic courts to examine and give reasons why, for example, the exception relied on could not be maintained on the facts of the case. There probably were good reasons, but we do not know what they were.[57]

It should be emphasised that the individual judges did not perceive any conflict between EU law and the ECHR in this instance; they rather hinted at the fact that national courts may not have applied EU law correctly.[58] The separate opinion stressed that

> the applicable EU law does not provide for blind automaticity as concerns the execution of judgments.[59]

---

53 See notably *Pellegrini v Italy*, n 27, identifying an obligation upon the State of enforcement to review the compatibility of foreign proceedings with Article 6 guarantees – in apparent contrast with the 'flagrant denial of justice' test applied in *Drozd and Janusek v France and Spain*, ECHR:1992:0626JUD001274787, para. 110. According to JJ Fawcett, 'Article 6(1)', n 24, 5, '[i]t is unclear whether *Pellegrini* applies where the judgment was granted in a ECHR State (which would include all the EC Member States), it is at least arguable that it does so'. Cf further P Kinsch, 'Droits de l'homme', n 23, 305; D Spielmann, 'La reconnaissance et l'exécution des décisions judiciaires étrangères et les exigences de la Convention européenne des droits de l'homme – Un essai de synthèse' (2011) 88 *Revue trimestrielle des droits de l'homme* 761, 765 ff.

54 *Avotiņš v Latvia*, n 36, para. 52.

55 Ibid, para. 37.

56 Ibid, para. 47; cf para. 112 of the Grand Chamber judgment. On *Bosphorus* see below, n 83 and corresponding text.

57 Ibid, separate opinion of Judges Ziemele, Bianku and De Gaetano, paras 4-5.

58 This was actually the applicant's contention: see ibid, judgment, para. 47.

59 Ibid, separate opinion of Judges Ziemele, Bianku and De Gaetano. Regulation 1215/2012 does not change much in this respect, notwithstanding the abolishment of the *exequatur* procedure:

Furthermore, it expressed concern that the judgment could amount to upholding a violation of EU law:

> Additionally, we are not sure that the implicit approval of the manner in which the Latvian Supreme Court applied the EU law is in fact consistent with EU law. While the Court is not competent to interpret EU law, we submit that it should not implicitly approve of domestic practices that may go against EU law. This is a new situation for the Court which merits very serious further reflection.

The opinion of the Grand Chamber on these issues, which is not identical, is discussed below. However, it emerges clearly from these and other pronouncements of the ECtHR, specifically where the principle of mutual trust is concerned, that whenever the requirements set out by EU law do leave some discretion to Member States to take into account considerations relating to human rights (or even oblige them to do so, as is the case with Article 34(2) Brussels I Regulation) and it is possible for a State to comply with both sets of obligations simultaneously, the ECtHR exercises full legal control over implementation of the guarantees set out in the ECHR. From the perspective of the ECHR, no 'conflict between systems' arises: the Contracting State takes full responsibility for its discretionary choices and is bound to take a course that harmonizes its different obligations. As the Strasbourg Court put it in *Nada*,

> When creating new international obligations, States are assumed not to derogate from their previous obligations. Where a number of apparently contradictory instruments are simultaneously applicable, international case-law and academic opinion endeavour to construe them in such a way as to coordinate their effects and avoid any opposition between them. Two diverging commitments must therefore be harmonised as far as possible so that they produce effects that are fully in accordance with existing law.[60]

The task of harmonizing apparently conflicting provisions is the Court's, provided that it is able to perform its task in full, namely 'to ensure the observance of the engagements undertaken by the High Contracting Parties' to the

---

see F Salerno, *Giurisdizione ed efficacia delle decisioni straniere nel Regolamento n. 1215/2012 (rifusione)* (4th ed, Cedam 2015), 347 ff.

60 *Nada v Switzerland*, n 44, para. 170. Difficulties in this respect have arisen with reference to UN Security Council resolutions, due to their special status under Article 103 UN Charter. However, according to the ECtHR, 'in the event of any ambiguity in the terms of a UN Security Council resolution, the Court must … choose the interpretation which is most in harmony with the requirements of the Convention and which avoids any conflict of obligations': *Al-Dulimi and Montana Managment inc. v Switzerland*, ECHR:2016:0621JUD000580908, para. 140.

Convention.[61] However, this obligation lies also and primarily with the ECHR Contracting Parties.

The situation may not be so simple from the perspective of the Court of Justice, as the parallel with the approach of the ECtHR to the so-called 'Dublin' system[62] shows. Under this system, which was first established under the Dublin Convention[63] and involves EU Member States and other countries,[64] the responsibility for examining requests of international protection is, in principle, allocated to only one State. Asylum seekers that happen to be in other States should hence be transferred to the State that is identified as being responsible in each case. However, participating States retain a significant measure of discretion thanks to the so-called 'sovereignty clause', which allows the State where the asylum seeker is located to take responsibility for examining his or her application.[65] As in the case of EU judicial cooperation in civil matters, the

---

61 *X v Latvia*, n 37, para. 94.

62 On this parallel, see M Weller, 'Mutual Trust', n 19.

63 Convention determining the State responsible for examining applications for asylum lodged in one of the Member States of the European Communities, signed in Dublin on 15 June 1990 [1997] OJ C 254/1. See also Regulation 343/2003/EC establishing the criteria and mechanisms for determining the Member State responsible for examining an asylum application lodged in one of the Member States by a third-country national [2003] OJ L 50/1, so-called 'Dublin II' Regulation; Regulation (EU) No 604/2013 establishing the criteria and mechanisms for determining the Member State responsible for examining an application for international protection lodged in one of the Member States by a third-country national or a stateless person [2013] OJ L 180/31 ('Dublin III' Regulation). A further amendment proposal was submitted by the Commission as regards determining the Member State responsible for examining the application for international protection of unaccompanied minors with no family member, sibling or relative legally present in a Member State (COM (2014) 382 final); more recently, the Commission also proposed a comprehensive reform in its Communication to the European Parliament and the Council, *Towards a Reform of the Common European Asylum System and Enhancing Legal Avenues to Europe* (COM (2016) 197 final).

64 Norway, Iceland, Switzerland and Liechtenstein: cf, respectively, Decision 2001/258 concerning the conclusion of an Agreement between the European Community and the Republic of Iceland and the Kingdom of Norway concerning the criteria and mechanisms for establishing the State responsible for examining a request for asylum lodged in a Member State or Iceland or Norway [2001] OJ L 93/38; 2008/147 on the conclusion on behalf of the European Community of the Agreement between the European Community and the Swiss Confederation concerning the criteria and mechanisms for establishing the State responsible for examining a request for asylum lodged in a Member State or in Switzerland [2008] OJ 53/3; Decision 2011/351 on the conclusion of a Protocol between the European Community, the Swiss Confederation and the Principality of Liechtenstein on the accession of the Principality of Liechtenstein to the Agreement between the European Community and the Swiss Confederation concerning the criteria and mechanisms for establishing the State responsible for examining a request for asylum lodged in a Member State or in Switzerland [2011] OJ L 160/37. Denmark is also participating in the Dublin system: see Council Decision 2006/188 on the conclusion of the Agreement between the European Community and the Kingdom of Denmark extending to Denmark the provisions of Regulation No 343/2003 and Regulation (EC) No 2725/2000 concerning the establishment of Eurodac for the comparison of fingerprints for the effective application of the Dublin Convention [2006] OJ L 66/37.

65 See Article 3(4) Dublin Convention; Article 3(2) Regulation No 343/2003; Article 17 Regulation No 604/2013.

Dublin system is based on the principle of mutual trust and on a presumption of compliance with fundamental rights by every participating State. However, the practical implementation of this presumption has proven problematic and, together with other factors, is at the origin of structural dysfunctions which were apparent even before the current refugee crisis.[66]

Claims that the Dublin system may affect fundamental rights, notably Article 3 ECHR, have been under scrutiny by the Strasbourg Court a number of times. The ECtHR decision in *K.R.S. v United Kingdom* affirmed the existence of a presumption that fundamental rights enshrined in the Convention would be respected in the recipient State;[67] however, in *M.S.S. v Belgium and Greece* the Grand Chamber of the Strasbourg Court determined that Belgium had breached Article 3 ECHR by expelling the applicant to Greece despite being aware of the systemic deficiencies of the asylum system in Greece at that time.[68] The Grand Chamber was only slightly more lenient in assessing the Italian asylum seekers' reception system in *Tarakhel v Switzerland*.[69]

The Court of Justice reacted to *K.R.S.* by confirming, in *N.S.*, that the principle of mutual trust is not absolute and the presumption of compliance by other Member States with EU law, particularly with fundamental rights, is rebuttable. More specifically,

> if there are substantial grounds for believing that there are systemic flaws in the asylum procedure and reception conditions for asylum applicants in the Member State responsible, resulting in inhuman or degrading treatment, within the meaning of Article 4 of the Charter, of asylum seekers transferred to the territory of that Member State, the transfer would be incompatible with that provision.[70]

However, under the ECHR risks of infringements of Article 3 rights must be avoided in individual cases even when no 'systemic flaw' appears to exist in

---

66 See only C Favilli, 'Reciproca fiducia, mutuo riconoscimento e libertà di circolazione di rifugiati e richiedenti asilo nell'Unione europea' (2015) 98 *Rivista di diritto internazionale* 701; V Mitsilegas, n 19, 126 ff.

67 ECHR:2008:1202DEC003273308. See already *T.I. v United Kingdom*, ECHR:2000:0307DEC004384498, where the ECtHR showed its readiness to pursue a full review of compatibility of a transfer made on the basis of the Dublin Convention with Article 3 ECHR. The application was considered to be manifestly ill-founded because of the assurances offered by Germany that the applicant would not be expelled to Sri Lanka.

68 ECHR:2011:0121JUD003069609, especially paras 342 ff.

69 Application No 29217/12, where the Court held that there would be a violation of Article 3 ECHR if the applicants, a family with young children, 'were to be returned to Italy without the Swiss authorities having first obtained individual guarantees from the Italian authorities that the applicants would be taken charge of in a manner adapted to the age of the children and that the family would be kept together' (para. 2 of the operative part). Cf also *Sharifi and others v Italy and Greece*, ECHR:2014:1021JUD001664309.

70 C-411/10 and C-493/10, *N.S. v. Secretary of State for the Home Department v Refugee Applications Commissioner*, EU:C:2011:865, para. 86. See also para. 94.

the recipient State. As the Supreme Court of the United Kingdom pointed out, transfers under the Dublin system should not take place in this kind of situation[71] – whereas systemic flaws may only be of relevance in terms of evidence that there is a risk connected to the transfer.[72] While the Supreme Court suggests a reading of *N.S.* in line with the obligations stemming from the ECHR, even a difference of position on this particular issue would not amount to an actual, positive conflict between the ECHR an EU law: although there would be no obligation, under *N.S.*, to rely on the alternative criteria set out in the Dublin Regulation,[73] Member States which cannot carry out the transfers would still be entitled to examine the asylum applications themselves.[74] From the ECtHR's perspective, those States are therefore fully responsible under the Convention if they choose not to rely on this discretionary power.

On the other hand, Opinion 2/13 shows that, from the perspective of the Court of Justice, this approach of the ECtHR poses a difficulty, as EU law – and more specifically the principle of mutual trust – cannot display its full effects.[75]

3.2.2. The Bosphorus *principle*

The situation discussed above, as seen from Luxembourg, would actually seem to be more problematic than those where EU law requires unconditional respect for the principle of mutual trust; this is due to the different approach adopted by the Strasbourg Court in the latter context.

EU legislation in the field of judicial cooperation, both in criminal matters (as was the case in *Melloni*), and in civil matters, often prescribes automatic implementation of the principle of mutual trust, although states still have broad discretion in setting forth the procedural aspects for that implementation.[76] As regards judicial cooperation in civil matters, discussion has focused especially on issues of parental responsibility and return orders under Regulation Brussels

---

71 *R (on the application of EM (Eritrea)) (Appellant) v Secretary of State for the Home Department (Respondent)* [2014] UKSC 12, per Lord Kerr, para. 37: 'A person applying for asylum in a Member State might be able to establish conclusively that he would be at substantial risk of being treated in a manner incompatible with his fundamental rights if returned to a listed country but because that risk did not arise from so-called systemic deficiencies it could not operate to prevent his enforced return to that country. That would be, to say the least, a remarkable conclusion'.

72 Ibid., para. 57: 'As it happened, in both those cases the existence of systemic deficiencies which had been extensively reported on by, among others, UNHCR was the means by which the transferring states were deemed to have that knowledge but there is nothing in the reasoning of CJEU nor is there, I believe, any reason in logic to suggest that, if the transferring state acquires the same knowledge through a different medium, that it should not have the same effect'. Compare Case C-394/07, *Gambazzi v Daimler Chrysler*, EU:C:2009:219.

73 Cf again *N.S.*, n 70, para. 95.

74 Cf ibid, para 96.

75 See again G Gaja, n 13.

76 See F Salerno, 'Cooperazione giudiziaria in materia civile', in G Strozzi (ed), *Diritto dell'Unione europea – Parte speciale* (4th ed, Giappichelli 2015), 496.

IIa.[77] In cases of this kind, the difficulty is making the automaticity of enforcement compatible with full respect of fundamental rights and, more specifically, with the principle of the 'best interest of the child'. As noted above, in *Povse* the Court of Justice held that

> Enforcement of a certified judgment cannot be refused in the Member State of enforcement because, as a result of a subsequent change of circumstances, it might be seriously detrimental to the best interests of the child. Such a change must be pleaded before the court which has jurisdiction in the Member State of origin, which should also hear any application to suspend enforcement of its judgment.[78]

In *Aguirre Zarraga*, the Court of Justice reiterated:

> In circumstances such as those of the main proceedings, the court with jurisdiction in the Member State of enforcement cannot oppose the enforcement of a certified judgment, ordering the return of a child who has been wrongfully removed, on the ground that the court of the Member State of origin which handed down that judgment may have infringed Article 42 [of the Brussels IIa Regulation], interpreted in accordance with Article 24 of the Charter of Fundamental Rights of the European Union, since *the assessment of whether there is such an infringement falls exclusively within the jurisdiction of the courts of the Member State of origin*.[79]

The same approach actually also characterizes more 'traditional' aspects of judicial cooperation in civil matters: for instance, in *Gasser* the ECJ interpreted what was then Article 21 of the Brussels Convention, on *lis pendens*, as a procedural rule based solely on the chronological order in which the courts involved are seised. In the ECJ's words,

> the Brussels Convention is necessarily based on the trust which the Contracting States accord to each other's legal systems and judicial institutions. It is that mutual trust which has enabled a compulsory system of jurisdiction to be established, which all the courts within the purview of the Convention are required to respect, and as a corollary the waiver by those States of the right to apply their internal rules on recognition and enforcement of foreign judgments in favour of a simplified mechanism for the recognition and enforcement of judgments

77 See H Muir Watt, 'Abolition of Exequatur and Human Rights', <http://conflictoflaws.net/2013/muir-watt-on-povse/>; P Beaumont, K Trimmings, L Walker and J Holliday, 'Child Abduction: Recent Jurisprudence of the European Court of Human Rights' (2015) 64 *International and Comparative Law Quarterly* 39.

78 *Povse*, n 32, para. 4 of the operative part.

79 Case C-491/10 PPU, *Aguirre Zarraga v Pelz*, EU:C:2010:828, operative part (emphasis added).

> ... In view of the foregoing, ... Article 21 of the Brussels Convention must be interpreted as meaning that it cannot be derogated from where, in general, the duration of proceedings before the courts of the Contracting State in which the court first seised is established is excessively long.[80]

Apparently, no room is left for the judge second seised to retain jurisdiction, even when systemic infringements of the right to a fair trial in the State of the judge first seised have emerged. It is only the State of origin that bears responsibility for ensuring full respect for fundamental rights, whereas the State of enforcement may not exercise any form of control in this regard.

Opinion 2/13 seems to imply that, as a consequence of this, there should be no possibility for the ECtHR to supervise the behaviour of the State of enforcement either, whereas no problem would seem to arise from an exercise of jurisdiction by the Strasbourg Court against the State that is competent to examine the case under EU law, as in *Šneersone and Kampanella v Italy*.[81]

As regards the Strasbourg Court, its *Povse* decision shows that the ECJ's approach is not perceived as *per se* problematic[82] and does not hinder the applicability of the *Bosphorus* 'equivalent protection' test, which addresses direct conflicts between the ECHR and EU law. According to this approach,

> the protection of fundamental rights afforded by the European Union is in principle equivalent to that of the Convention system as regards both the substantive guarantees offered and the mechanisms controlling their observance.[83]

This presumption of compliance applies whenever national authorities merely implement legal obligations flowing from EU law, without exercising any discretion.[84] However,

> any such presumption can be rebutted if, in the circumstances of a particular case, it is considered that the protection of Convention rights was manifestly deficient. In such cases, the interest of international cooperation would be outweighed by the Convention's role as a 'constitutional instrument of European public order' in the field of human rights.[85]

---

80 Case C-116/02, *Erich Gasser GmbH v MISAT Srl*, EU:C:2003:657, paras 72-73.

81 ECHR:2011:0712JUD001473709. Cf also *Manic v Lithuania*, ECHR:2015:0113JUD004660011. The Court of Justice recently modified this stance in Joined Cases C-404/15 and C-659/15 PPU, *Aranyosi and Caldararu*, EU:C:2016:198, upon pressure from national jurisdictions. See further below, n 105 and corresponding text.

82 *Povse v Austria*, n 33, paras 86-87.

83 *Bosphorus Hava Yollari Turizm ve Ticaret Anonim Şirketi v Ireland*, ECHR:2005:0630JUD004503698.

84 *Povse v Austria*, n 33, para. 78; see also *Bosphorus*, n 83, para. 156.

85 Ibid.

The finding, which was reached unanimously by the Grand Chamber,[86] has been read both as an expression of (possibly excessive) comity[87] and as an attempt to push for a 'forced accession' to the ECHR.[88] Although the fact that the UN sanction system was involved helps to explain this stance,[89] the Grand Chamber's position is in line with the case law of the European Commission of Human Rights on the issue;[90] after *Bosphorus*, the ECtHR has shown willingness to 'reduce the intensity of its supervisory role'[91] in a number of cases that had nothing to do with the United Nations.[92]

Moreover, in *Michaud* the Strasbourg Court made clear that the principle of equivalent protection applies only when the 'full potential of the relevant international machinery for supervising fundamental rights ... [has] been deployed'[93] – that is, provided that the Court of Justice has previously been asked to rule on the issue, whenever possible under EU law.[94] This sort of 'prior involvement' mechanism adds a further element of judicial comity vis-à-vis the Court of Justice.[95] In light of Opinion 2/13, this solution is apparently more satisfactory in the view of the Court of Justice, in terms of safeguarding the autonomy of the EU legal order, than the option of accession – which would have led to the ECtHR exercising full supervision over the compatibility of EU law

---

86 See, however, the joint concurring opinion of Judges Rozakis, Tulkens, Traja, Botoucharova, Zagrebelsky and Garlicki, emphasising the risks of double standards and that 'the Union has not yet acceded to the European Convention on Human Rights and that full protection does not yet exist at European level'. Cf also the concurring opinion of Judge Ress. On the judgment and its background see O De Schutter, 'Bosphorus Post-Accession: Redefining the Relationships between the European Court of Human Rights and the Parties to the Convention', in V Kosta, N Skoutaris, VP Tzevelekos (eds), *The EU Accession to the ECHR* (Hart 2014), 177.

87 For a criticism see G Gaja, 'The Review by the European Court of Human Rights of the Member States' Acts Implementing European Union Law. "Solange" Yet Again?' in P-M Dupuy et al (eds), *Common Values in International Law: Essays in Honour of Christian Tomuschat* (Norbert Paul Engel 2006), 517.

88 G Cohen-Jonathan and J-F Flauss, n 44, 687.

89 VP Tzevelekos, n 12, fn 10 and corresponding text.

90 *M. & Co. v the Federal Republic of Germany*, ECHR:1990:0209DEC001325887.

91 *Michaud v France*, ECHR:2012:1206JUD001232311, para. 104.

92 See O De Schutter, n 86, 178 ff., also as regards the relationship between the ECHR and obligations stemming from participation in international organizations other than the EU.

93 Ibid, para. 115; compare *Povse*, n 33, para. 83.

94 Precisely the fact that the French courts had not asked for a preliminary ruling by the Court of Justice led the Strasbourg Court not to apply the presumption of equivalent protection in *Michaud*, n 87: see para. 115. Cf *Povse*, n 33, para. 83. Cf further the Grand Chamber judgment in *Avotiņš*, para. 111, suggesting that there is an onus on applicants to raise the issue in their defences before national courts.

95 The 'prior involvement' mechanism is one of the aspects of the Draft Accession Agreement that the Court of Justice deemed to be critical: see 'Joint Communication by Presidents Costa and Skouris', 17 January 2011, para. 2, <http://www.echr.coe.int/Documents/UE_Communication_Costa_Skouris_ENG.pdf>. See also R Baratta, 'Accession of the EU to the ECHR: The Rationale for the ECJ's Prior Involvement Mechanism' (2013) 50 *Common Market Law Review* 1305.

with the Convention.[96] Some have argued that Opinion 2/13 should induce the ECtHR to review its position on the relationship between the European Convention and the EU legal order.[97] The Grand Chamber's ruling in *Avotiņš* shows, on the contrary, that the ECtHR will not abandon its 'spirit of complementarity'. The Grand Chamber, however, did emphasise that the principle of mutual trust should not be applied 'automatically and mechanically ... to the detriment of fundamental rights' and highlighted that a 'literal and automatic application' of EU law by national courts

> could in theory lead to a finding that the protection afforded was manifestly deficient such that the presumption of equivalent protection of the rights of the defence guaranteed by Article 6 § 1 is rebutted.[98]

4. CONCLUSIONS

The ECtHR usually adopts a positive attitude towards EU law and exercises self-restraint in its relationship with the ECJ. In most situations, it relies on EU law as a tool for specifying the positive obligations stemming from the ECHR; moreover, it uses great caution in assessing possible conflicts between the two legal systems. In this context, any infringement of the Convention has been ascribed to discretionary choices of Member States – for instance, as regards the decision not to rely on a 'sovereignty clause' in order to take responsibility for asylum applications, as in *M.S.S.*, or because national courts did not avail themselves of the possibility to seek a ruling by the ECJ on the interpretation of obligations stemming from EU law, as in *Michaud*. Direct conflicts between legal rules are addressed by relying on the 'equivalent protection' principle set out in *Bosphorus*, which can be rebutted only in case of a 'manifestly deficient' protection of Convention Rights. Nonetheless, Opinion 2/13 shows that the relationship between the EU legal system and the ECHR remains problematic. Neither Article 6(2) TEU[99] nor the formal encouragement to resume negotiations by the Brussels Conference[100] can avoid the impression that formal accession of the EU

---

96 G Gaja, n 87; FG Jacobs, 'The Lisbon Treaty and the Court of Justice', in A Biondi, P Eeckhout and S Ripley (eds), *EU Law after Lisbon* (Oxford University Press 2012), 205. Cf however O De Schutter, n 86, 182 ff., and C Timmermans, 'Some Personal Comments on the Accession of the EU to the ECHR', in V Kosta, N Skoutaris, VP Tzevelekos (eds), n 86, 333, 337.

97 The AIRE Centre maintained this position in *Avotiņš*, n 36: see the Grand Chamber judgment, para. 95.

98 Ibid, paras 116, 121.

99 On the interpretation of Article 6(2) see R Baratta, n 95, 1305, fn 1 and corresponding text.

100 See High-level Conference on the 'Implementation of the European Convention on Human Rights, our shared responsibility', Brussels Declaration of 27 March 2015, <http://www.coe.int/t/dghl/monitoring/execution/Source/Documents/Declaration_Bruxelles_EN.pdf>, para. 15,

to the ECHR will not be possible anytime soon. The 'disconnection clause' that the ECJ has sought would appear to be highly problematic as regards both the inter-State relationships with non-EU Contracting Parties and in terms of respect of the individual rights that the ECHR protects;[101] at the same time, the conclusion of a 'Notwithstanding Protocol'[102] does not seem to be attainable either.

While avoiding accession leaves the ECJ more scope for manoeuvre in upholding the autonomy of the EU legal order and, specifically, the principle of mutual trust, after Opinion 2/13 the ECtHR may be less inclined to comity whenever issues involving EU law are at stake. Firstly, it is unlikely that it will renounce to exercising full control of compatibility with the ECHR in situations where EU Member States retain some discretion under EU law, notwithstanding the adverse impact this control may have on the principle of mutual trust. Secondly, although *Avotiņš* confirms that the *Bosphorus* principle as such will not be set aside, the Strasbourg Court may become stricter in assessing the applicability of the proviso whereby the presumption of equivalent protection is rebutted if a manifest infringement of Convention rights appears to be at stake. As noted above, this situation could also arise in the absence of a pattern of 'systemic flaws' in the protection of those rights in the Member State that, according to EU law, is competent to address a given case. Moreover, a problem of systemic failure could arise, also in the context of judicial cooperation in civil matters. Italy's difficulties in respecting the right to a hearing 'within a reasonable time' under Article 6(1) ECHR, which was the issue addressed in *Gasser*, comes to mind. Should a similar case be brought before the Strasbourg Court, there seems to be no reason why its approach would change, as compared to the 'Dublin' cases, only because Article 6 ECHR is at stake, rather than Article 3.

Even if there is no shift in the attitude of the ECtHR towards the EU legal order, the present situation leads to potential uncertainties for Member States (and, specifically, national courts). As Baratta notes,

> EU States may not like being held (jointly or individually) liable for conduct over which, in some cases at least, they exercised no effective or factual control or, more generally, for an act that does not strictly relate to their jurisdiction within the meaning of Article 1 ECHR.[103]

A second, and perhaps more serious difficulty, is that EU Member States are left alone in bearing the risk that their duty of 'double loyalty' entails, and still

where the Conference 'Reaffirms the importance of the accession of the European Union to the Convention and encourages the finalisation of the process at the earliest opportunity'.

101 See O De Schutter and F Tulkens, n 13.

102 See LFM Besselink, 'Acceding to the ECHR notwithstanding the Court of Justice Opinion 2/13', Verfassungsblog, 23 December 2014 <http://www.verfassungsblog.de>.

103 R Baratta, n 95, 1309.

face the dilemma of choosing whether to respect the European Convention of Human Rights or EU law (notably, the principle of mutual trust). The problem does not change much as regards EU external relations in the field of private international law, as the principle of mutual trust is clearly at the basis of most forms of cooperation between the EU and third countries in this field[104] – although, admittedly, it is not as central as in intra-EU relations and elements of discretion are usually stronger.

Now that the goal of accession is set aside, at least for the time being, the risk of such a conflict between treaty obligations may discourage further integration, or at least fully uniform rules, at the EU level. Member States will be inclined to keep broad discretion in enacting EU legislation in this area so as to be able to accommodate the requirements stemming from the European Convention without impairing the functioning of EU law. Domestic courts and other national authorities may seek to justify a failure to implement EU law by invoking the need to respect the ECHR. This is not necessarily likely to happen frequently (especially in countries where EU law enjoys higher status than the ECHR); moreover, domestic courts – notably constitutional courts due to their specific mandates – rely on national constitutions, rather than on the ECHR, when addressing possible conflicts between EU law and fundamental rights. This was actually the case of the ruling of the German Constitutional Court[105] that has led the Court of Justice to modify its approach to the relationship between mutual trust and fundamental rights in *Aranyosi*. Albeit with some *caveats*, the Court of justice has come to accept that an European arrest warrant may not be executed if there are substantial grounds to believe that individual concerned could be subject to treatments contrary to Article 4 of the EU Charter of fundamental rights.[106] While this finding has a bearing on the whole Area of Freedom, Security and Justice and ultimately implies an alignment of the Court of Justice with the perspective of the ECtHR, Opinion 2/13 has come at a time where judicial comity is growingly replaced by confrontation also in the relationship between national and international courts.[107] It is difficult to see how, in this context, the Opinion could contribute to enhancing the principle of mutual trust in the EU legal order.

---

104 As the Swiss Government observed in *Neulinger*, n 37, para. 121, 'the Hague Convention system [is] based on mutual confidence between the States Parties to that instrument and that if a State should fail to comply with its assurances, it would run the risk that the other States might not cooperate with it in the fashion envisaged'.

105 Order 2 BvR 2735/14 of 15 December 2015, available at <www.bundesverfassungsgericht.de>, especially para. 125.

106 *Aranyosi*, n 81, operative part.

107 Cf, for instance, Italian Constitutional Court, judgment No 238/2014, *Gazzetta Ufficiale della Repubblica Italiana*, Prima Serie Speciale, No 45, of 29 October 2014 (unofficial English translation available at <www.cortecostituzionale.it>.

PART II

OPINION 1/13 AND ITS IMPLICATIONS

A CRITICAL ANALYSIS OF THE JUDICIAL ACTIVISM OF THE COURT OF JUSTICE OF THE EUROPEAN UNION IN OPINION 1/13

Paul BEAUMONT *
University of Aberdeen

1. INTRODUCTION

On 14 October 2014 the Grand Chamber of the Court of Justice of the European Union (CJEU) decided that the EU has exclusive competence to accept the accession of a non-EU State to the Hague Convention on the Civil Aspects of International Child Abduction of 25 October 1980. The Court's judgment coincides with the views of AG Jääskinen, the Commission, the European Parliament and the Italian Government. The French, Greek and Polish Governments argued before the Court that the EU has no external competence in this matter whilst sixteen Governments (Austria, Belgium, Cyprus, Czech Republic, Estonia, Finland, Germany, Ireland, Latvia, Lithuania, Portugal, Romania, Slovakia, Spain, Sweden and United Kingdom) and the Council argued that the EU does not have exclusive external competence in this matter.

Given the weight of advice to the Court against exclusive external competence it is reasonable to expect a carefully reasoned opinion from the Court justifying its 'minority' decision. Sadly the Court fails to meet this legitimate expectation. On the question of the existence of EU competence the Court devotes two paragraphs of its Opinion.[1] The Court does not properly set out the criteria for external competence found in Article 216 TFEU and it does not clarify under which aspect of Article 216(1) TFEU the competence arises. It does not set out, far less address, the arguments of France, Greece and Poland as to why the EU has no external competence. In relation to exclusive external com-

* The author is grateful for the helpful comments of Professor Joanne Scott and Dr Justin Borg Barthet on an earlier version of this paper. The author is solely responsible for the final content.

1 Opinion 1/13, EU:C:2014:2303, paras 67-68.

petence the Court does at least set out the three criteria in Article 3(2) TFEU and makes it clear that the case turns on the third criterion: whether the acceptance of third State accessions to the Hague Child Abduction Convention 'may affect common rules [of EU law] or alter their scope'.[2] However, the Court fails to give reasons as to why its pre-Lisbon case law on 'largely covered area' and 'foreseeable future developments' is still relevant to determining this third criteria now that the Treaty (since Lisbon) defines exclusive external competence rather than the matter being one that had purely and simply been created by the Court through its case law. The Court merely asserts that its earlier case law is still relevant.[3] The continued relevance of these features of the Court's case law which are not codified in the TFEU is, in a technical sense, 'unjustified' by the Court. Likewise in relation to the question of whether the Brussels IIa rules may be affected by the Member States declaring their acceptance of the accession of third States to the Child Abduction Convention the Court indulges in mere assertion that this is likely to happen with no evidence presented of how such acceptance of the accession of third States could possibly 'affect' the application of Brussels IIa or alter its scope.[4] This is despite the Court's continued rhetorical flourish (taken over from Opinion 1/03) that 'since the EU has only conferred powers, any competence, especially where it is exclusive, must have its basis in conclusions drawn from a comprehensive and detailed analysis of the relationship between the envisaged international agreement and the EU law in force.'[5]

2. BACKGROUND TO OPINION 1/13

The Brussels IIa Regulation entered into force on 1 August 2004. In practice it made it a prerequisite of its application that EU Member States be a party to the Hague Child Abduction Convention and therefore that Convention became part of the EU *acquis*. However, it did not incorporate the Convention into EU law in any classical sense of the word 'incorporate'. Instead it assumed the application of the Convention between EU Member States and added some new interpretations of existing Hague Convention provisions (e.g. in relation to the Article 13 exceptions strengthening the right of a child to be heard and regulating how the grave risk of harm exception should be applied) for such intra-EU cases. Recital 17 says that: 'the Hague Convention of 25 October 1980 would continue to apply as complemented by the provisions of this Regulation, in particular Article 11.' So even for intra-EU cases the Regulation does not cre-

2 Ibid, para. 70.
3 Ibid, paras 73 and 74.
4 Ibid, paras 85-89.
5 Ibid, para. 74. See Opinion 1/03, EU:C:2006:81, para. 124.

ate a complete system for child abduction cases but rather presumes that all EU Member States will be parties to the Convention and that the Regulation creates some complementary additional provisions for intra-EU child abduction cases. For the purposes of external competence the key sense in which Brussels IIa did not incorporate the Convention into EU law is that the Regulation does not touch at all upon the application of the Convention between EU Member States and Contracting States to the Convention which are not Member States of the EU. The intra-EU scope of Brussels IIa as regards child abduction cases is key to understanding why the vast majority of EU Member States did not think it created exclusive external competence in relation to Hague Convention cases between EU and non-EU States. Even though the Regulation entered into force on 1 August 2004 and the Commission argued before the Court that the EU had exclusive external competence to accept the accession to the Convention of third States from that date on, the Commission allowed the Member States to deposit a total of more than 300 declarations of acceptance of accession before making its proposals on 21 December 2011 for the EU to accept the accession of 8 third States.[6] When the Council failed to adopt the Commission proposals in relation to the 8 third States the Commission, on 21 June 2013, requested an opinion of the Court pursuant to Article 218(11) TFEU on whether the EU has exclusive competence to accept the accession of a non-Union country to the Hague Abduction Convention.[7]

3. BACKGROUND TO JUDICIAL ACTIVISM

Judicial activism by the Court has been criticised historically by a number of academics on the basis that the Court sometimes departs from an interpretation of the legal text which is consistent with the intention of the drafters or even with a reasonable purposive interpretation of the text.[8] Recently the literature

---

6 See Opinion 1/13, n 1, para. 52. It is not really a question of accepting the accession of third States to the Hague Convention. Article 38 of the Convention makes it clear that any State that was not a member of the Hague Conference at the time of its Fourteenth Session (October 1980) may accede to the Convention. However, if the Convention is to have any effect between an acceding State and an existing Contracting State then the existing Contracting State must declare their acceptance of the accession (see Article 38(4) and (5)).

7 For a useful overview of the development of EU external competence by the CJEU and of the significant Treaty changes on external competence made by the Lisbon Treaty see M Cremona, 'External Relations and External Competence of the European Union: The Emergence of an Integrated Policy', in P Craig and G de Búrca (eds), *The Evolution of EU Law* (2nd ed, Oxford University Press 2011), 217.

8 See H Rasmussen, *On Law and Policy in the European Court of Justice. A Comparative Study in Judicial Policy-Making* (Martinus Nijhoff 1986), and *European Court of Justice* (GadJura 1998); T Hartley, *Constitutional Problems of the European Union* (Hart 1999); S Weatherill and P Beaumont, *EU Law* (Penguin 1999), 193-201.

on this topic has expanded again with critiques of the Court exceeding its role as an institutional actor in the EU in the development of EU law because it does not give sufficient respect to the roles of the other institutional actors in the EU when interpreting the Treaties or EU legislation.[9] Others have highlighted concerns with the extent to which the CJEU is creating case law that may be ignored by national courts and to prevent this have suggested that the Court should pay more attention to young European Union law academics who are pro-European Union but feel the need to critique the Court when it seems to be going too far.[10] One very prominent pro-European Union law academic, Joseph Weiler, has warned the CJEU in surprisingly, but nonetheless welcome, cogent terms about the paucity of the reasoning in a number of important judgments and the tendency to interfere in the EU political process by effectively rewriting legislation.[11]

Some senior judges in the UK Supreme Court are extra-judicially[12] and judicially (albeit *obiter*)[13] firing very severe warning shots across the bow of the CJEU that the reasoning of the latter is often inadequate and that it does not pay sufficient deference to the intentions of the Treaty makers and of the EU legislature (instead turning Treaty or legislative objectives into overriding principles that abolish the nuances and exceptions built into the Treaties and the

9 See eg T Horsley, 'Reflections of the Role of the Court of Justice as the 'Motor' of European Integration: Legal Limits to Judicial Lawmaking' (2013) 50 *Common Market Law Review* 931.

10 See M Bobek, 'Of Feasibility and Silent Elephants: The Legitimacy of the Court of Justice through the Eyes of National Courts', in M Adams, H de Waele, J Meeusen and G Straetmans (eds), *Judging Europe's Judges* (Hart 2013), 197.

11 JHH Weiler, 'Epilogue: Judging the Judges – Apology and Critique' in M Adams, H de Waele, J Meeusen and G Straetmans (eds) *Judging Europe's Judges* (Hart 2013), 235. See the cogent critique he gives, at pp.242-246, of the Court's reasoning, and the then Vice President of the CJEU (Koen Lenaerts)'s defence of it in the first chapter of the book, in Case C-236/09 *Test-Achats*, EU:C:2011:100, and in Cases C-402 and 432/07 *Sturgeon*, EU:C:2009:716. See also Catherine Barnard's suggestion to the Court of Justice to reposition itself 'from standard bearer of EU integration to ensuring that the EU is able to function in its new, more fragmented reality ... to develop a new kind of doctrine of effectiveness, one that might mean endorsing the devolution of more decision-making power to the Member States or other actors:' 'Van Gend en Loos to(t) the future' in A Tizzano, J Kokott and S Prechal (eds), *50th Anniversary of the Judgment in Van Gend en Loos* (Court of Justice of the EU 2013) 117, 122, <http://curia.europa.eu/jcms/upload/docs/application/pdf/2013-12/qd30136442ac_002.pdf>.

12 J Mance, 'The Interface Between National and European Law' (2013) 38 *European Law Review* 437.

13 Lord Mance and Lord Neuberger, on behalf of a UK Supreme Court bench of 7 judges, in *R (Buckinghamshire County Council and Others) v Secretary of State for Transport (the HS2 case)* [2014] UKSC 3; [2014] 1 WLR 324; paras 158-211. See also Lord Mance (whose views on the issue were concurred with by Lords Neuberger, Hale, Wilson, Reed and Sumption) on the relationship between British citizenship and EU citizenship in *Pham v Secretary of State for the Home Department* [2015] UKSC 19; *The Times* April 9, 2015; paras 68-92. It is worth noting that Lord Mance is a Europhile, an excellent linguist, with a strong interest in the EU who sits on the Article 255 TFEU panel that reviews nominations by Member States of CJEU judges and Advocates General.

EU legislation to limit the achievement of the stated objective in what amounts to a threat to the democratic will). A unanimous UK Supreme Court in the *HS2* case has recently reminded the CJEU to pay more attention to the text of EU laws,[14] to 'respect' the balance of interests inherent in the EU legislative structure which often leads to 'objectives' not being fully achieved in legislation in order to reach political agreement[15] and thus:

> When reading or interpreting legislation, it can never therefore be assumed that particular objectives have been achieved to the fullest possible degree. Limitations on the scope or application of a legislative measure may have been necessary to achieve agreement. There may also have been good reasons for limitations, of which courts are unaware or are not the best to judge. Where the legislature has agreed a clearly expressed measure, reflecting the legislator's choices and compromises in order to achieve agreement, it is not for courts to rewrite the legislation, to extend or 'improve' it in respects which the legislator clearly did not intend.[16]

The UK Supreme Court warned the CJEU that failure to heed its advice will lead to a 'loss of confidence at national level in European Union law'[17] which may impair the dialogue between national courts and the CJEU and risk States being reluctant to reach agreement on new legislation in the EU (or where relevant make it more likely that an EU State will exercise its right not to opt in to EU law – a point relevant for Denmark, Ireland and the UK in some areas, including private international law).[18] In the recent *Pham* case Lord Mance, in an observation that was concurred in by a majority and not opposed by any of the Justices, reminded the CJEU that if

> the Court of Justice reaches a decision which oversteps jurisdictional limits which Member States have clearly set at the European Treaty level and which are reflected domestically in their constitutional arrangements... a domestic court must ultimately decide for itself what is consistent with its own domestic constitutional arrangements, including in the case of the 1972 Act [European Communities] what jurisdictional limits exist under the European Treaties and upon the competence conferred on European institutions including the Court of Justice.[19]

---

14 *R (Buckinghamshire County Council and Others) v Secretary of State for Transport (the HS2 case)* [2014] UKSC 3; [2014] 1 WLR 324; para. 169.

15 Ibid, para. 170.

16 Ibid, para. 171.

17 Ibid, para. 172.

18 Ibid, para. 174.

19 *Pham v Secretary of State for the Home Department* [2015] UKSC 19, para 90 (his judgment was concurred with by Lord Neuberger, Lady Hale and Lord Wilson; Lord Sumption said at para.

4. OPINION 1/13 – ADMISSIBILITY

The Council and some Member States argued that the request for an opinion was inadmissible on a number of grounds. Two of these grounds merit analysis because of the Court's unclear reasoning or departure from the views of the Advocate General.

A. MISUSE OF THE OPINION PROCEDURE

The Council and some Member States argued that it was a misuse of the opinion procedure by the Commission to bring such a procedure after such a long delay when the Commission should instead have been bringing infringement proceedings under Article 258 TFEU against those Member States who had declared their acceptances of third State accessions to the Hague Convention in violation of exclusive EU external competence. The Court of Justice said that it was not presented with any 'specific and objective evidence which could lead it to conclude that, in making this request, the Commission has acted exclusively, or at the least primarily, with the aim of circumventing the procedure laid down in Article 258 TFEU.'[20] This quotation gives the impression that a 'misuse of the opinion procedure' could be sustained if enough evidence were to be presented to the Court. The next paragraph of the Court's reasoning seems to refute this impression by saying that: 'In any event' the fact that the Commission could bring Treaty infringement proceedings to give the Court the opportunity to address the same questions does not 'preclude' the Commission from asking the Court to give an Article 218(11) Opinion.[21] This is very unsatisfactory reasoning. Either a misuse of the opinion procedure is possible (when the requisite amount of evidence is presented to the Court) on the basis that the Commission is evading bringing infringement proceedings or it is not. If it is not, the Court should not make spurious references to the amount of evidence presented before it. It should simply say it can never be a misuse of the opinion procedure when it is used as an alternative to bringing infringement proceedings. The fact that the Court has to act collegially in a single judgment can make it difficult for it to always produce logically coherent judgments, given internal disagreements among the judges as to the reasoning by which the majority decision is reached, but the collective responsibility of the Court is to ensure that it does.

111 that he agreed with Lord Mance's 'important reservations ... about the relevance of EU law to questions of national citizenship'; and Lord Reed said, at para 112, that there was 'much' in the judgment of Lord Mance that he agreed with including his 'observations about EU law and British nationality'.

20 Opinion 1/03, n 5, para. 53.

21 Opinion 1/13, n 1, para. 54.

B. THE AGREEMENT WITH THIRD STATES IS NO LONGER 'ENVISAGED' AS IT HAS ALREADY TAKEN PLACE AT LEAST FOR SOME MEMBER STATES

Article 218(11) TFEU requires that an agreement is 'envisaged' when an Opinion from the Court is sought and this is made abundantly clear by the last sentence of the Article which says that: 'Where the Opinion of the Court is adverse, the agreement envisaged must not enter into force unless it is amended or the Treaties are revised.' The problem is that in this case a number of EU Member States had already accepted the accession to the Hague Abduction Convention of some or all of the eight third States referred to in the Commission's proposals of December 2011. For those States the Hague Abduction Convention was already in force between those States and the relevant third States under public international law. Therefore the Council and some of the Member States argued that at least for those EU States the potential EU 'agreement' to accept the accession of the relevant third States was no longer 'envisaged' at the time of the request for an Opinion by the Commission and therefore was inadmissible. This was an argument that found favour with AG Jääskinen.[22]

The Court, however, does not 'engage' with this argument, or the View of the Advocate General on it, at all. Instead it resorts again to mere unreasoned assertion as follows:

> Although it follows from the objective of the opinion procedure referred to in paragraph 47 above that the agreement concerned – in order to be classified as 'envisaged' – must not be concluded before the Court gives the opinion requested, the abovementioned circumstance [certain Member States have already deposited declarations of acceptance of accession with the depositary of the 1980 Hague Convention] alone is not such as to render the request redundant.[23]

The Court does not make clear what, if any, effect its Opinion is intended to have on the acceptance by some EU Member States of the third States referred to in the Commission proposals which envisage an EU 'agreement' with these third States. One can only assume that the Opinion has no effect on these matters because it has come too late to deal with them and cannot reverse what is already true in public international law (certainly Article 218(11) does not confer any power on the Court to (retrospectively) annul an international agreement that has already entered into force between an EU State and a third State).

The Court's style gets in the way of a clear understanding of its decision, of the reasons for its decision and of the consequences of its decision. The Court's

---

22 View of AG Jääskinen on Opinion 1/13, EU:C:2014:2292, paras 42-47.

23 Opinion 1/13, n 1, para. 51.

reluctance to refer to an Advocate General's View when the Court is disagreeing with that View makes it very hard to see what the basis for the Court's Opinion on this point is. Is the Court saying that because the request for an Opinion is still relevant for some EU States (those that have not accepted the accession of the 8 third States) it is admissible and there is no need to rule on the effects of the Opinion in relation to those States that have accepted the accession of the relevant third States? Or is the Court saying that the request is admissible but that it is irrelevant in relation to the EU States that have accepted the accession of the third States? Merely stating the negative proposition that 'the abovementioned circumstance alone is not such as to render the request redundant' does not create sufficient clarity.

5. OPINION 1/13 – SUBSTANCE

A. EXISTENCE OF EU COMPETENCE TO DECLARE THE ACCEPTANCE OF THIRD STATES ACCEDING TO THE HAGUE CHILD ABDUCTION CONVENTION

Article 216(1) TFEU sets out the criteria for the EU having external competence. This is a new provision introduced by the Lisbon Treaty that has its origins in the failed Constitutional Treaty.[24] Article 216(1) TFEU says:

> The Union may conclude an agreement with one or more third countries or international organisations where the Treaties so provide or where the conclusion of an agreement is necessary in order to achieve, within the framework of the Union's policies, one of the objectives referred to in the Treaties, or is provided for in a legally binding Union act or is likely to affect common rules or alter their scope.

However, in the Court's Opinion 1/13 the Grand Chamber declines to start with Article 216 TFEU in determining whether the EU has competence to accept the accession of third States to the Hague Child Abduction Convention. In a clear assertion of its own case law transcending the Treaty it sets out the competence

[24] See European Convention, 'Final Report Working Group VII – External Action' (CONV 459/02) Brussels 16 December 2002, Part A, para. 4, and Part B, para. 18, at <http://www.europarl.europa.eu/meetdocs/committees/deve/20030218/489393EN.pdf> and the IGC 2007 Mandate POLGEN 74 (26 June 2007), para. 18, fn 10, at <http://register.consilium.europa.eu/doc/srv?l=EN&f=ST%20 11218%202007%20INIT>. For such an important topic (external competence of the EU) these preparatory resources from the failed constitutional convention and from the Lisbon IGC tell us practically nothing about the intentions of the drafters. This suggests a casualness on the part of the drafters that is deeply worrying from the point of view of EU Member States caring about and exercising their sovereign rights properly.

of the EU from its own case law[25] and then dismissively says: 'The last-mentioned possibility is also referred to in Article 216(1) TFEU'.[26]

This is a small but vivid example of the Court thinking it is master of the Treaties rather than it being the servant of the Treaties. In the Court's view it would seem that the idea of conferred powers encompasses the notion of conferred by earlier case law of the Court of Justice.

So having partially stated the law on EU external competence based on its own case law in one paragraph the Court then applies the law to the case in the next paragraph saying that the Hague Convention:

> falls within the area of family law with cross-border implications in which the EU has internal competence under Article 81(3) TFEU. Moreover, the EU has exercised that competence by adopting Regulation 2201/2003. In those circumstances, the EU has external competence in the area which forms the subject matter of the Convention.[27]

So the Court asserts that the EU has external competence without clarifying on which basis of Article 216(1) TFEU the competence arises. The impression is that the Court thinks the EU has external competence whenever a matter falls within an area over which the EU has internal competence to legislate. However, this is not the test in Article 216(1) TFEU. Article 216(1) TFEU requires that the Treaty or a legally binding Union act must confer external competence (clearly not the case here), or that the external agreement is 'likely to affect common rules or alter their scope' (not considered by the Court here but only later in relation to exclusive external competence), or that the 'conclusion of an agreement is necessary in order to achieve, within the framework of the Union's policies, one of the objectives referred to in the Treaties' (but the Court does not discuss this either as it does not refer to an 'objective' of the Treaty nor to whether declaring the acceptance of the accession of third States to the Hague Child Abduction Convention is 'necessary' to achieve that objective).[28]

---

25 Opinion 1/13, n 1, para. 67: 'The competence of the EU to conclude international agreements may arise not only from an express conferment by the Treaties but may equally flow implicitly from other provisions of the Treaties and from measures adopted, within the framework of those provisions, by the EU institutions. In particular, whenever EU law creates for those institutions powers within its internal system for the purpose of attaining a specific objective, the EU has authority to undertake international commitments necessary for the attainment of that objective even in the absence of an express provision to that effect (Opinion 1/03, EU:C:2006:81, paragraph 114 and the case-law cited)'.

26 Ibid, end of para. 67.

27 Ibid, para. 68.

28 When dealing with exclusive external competence the Court decided that the slightly different test in Article 3(2) TFEU was not met in this case – acceptance of the declaration of accession to the Hague Convention by a third State 'is not necessary to enable the EU to exercise its internal competence' (para. 70). The test for external competence is the necessity of achieving a Treaty

Perhaps the reason that the Court does not allow Article 216(1) TFEU to govern its decision on whether the EU has external competence is that it would have to apply an even higher standard than in determining whether the EU has exclusive external competence under Article 3(2) TFEU. Article 3(2) TFEU says:

> The Union shall also have exclusive competence for the conclusion of an international agreement when its conclusion is provided for in a legislative act of the Union or is necessary to enable the Union to exercise its internal competence, or in so far as its conclusion may affect common rules or alter their scope.

The only possible criterion that justifies, 'under the Treaty', EU external competence to decide on the acceptance of third State accessions to the Hague Child Abduction Convention is that such an acceptance '*is likely* to affect common rules or alter their scope' (Article 216(1) TFEU) and not just that such an acceptance '*may* affect common rules or alter their scope' (Article 3(2) TFEU).[29] A sensible construction of the Treaty is surely that exclusive external competence cannot arise unless there is external competence. Therefore the higher standard of 'is likely to', rather than the lower standard of 'may', affect should apply to both issues. Instead the Court of Justice runs away from such textual analysis of the Treaty. It does not replace the Treaty standard with a clear standard of its own which could readily be followed in subsequent cases. So the Court's approach is bad judicial activism in policy terms – a Court not acting within the powers conferred on it – and in process terms – a Court creating the law but not making it clear what the new law is.

The Court's standard for the existence of EU external competence may be simply that the external agreement falls within an area of internal EU competence whether or not that competence has been exercised internally (a very radical position) or it may be that external competence exists when the external agreement falls within an area of EU internal competence and the EU has already exercised 'that competence' internally (less radical but still not what the Treaty requires). The reason for the confusion is that the Court is not clear whether the sentence beginning 'Moreover' is a necessary precondition for the creation of external competence in this case or is just a happy fact that the Court can emphasise to reinforce the correctness of awarding external competence to the EU.

---

objective rather than the necessity of exercising its internal competence.

29 Emphasis added. AG Sharpston has said that the distinction noted in the text 'cannot be right', see Opinion in Case C-114/12, *Commission v Council*, EU:C:2014:224, para. 88. Her Opinion then focuses on how to interpret Article 3(2) TFEU and does not really help with an analysis of the interpretation of Article 216(1) TFEU.

B. EXISTENCE OF EXCLUSIVE EXTERNAL COMPETENCE FOR THE EU TO DECLARE THE ACCEPTANCE OF THIRD STATES ACCEDING TO THE HAGUE CHILD ABDUCTION CONVENTION

The Court immediately goes to the relevant Treaty provision on exclusive external competence (Article 3(2) TFEU quoted above) in its opening paragraph[30] on the topic of exclusive external competence. However, it sees Article 3(2) as only a partial statement of exclusive external competence. The Grand Chamber says that the TFEU 'specifies the circumstances in which the EU has exclusive external competence' and only adds 'in particular in Article 3(2)'. The reader is left wondering as to where else in the TFEU there is material on exclusive external competence.

In the next paragraph the Court recognises that 'it is common ground' that the first two possibilities for exclusive external competence in Article 3(2) TFEU are not applicable in this case and focuses on the final condition in that provision – whether the acceptance of a declaration of accession 'may affect common rules or alter their scope'.[31]

The Grand Chamber then refers back in the next paragraph to its own case law on affecting common rules or altering their scope as originally developed in the *ERTA* case,[32] elaborated upon in the *Open Skies* case[33] and then, post-Lisbon, discussed by another Grand Chamber in the *Council of Europe Broadcasting* case shortly before Opinion 1/13.[34] The Grand Chamber in Opinion 1/13 does not make any attempt to justify why the Court's old case law on this topic is still relevant to interpreting the words of the Treaty.[35] The *travaux préparatoires* are not very helpful on this point.[36] If we go back to the European Convention Working Group on External Action that prepared the text of the failed Con-

30 Opinion 1/13, n 1, para. 69.

31 Ibid, para. 70.

32 Case 22/70, *Commission v Council* ('*ERTA*'), EU:C:1971:32, para. 30.

33 Case C-467/98, *Commission v Denmark*, EU:C:2002:625, para. 82.

34 Case C-114/12, *Commission v Council*, EU:C:2014:2151, para. 69.

35 In Case C-114/12, paras 66 and 67, the Grand Chamber does deal with this point by saying that the wording of the Court in para 22 of its judgment in *ERTA* is used in the Lisbon Treaty amendments and therefore should be interpreted in the light of the Court's explanation of those words in the judgment in *ERTA* 'and in the case-law developed as from that judgment'.

36 See the very brief discussion of them by AG Sharpston in her Opinion in the *Council of Europe Broadcasting* case, n 29, paras 94-96. She rightly sees the last clause in Art 3(2) TFEU as 'evidently taken from *ERTA*' (para. 95) and she very reasonably concludes that: 'If the negotiating history of Article 3(2) TFEU shows anything, it is that there was no intention to depart from the *ERTA* principle' (para. 96).

stitutional Treaty its Final Report has this rather unclear observation on the Court's case law on external competence:

> The Group saw merit in making explicit the jurisprudence of the Court to facilitate the action of the Union in a globalised world, in particular when dealing with the external dimension of internal policies and action.[37]

This leaves open the question of how much of the Court's jurisprudence should be made explicit and whether some of it should in fact be left behind. Both in this Opinion and in the *Council of Europe Broadcasting* case there is a sharp disagreement between the Commission and the Council of the European Union as to whether some of the developments of the ERTA principle (that the EU has exclusive competence when the EU has created common rules internally and the Member States can no longer undertake obligations with third countries which affect those common rules)[38] in the Court's subsequent case law are still relevant. The two controversial concepts are 'the largely covered area' and 'foreseeable future developments'. The Court of Justice retains both these features of its pre-Lisbon case law without giving any justification for doing so[39] after the Treaty makers have used wording that solely reflects the *ERTA* principle and not any of its subsequent accretions.

(i) Largely Covered Area

The Court in Opinion 1/13 reiterates its case law from Opinion 2/91[40] that 'the scope of EU rules may be affected or altered by international commitments where such commitments are concerned with an area which is already covered to a large extent by such rules'.[41] The Court asserts that this concept remains relevant after the Lisbon Treaty in interpreting the last clause of Article 3(2) TFEU contrary to the views of the Council and some Member States. The Grand Chamber does not give any reasons as to why the largely covered area concept is still relevant in an era when the external competence of the EU has been clarified in the Treaty and it is not obvious from the wording of the Treaty that the concept is still relevant. The Court does, however, refer to its very recent judgment in the *Council of Europe Broadcasting* case where further enlightenment may be sought on this issue. However, the decision of the Grand Chamber in

---

37 See European Convention, 'Final Report Working Group VII – External Action' (CONV 459/02) Brussels 16 December 2002, Part B, para 18, see http://www.europarl.europa.eu/meetdocs/committees/deve/20030218/489393EN.pdf, last accessed 16 October 2015.

38 Using here the definition of the *ERTA* principle given by AG Sharpston in her Opinion in the *Council of Europe Broadcasting* case, n 29, para. 95.

39 Opinion 1/13, n 1, paras 73 and 74.

40 EU:C:1993:106, paras 25 and 26.

41 Opinion 1/13, n 1, para. 73.

the latter case also deals with this question simply by asserting the continued validity of the Court's case law on the largely covered area with no rationale as to why the case law is still relevant.[42] The Grand Chamber in the *Council of Europe Broadcasting* case dismissed arguments to the contrary:

> The above analysis is not affected by the argument of the Council, the Kingdom of the Netherlands and the United Kingdom that, since the entry into force of the Lisbon Treaty, the exclusive external competence of the European Union is viewed in a more restrictive manner.[43]

The Grand Chamber seems to believe that it is acceptable to reject the arguments in favour of a narrower textual construction of the last part of Article 3(2) TFEU by refuting a different argument put forward by the Council and some Governments relating to the effect of Protocol (No 25) on the exercise of shared competence under the Lisbon Treaty.[44] The Court should deal with the arguments of the body that represents the interests of all EU Member States properly. An argument by inference from Protocol No 25 was not the only argument made by the Council but merely a support of an argument to construe the actual words of Article 3(2) TFEU and not parts of the Court's pre-Lisbon case law which cannot be reconciled with those words. Protocol No 25 is not a knock-out blow to the Court's case law on largely covered area in the field of exclusive competence because the protocol does indeed relate to shared competence. However, a more modest Court might pay more attention to Protocol No 25 as a sign of the fact that the Member States are anxious to ensure that the exercise of competence in part of an area is not deemed to be the exercise of competence over the whole area. The fact that there is no Protocol on exclusive external competence may be because the Member States felt that it was enough to expressly limit the external competence to cases where the conclusion of an international agreement 'may affect common rules or alter their scope'.

This condition seems to require that only aspects of the international agreement which have a direct effect on a binding internal EU instrument create exclusive EU external competence. Therefore in relation to parts of an international agreement that are not covered by a binding EU instrument there can be no effects by the former on the latter and therefore no exclusive external competence in relation to those parts of the international agreement (thus leading to a mixed agreement). Something of this idea is evident in AG Sharpston's Opinion in the *Council of Europe Broadcasting* case. She did not reject the largely covered

42 Case C-114/12, n 34, para. 70.

43 Ibid, para. 72.

44 Ibid, para. 73.

area concept in theory.[45] However, in practice she gave it no weight because she decided that the EU did not have exclusive competence to enter into the proposed Council of Europe Convention because there was at least one area of that Convention which was not covered by the internal EU instrument and therefore that area of the proposed Convention could not have an effect on the EU instrument.[46] The Grand Chamber in *Council of Europe Broadcasting* did not follow AG Sharpston on this point. It did not find any area of the future Convention which might not affect an existing EU instrument.[47] However, the Grand Chamber in the *Council of Europe Broadcasting* case is to be congratulated for its thorough reasoning even if it errs on the side of finding exclusive external competence by putting the onus of proof on those who are asserting that there is not exclusive competence. Given that the Council of the EU – representing a substantial proportion of the Contracting States to the Council of Europe – was arguing that there could well be protection of pre-broadcast signals in the new Council of Europe Convention that would be achieved without affecting EU law it seems rather unreasonable to describe this as a 'hypothetical' possibility.

The fact that the Court retained the largely covered area concept had a material bearing on the outcome of Opinion 1/13. It compared the provisions of the Hague Child Abduction Convention with those of the Brussels IIa Regulation and decided that the latter 'cover to a large extent the two procedures governed by the 1980 Hague Convention, namely the procedure concerning the return of children who have been wrongfully removed and the procedure for securing the exercise of access rights.'[48] This led the Court to conclude that: 'Thus, the whole of the Convention must be regarded as covered by the EU rules.'[49] This is a huge leap given that on one view Brussels IIa does not even largely cover the Hague Convention primarily because Brussels IIa has nothing to say about cases between EU States and non-EU Contracting States to the Hague Convention but also because the whole system of cooperation between Central Authorities in relation to Hague Child Abduction cases even in intra-EU cases is not regulated by the Regulation but rather by the Convention itself. The Brussels IIa Regula-

---

45 Opinion of AG Sharpston, n 29, paras 104-110.

46 Ibid, paras 141-145, 153-155 and 166. In particular the protection of pre-broadcast signals is not covered by EU law.

47 Case C-114/12, *Commission v Council*, n 34, paras 78-103. In particular the Grand Chamber decided that although pre-broadcasting signals are not covered by EU law (para. 97) one of the 'possible' approaches being considered for the Council of Europe Convention, to extend the term 'broadcasts' to pre-broadcast signals, 'would undeniably be capable of altering in a horizontal manner, the scope of the common EU rules in the area concerned' (para. 98) and that any of the other suggested ways of handling pre-broadcast signals suggested to the Court (which would not affect EU law) were 'hypothetical' and not relevant due to the lack of evidence that they were being considered for the future Council of Europe Convention (para. 99).

48 Opinion 1/13, n 1, para. 83.

49 Ibid.

tion's provision on co-operation between Central Authorities is confined to the Article 11(6)-(8) procedure permitting the courts of the habitual residence of the child immediately before the abduction of the child to insist on the return of the child to that country when the courts of refuge have issued an order under Article 13 of the Hague Child Abduction Convention refusing to return the child. The Article 11(6)-(8) Brussels IIa procedure is not an implementation of the Convention in EU law but rather a wholly new addition created by EU law.

(ii) Foreseeable future developments

While it was not a big issue in this case it is regrettable that the Court continues to argue that it can assess whether or not the EU rules may be affected by the international agreement by considering the 'foreseeable future development' of the EU rules. This cannot be consistent with a system of conferred powers. Why should the Court be allowed to restrict the external competence of Member States on the basis of what the Court thinks might be decided in internal EU instruments in the foreseeable future? This can, at best, only be fair where the binding EU instrument has already been agreed and its entry into force is pending. It is surprising to see the kind of speculation resorted to by Advocate General Jääskinen in this case relying on this concept.[50]

(iii) The risk that common rules may be affected

The Court's reasoning on the possible effects on Brussels IIa of declaring the acceptance of the accession of third States to the Hague Convention is given in positive terms in paragraphs 85, 88 and 89 of its judgment. In negative terms the Court asserts that the consistency of many of the provisions of the Regulation and the Convention does not mean that there may be no affect of the latter on the former and the fact that the Regulation gives priority to the Regulation over the Convention in Article 60 does not prevent an affect of the latter on the former.[51]

---

50 View of AG Jääskinen on Opinion 1/13, n 22, para. 100. The Advocate General's speculation, at para 102, about an adverse effect of accepting third States into the Hague Convention because they will make it harder to agree amendments to the Convention misses the point that the EU cannot prevent third States from acceding to the Convention and from having to consent to amendments to the Convention in a Protocol. In any case no Protocol to the Child Abduction Convention is foreseeable given it was shelved *sine die* at the last Special Review Commission in 2011-12 (compare preliminary doc. No 7 of 2011 on the 'desirability and feasibility of a Protocol' to the Child Abduction Convention with the conclusions and recommendations of the Special Commissions in 2011-12 which only recommend creating guides to good practice, see <http://www.hcch.net/index_en.php?act=publications.details&pid=6224&dtid=57>) and the Hague only adopts new instruments by consensus of all its members, see Article 8(2) of the Hague Statute as amended in 2005 and entered into force on 1 January 2007 (see <http://www.hcch.net/index_en.php?act=conventions.text&cid=29>).

51 Opinion 1/13, n 1, paras 86-88. But the Court does not say what the 'affect' might be.

The Court's first positive assertion of possible effect of the Convention on the Regulation is stated as follows:

> because of the overlap and the close connection between the provisions of Regulation 2201/2003 and those of the Convention, in particular between Article 11 of the regulation and Chapter III of the Convention, the provisions of the Convention may have an effect on the meaning, scope and effectiveness of the rules laid down in Regulation No 2201/2003.[52]

Chapter III of the Convention and Article 11 of the Regulation both contain provisions governing the return of a child who has been abducted but their material scopes are completely different in relation to the issue in hand (whether the declaration of the acceptance of a third State to the Hague Convention can affect the provisions in Brussels IIa or alter their scope). The question is how can the application of the return provisions in the Convention in cases between an EU State and a third State have any bearing on the meaning, scope or effectiveness of the provisions in the Regulation on the return of a child in cases between EU Member States? The Court makes no attempt to address this point and therefore its statement is a mere assertion and not a reasoned opinion.

The next positive statement on the issue of possible affects on the Regulation is as follows:

> Despite the precedence afforded to Regulation No 2201/2003, the scope and effectiveness of the common rules laid down by the regulation are likely to be affected when the Member States individually make separate declarations accepting third-State accessions to the 1980 Hague Convention.[53]

Once again one is left asking the Court the question 'why is the Regulation likely to be affected by the EU Member States making individual declarations of acceptance of the accession of third States?'. The application of the Convention between, eg, France and Russia will have no direct bearing on the application of the Regulation as the latter does not apply to cases between France and any third State. It is for the Court to say what these possible affects might be as they are not inherently obvious.

Finally the Court adds the following paragraph connected to the above point:

> In that regard, as the Parliament and the Commission have submitted, if the Member States, rather than the EU, had competence to decide whether or not to accept the accession of a new third state to the 1980 Hague Convention,

---

52 Opinion 1/13, n 1, para. 85.

53 Ibid, para. 88.

> there would be a risk of undermining the uniform and consistent application of Regulation No 2201/2003 and, in particular, the rules concerning cooperation between the authorities of the Member States, whenever a situation involving international child abduction involved a third state and two Member States, one of which had accepted the accession of that third State to the Convention whilst the other had not.[54]

The first problem with this paragraph is that the provisions on cooperation between Central Authorities are found in the Convention (Article 7) and not in the Regulation (apart from one tiny point in Article 55(c) which relates to the override provisions in Article 11 of the Regulation that have no equivalent in the Convention and therefore seem to be irrelevant for present purposes) so it is hard to say that the Convention could 'affect' the Regulation in relation to cooperation between the authorities of Member States as it is a matter for these purposes which is exclusively governed by the Convention and not the Regulation.

The second problem is that the Court does not set out in its Opinion what are the examples submitted by the Commission and the European Parliament and neither does the Advocate General in his View.[55] This lack of transparency means that the reader is unable to fully test the veracity of the Court's assertion or, to be more positive, is unable to be convinced by the Court's reasoning because the examples are not given but merely referred to in submissions that are not easy for the reader to find.

It is very difficult to imagine how the cooperation between Central Authorities in relation to intra-EU cases might be affected by the fact that one of the EU Central Authorities involved also has responsibilities in relation to cases with a third State and this point is well made by the Council in its observations as reported by the Court at paragraphs 61 and 62. The Court refers to a scenario where two EU Member States are involved in the same case involving a third State but only one of the EU Member States has accepted the accession of the third State. But how might this have any affect on the Regulation? The Member State that has Convention obligations with the third State will carry out those obligations and the Member State that has no such Convention obligations will not be obliged to do anything. If the issue arises because it is not clear whether the child has been abducted to one or the other of the EU Member States this cannot affect the Regulation. Neither EU Member State will act under the Regulation and one EU Member State will act under the Convention.

54 Ibid, para. 89.

55 The latter merely refers to examples without setting them out, see Opinion 1/13, n 1, para. 93, and View of AG Jääskinen, n 22, fn 134.

6. CONCLUSION

The Court of Justice of the European Union has relied too much on assertions and spent too little time giving cogent reasons for those assertions in Opinion 1/13. The Court does not appear to be concerned to convince its readers of the correctness of its decision but seems to be content to ask its readers to trust in dogmatic assertions. In the area of external competence where the sovereign rights of States are at stake and the practical possibilities of the Hague Child Abduction Convention applying between EU States and third States may be limited (given the requirement of unanimity in the Council) the Court should have been much more thorough and careful. The European Union would be more democratic and gain the trust of its citizens more if the Court were to be much more deferential to the intentions of the Treaty makers and pay careful attention to the wording of the Treaty (consistent with its declared acceptance of the principle of conferred powers) rather than to its own case law when that case law is not clearly supported by the wording of the Treaty.

An appropriate reading of Article 3(2) and 216(1) TFEU together should be that the *ERTA* principle on exclusive external competence has been codified in EU law in the final words of Article 216(1) TFEU. Therefore exclusive EU external competence only arises under that principle where every aspect of the international agreement is 'likely to affect' common EU rules or alter their scope. There should be no room for the largely covered area doctrine or the foreseeable future developments doctrine from the pre-Lisbon case law of the CJEU. These are not consistent with the principles of conferred powers and legal certainty. They give too much discretion to the CJEU to decide when the area of the international agreement is sufficiently largely covered by existing EU laws or even worse by what the Court regards as a foreseeable future EU law. These concepts were not explicitly preserved by the drafters of the Lisbon Treaty and are not clearly supported by the words of the Treaty. These vague criteria encourage litigation in the Court over external competence rather than Member States and the EU knowing where they stand on external competence. Clarity would be provided and the Treaty regime fully respected if the last parts of Articles 3(2) and 216(1) TFEU were only to be applicable when the whole of the international agreement affects already existing binding EU laws.

In relation to the existence of EU external competence the Court must restrict this to what is provided by Article 216(1) TFEU unlike its approach in Opinion 1/13 where it was prepared to rely on its case law as a legal basis for external competence. It must only find external competence under the second limb of that provision if it can clearly demonstrate that the conclusion of the international agreement is 'necessary in order to achieve, within the framework of the Union's policies, one of the objectives referred to in the Treaties'. In order to do this it must analyse the relevant Treaty objective and determine whether it is necessary for the EU to enter into the international agreement to achieve that objective. The Court avoided any analysis of Treaty objectives and the necessity of achieving them in Opinion 1/13 while concluding that the EU had external competence.

THE IMPLICATIONS OF THE EUROPEAN UNION'S EXCLUSIVE COMPETENCE WITH REGARD TO THE CHILD ABDUCTION CONVENTION

Giorgio GAJA
University of Florence
Judge at the International Court of Justice

1. THE BASIS AND EXTENT OF THE EXCLUSIVE COMPETENCE OF THE EU CONCERNING INTERNATIONAL CHILD ABDUCTION

The jurisprudence of the Court of Justice has significantly expanded the role played by the EU in its external relations in the field of private international law. In Opinion 1/03, the Court stated that the European Community (now the Union) had exclusive competence to conclude the revised Lugano Convention on jurisdiction and the recognition and enforcement of judgments in civil and commercial matters, notwithstanding the fact that this Convention also covers matters that are not regulated by EC rules, such as the recognition of judicial decisions rendered in non-Member States. The Court of Justice gave as a reason for the exclusive competence of the European Community the fact that the Lugano Convention may affect common rules or alter their scope.[1] This criterion for exclusive competence, which had first been expressed in the *ERTA* judgment,[2] has since been incorporated by the Lisbon Treaty in Article 3(2) of the TFEU.

In Opinion 1/13, the Court of Justice relied on the latter provision of the TFEU to assert the exclusive competence of the EU as regards the acceptance of accessions to the 1980 Hague Convention on the civil aspects of international child

1 Opinion 1/03, EU:C:2006:81, para. 116.

2 Case 22/70, *Commission v. Council* ('*ERTA*'), EU:C:1971:32, paras 77-81.

abduction by non-Member States ('third States').[3] The reference to 'third States', which appears in the operative part of Opinion 1/13, corresponds to the meaning of the Commission's request, which referred to 'accession of a non-Union country'.[4] Both the request and the operative part of Opinion 1/13 could have been more precise. Articles 37 and 38 of the Convention state that an acceptance of the accession is not required for any acceding State which, unlike the Member States of the Union, is not yet a party to the Convention, but only for those acceding States that were not 'Members of the Hague Conference on Private International Law at the time of its Fourteenth Session'.

Since this Hague Convention is open only to the ratification by States, the EU has not taken any steps towards becoming a party to it. Moreover, given that all the Member States were already parties to the Convention when Regulation (EC) No 2201/2003 concerning jurisdiction and the recognition and enforcement of judgments in matrimonial matters and the matters of parental responsibility (Brussels IIa) was adopted,[5] no opportunity has arisen for the EU to prompt Member States to ratify the Convention on behalf of the Union. Furthermore, it is clear from the position taken by twenty Member States which intervened in the proceedings relating to Opinion 1/13[6] that the Council would not have considered that the Union has exclusive competence to conclude the Child Abduction Convention.

The Brussels IIa Regulation takes into account the obligations accepted by all the Member States under the Convention and makes use of the instruments provided by the Convention, in particular the establishment and functions of central authorities, for facilitating the return of the child and access for visits. The Regulation makes some express references to the Convention in paragraphs 17 and 18 of the Preamble and especially in Article 11, which is designed to implement, but also to supplement, in the relations among Member States the rules laid down in the Convention to deal with the return of a child. As the Court noted,[7] several other provisions of the Regulation are modelled on the Convention. However, Article 60 of the Regulation also states that the Regulation itself prevails over the Convention.

The Court of Justice observed that, 'because of the overlap and the close connection between the provisions of Regulation 2201/2003 and those of the Convention', 'the provisions of the Convention may have an effect on the meaning, scope and effectiveness of the rules laid down in Regulation No 2201/2003'.[8]

---

3 Opinion 1/13, EU:C:2014:2303, paras 69-73.

4 Ibid, para. 1.

5 [2003] OJ L 338/1.

6 All the States that intervened except Italy argued against the Union's exclusive competence.

7 Opinion 1/13, n 3, paras 75-83.

8 Ibid, para. 85.

On the specific question that was the object of the request for an opinion, the Court of Justice added that

> [d]espite the precedence afforded to Regulation No 2201/2003, the scope and effectiveness of the common rules laid down by the regulation are likely to be affected when the Member States individually make separate declarations accepting third-State accessions to the 1980 Hague Convention[9]

and that,

> if the Member States, rather than the EU, had competence to decide whether or not to accept the accession of a third State to the Child Abduction Convention, there would be a risk of undermining the uniform and consistent application of Regulation No 2201/2003 and, in particular, the rules concerning cooperation between the authorities of the Member States, whenever a situation involving international child abduction involved a third State and two Member States, one of which had accepted the accession of that third State to the Convention whilst the other had not.[10]

The exclusive competence of the Union thus derives from the enactment by the Union of a regulation concerning international child abduction.[11] Although this act only governs relations among Member States, according to the Court of Justice it may be significantly affected by a treaty covering relations of a Member State with a non-Member State. This does not seem to depend on the relations existing between the regulation and the Hague Convention. The common rules enacted by the regulation would be similarly affected by any other treaty covering the same matter. In other words, while Opinion 1/13 focuses on the Child Abduction Convention, the existence of an exclusive competence on the part of the Union rules out any competence of a Member State to conclude a treaty on international child abduction.

Logically, the asserted exclusive competence of the Union runs from the date when the Brussels IIa Regulation entered into force (1 August 2004). Thus the need for an acceptance by the Union of the accession of States that were not members of the Hague Conference at the time of its Fourteenth Session does not only concern the more recent accessions. Opinion 1/13 has not addressed this issue, which is likely to cause uncertainties, because the effects of acceptances unilaterally given by Member States could be contested.

---

9 Ibid, para. 88.

10 Ibid, para. 89.

11 In his note on the *Intertanko* judgment, (2009) 46 *Common Market Law Review* 2041, 2051-2, P Eeckhout had already observed that '[i]t is not inconceivable that a "full transfer of powers" could result from a complete harmonization of a subject also regulated in an international agreement concluded by the Member States'.

2. THE SCOPE OF THE EXCLUSIVE COMPETENCE OF THE EU AS REGARDS ACTIONS RELATING TO THE CHILD ABDUCTION CONVENTION

At the international level the acceptance of an accession of a non-Member State is not the only action that a Member State could take with regard to the Child Abduction Convention. However, in Opinion 1/13 the Court of Justice only addressed the question posed by the Commission, reaching the conclusion that

> [t]he exclusive competence of the European Union encompasses the acceptance of the accession of a third State to the Convention on the civil aspects of international child abduction concluded in The Hague on 25 October 1980.[12]

Although Opinion 1/13 does not refer to any other action that Member States could take with regard to the Child Abduction Convention, what applies to acceptances of accession should apply *a fortiori* to withdrawal from the Convention under its Article 44.[13] It is clear that 'the uniform and consistent application' of Regulation No 2201/2003 would be affected by the termination of the Convention by a Member State, or by the suspension of its operation, even more than by the Member State's acceptance or not of the accession of a non-Member State. The Regulation relies on the Convention for the relations involving Member States. One can refer in particular to the establishment of a central authority in each State with the functions outlined in Article 7 of the Convention. It follows that Member States would be free to withdraw from the Convention or to suspend its operation only if they were so required, or at least authorised, by the Union.

The adoption of amendments to the Convention would generally cover matters governed by common rules and would therefore also require a decision by the Union.[14]

3. THE PROCEDURE FOR EXERCISING THE COMPETENCE OF THE EU AS REGARDS THE CHILD ABDUCTION CONVENTION

Although the Court did not state this explicitly, it is clear that acceptances may be made only by the Member States, who alone are parties to the Convention.

---

12 Opinion 1/13, n 3, para. 90.

13 A Dutta, 'Anmerkung', (2015) 1 *Zeitschrift für das gesamte Familienrecht* 24.

14 See S Peers, 'Child Abduction: a further extension of EU exclusive external powers', <http://eulawanalysis.blogspot.nl/2014/10/child-abduction-further-extension-of-eu.html>.

The role of the Union in the exercise of its exclusive competence would be to decide whether Member States should give their acceptances, 'acting jointly in the [Union's] interest'.[15]

This raises the problem of the procedure to be followed within the Union for that purpose. The general rule set out in Article 218(6) TFEU should apply also to the decisions concerning these acceptances, which have been defined by the Court as part of international agreements with the acceding States.[16] According to this rule, the Council should take a decision relating to each acceptance after consulting the Parliament. Unanimity is required in the Council according to Article 218(8) TFEU on the basis of Article 81(3) TFEU.[17]

Since the acceptance of amendments is also a form of concluding an international agreement supplementing the treaty to be amended, the same procedure outlined for the acceptance of accessions to the Child Abduction Convention should apply to the acceptance of amendments modifying the Convention.

Article 218(9) TFEU gives the Council the power to suspend the operation of a treaty, but does not specify whether unanimity is required. Nothing is said in the TFEU about the termination of treaties.

The analogy between the conclusion of a treaty and the withdrawal from the same treaty or the suspension of its operation is not such as to necessarily require a parallel solution, also in view of the practice of many States which imposes less stringent conditions in the procedure concerning withdrawals from treaties or suspension of their operation than in the procedure applying to the conclusion of treaties. However, with regard to the Child Abduction Convention, the close link existing between the Convention and the Brussels IIa Regulation would make it difficult to justify an authorisation to withdraw from the Convention or to suspend its operation that does not involve a unanimous decision by the Council.

4. DOES THE CHILD ABDUCTION CONVENTION BIND THE EU?

The fact that a treaty concluded by all the Member States comes under the exclusive competence of the EU does not necessarily imply that the Union is bound by the treaty.

It is well known that according to the Court of Justice the Union may be bound by a treaty to which it is not a party. With regard to GATT 1947, a treaty which had been concluded by all the Member States before the relevant transfer

[15] These words are taken from Opinion 2/91, EU: C:1993:106, para. 5.

[16] Opinion 1/13, n 3, paras 37-42.

[17] In this sense also A Dutta, n 13.

of powers to the Community, the Court of Justice had observed in *International Fruit* that, '[b]y conferring those powers on the Community, the Member States showed their wish to bind it by the obligations entered into under the General Agreement'.[18]

In *Intertanko* the Court explained that:

> it does not appear that the Community has assumed, under the EC Treaty, the powers previously exercised by the Member States in the field to which Marpol 73/78 [the International Convention for the Prevention of Pollution from Ships] applies, nor that, consequently, its provisions have the effect of binding the Community ... In this regard, Marpol 73/78 can therefore be distinguished from GATT 1947 within the framework of which the Community progressively assumed powers previously exercised by the Member States, with the consequence that it became bound by the obligations flowing from that agreement.[19]

In respect of Marpol 73/78, the Court noted 'the absence of a full transfer of the powers previously exercised by the Member States to the Community'.[20] Many matters remained which were not covered by common rules.

Similarly, in *Bogiatzi* the Court found that:

> In the absence of a full transfer of the powers previously exercised by the Member States to the Community, the latter cannot, simply because at the material time all those States were parties to the Warsaw Convention [for the Unification of Certain Rules Relating to International Carriage by Air], be bound by the rules set out therein, which it has not itself approved.[21]

Again in *Air Transport Association of America* the Court observed that:

> in order for the European Union to be capable of being bound, it must have assumed, and thus had transferred to it, all the powers previously exercised by the Member States that fall within the convention in question.[22]

---

18 Joined Cases 21 to 24/72, *International Fruit Company NV and others v Produktschap voor Groenten en Fruit*, EU:C:1972:115, para. 15.

19 Case C-308/06, *The Queen, on the application of International Association of Independent Tanker Owners (Intertanko) and Others v Secretary of State for Transport*, EU:C:2008:312, para. 48.

20 Ibid, para. 49.

21 Case C-301/08, *Irène Bogiatzi, married name Ventouras v Deutscher Luftpool and Others*, EU:C:2009:649, para. 33. As observed by R Schütze, 'The 'Succession Doctrine' and the European Union', in A Arnull, C Barnard, M Dougan and E Spaventa (eds), *A Constitutional Order of States? Essays in EU Law in Honour of Alan Dashwood* (Hart 2011), 459, 481, the Court, in this judgment, regarded '[l]egislative exclusivity ... as capable of triggering functional succession'.

22 Case C-366/10, *Air Transport Association of America and Others v Secretary of State for Energy and Climate Change*, EU:C:2011:864, para. 63, referring to the Chicago Convention on International Civil Aviation.

Nowhere in Opinion 1/13 does the Court of Justice say that the EU has become bound by the Child Abduction Convention. The Court may not have found it necessary to dwell on this issue because the proceedings concerned a question relating to the competences of the Union and the Member States, and no question of the validity of legislative acts had been raised in relation to this Convention.

Given the wide scope of the Brussels IIa Regulation, one could probably reach the conclusion that there had occurred, with regard to the matters covered by the Child Abduction Convention, a 'full transfer of the powers previously exercised by the Member States'. However, it would be difficult to conclude that the Union showed a will to bind itself to the Convention. One element that is very significant in order to rule out the existence of such a will is that Article 60 of the regulation states that the provisions of the regulation 'shall take precedence over' certain treaties, among which letter (*e*) includes the Child Abduction Convention. This provision is inconsistent with the idea that the Union should regard itself as being bound by the Convention, because in the latter case the treaty would prevail over the regulation on the basis of Article 216(2) TFEU.

If the Union cannot be regarded as being bound by the Convention, the Member States, when they comply with a decision by the Council concerning the acceptance of accession of a non-Member State, would not act on behalf of the Union. The same would apply to actions by Member States complying with Council decisions concerning amendments to the Convention or withdrawals from it. The purpose of decisions that the Union may take in this field of exclusive competence in external relations would be only to safeguard a certain uniformity in the attitude of States with regard to matters concerning child abduction.

5. THE ROLE OF THE COURT OF JUSTICE IN THE INTERPRETATION OF THE CHILD ABDUCTION CONVENTION

Should one reach the conclusion that the Union is not bound by the Child Abduction Convention, the validity of legislative acts of the Union cannot be challenged in case of conflict with the provisions of this Convention.

The question remains whether the interpretation of the Child Abduction Convention may give rise to preliminary rulings by the Court of Justice.

If one considers that the Convention does not bind the Union, the Convention cannot *per se* be the object of a preliminary ruling. Only the interpretation of common rules enacted by secondary legislation may be requested from the Court, when the interpretation of the Convention is indirectly relevant for the interpretation of the legislative act.

In so far as a provision in a legislative act refers to a treaty, whether or not the Union is a party to it, the interpretation of the treaty may affect the meaning of the provision in question. The interpretation of the treaty may also be relevant in more general terms, as was suggested in *Intertanko*, where the Court noted that 'the provisions of secondary law which fall within the field of application of Marpol 73/78', which 'binds the Member States', have to be interpreted 'taking account of Marpol 73/78'.[23]

For the Child Abduction Convention, this would mean that the Court is competent to interpret the Convention when provisions like Article 11 of Regulation No 2201/2003 refer to the Convention, but also when other provisions of the same regulation reflect the content of the Convention. This is acknowledged by Opinion 1/13. It does say that 'the provisions of the Convention may have an effect on the meaning' of the provisions of the regulation,[24] although it does not specify when this occurs.

---

23 Case C-308/06, *Intertanko*, n 19, para. 52.

24 See above, n 8.

CONSEQUENCES OF OPINION 1/13 ON THE ACCEPTANCE IN THE EU OF ACCESSIONS TO THE HAGUE CHILD ABDUCTION CONVENTION

Karen VANDEKERCKHOVE *

Acting Head of Unit in the European Commission

1. INTRODUCTION

Opinion 1/13 of the Court of Justice of the European Union[1] clarified that the exclusive competence of the European Union encompasses the acceptance of the accession of non-EU States to the 1980 Hague Convention on the Civil Aspects of International Child Abduction (hereafter referred to as the 1980 Hague Child Abduction Convention or the 1980 Hague Convention). As a consequence, EU Member States cannot accept the accession of non-EU States to the Convention without the Union's authorisation. This contribution does not aim at analysing Opinion 1/13 nor does it aim at expressing an opinion on this Opinion. It rather aims at examining, from a pragmatic point of view, what are the practical consequences of Opinion 1/13 on the acceptance, in the European Union, of accessions to the 1980 Hague Child Abduction Convention.

There were many different legal and political reasons why Member States were generally opposed to accepting exclusive external competence of the European Union in the area of child abduction generally or on the matter of the acceptance of accessions of non-EU States to the 1980 Hague Child Abduction Convention. The decision-making procedure in the European Union in family law matters was undoubtedly one of the matters which caused concern. Accord-

* Any views expressed in this contribution are personal and should not be attributed to the European Commission.

1 Opinion 1/13, EU:C:2014:2303.

ing to Article 81(3) TFEU, measures concerning family law with cross-border implications shall be adopted by the Council, acting unanimously after consulting the European Parliament. While several instruments in the area of family law have been adopted by unanimity,[2] other instruments had to be adopted in enhanced cooperation following a failure to reach the necessary unanimity,[3] showing the difficulty in finding unanimity among Member States in this sensitive area of family law.

More concretely, with respect to the acceptance of non-EU States to the 1980 Hague Child Abduction Convention, Member States take diverging positions. A number of Member States take a liberal approach towards accepting new acceding States, proceeding from a presumption in favour of acceptance. The rationale behind this liberal approach is that it is preferable to have a common legal framework in place rather than no legal framework at all to deal with child abductions and that, even if doubts may exist on the capability of the acceding State to apply the Convention properly, the inclusion of the acceding State in the cooperation system of the Convention will gradually improve the situation. The process of implementation is seen as a continuing process of development and improvement. Other Member States take a more restrictive approach. In their view, it may be risky to create international obligations towards a State in the highly sensitive area of child abduction which may attract political attention. In addition, it is also feared that the acceptance of third States to the Convention might in some instances create a false impression for citizens that relations with parents in such States may be considered 'safe' from the point of view of legal protection against child abduction. Therefore, before accepting a non-EU acceding State into the system of cooperation of the Convention, these Member States will evaluate such accession, considering the general legal and political environment in the country concerned as well as the requirements of the Convention and the measures and institutions that the accession State has in place to enable it to operate the Convention effectively.

In the light of this, apart from any considerations on the existence of exclusive external competence generally in this area or on the matter of accepting ac-

---

2 For example Regulation (EC) No 2201/2003 concerning jurisdiction and the recognition and enforcement of judgments in matrimonial matters and the matters of parental responsibility (covering, among others, the matter of international child abduction) [2003] OJ L 338/1, and Regulation (EC) No 4/2009 on jurisdiction, applicable law, recognition and enforcement of decisions and cooperation in matters relating to maintenance obligations [2009] OJ L 7/1.

3 Regulation (EU) No 1259/2010 implementing enhanced cooperation in the area of the law applicable to divorce and legal separation [2010] OJ L 343/10; Regulation (EU) 2016/1103 implementing enhanced cooperation in the area of jurisdiction, applicable law and the recognition and enforcement of decisions in matters of matrimonial property regimes [2016] OJ L 183/1; Regulation (EU) 2016/1104 implementing enhanced cooperation in the area of jurisdiction, applicable law and the recognition and enforcement of decisions in matters of the property consequences of registered partnerships [2016] OJ L 183/30.

cessions, it is understandable that Opinion 1/13 created concern among Member States. It was generally feared that no new international obligations towards acceding States under the 1980 Hague Convention could be established. This would not only be highly regrettable from the point of view of citizens confronted with problems of international child abduction, but it would also be detrimental for the further operation of the Convention. In addition, a failure on the part of the European Union to accept accessions to the Convention would damage the image of the European Union and its Member States as strong supporters of civil judicial cooperation at the international level.

2. ACCEPTANCE OF ACCESSIONS TO THE 1980 HAGUE CHILD ABDUCTION CONVENTION – THE WAY FORWARD

In the midst of the political turmoil following the issuing of Opinion 1/13 by the Court, it was for the European Commission to take action so as to ensure that accessions of non-EU States to the 1980 Convention would remain feasible in the light of the clarified legal situation regarding the competence to decide on such accessions. In addition, the Commission wished to facilitate the adoption of its eight pending proposals regarding the accessions of Albania, Andorra, Armenia, Gabon, Morocco, Seychelles, Singapore, and Russia.[4]

As a first step, the Commission engaged in discussions with experts from the governments of the Member States. The aim of such discussions was to exchange views on the current practice in Member States regarding the acceptance of non-EU acceding States to the 1980 Hague Convention. In particular, the discussions aimed at sharing the practical experience and the process in accepting or not accepting non-EU States, in particular considering the elements, if any, which Member States have traditionally taken into account when deciding whether or not to accept the accession of a non-EU State to the Convention, and at finding common ground for a common methodology to handle the acceptance of accessions to the Convention.

Many varying elements are taken into account by at least a number of Member States when considering the appropriateness of accepting the accession of a particular non-EU State to the 1980 Convention. In this respect, it should be noted that certain information relevant to considering the acceptance of an accession is gathered by the Permanent Bureau of the Hague Conference itself. In particular, the Conference developed a standard questionnaire which provides a means for newly acceding States to describe the measures taken in their

---

4 COM (2011) 904 final, COM (2011) 908 final, COM (2011) 909 final, COM (2011) 911 final, COM (2011) 912 final, COM (2011) 915 final, COM (2011) 916 final, and COM (2011) 917 final.

State to ensure compliance with their Convention obligations and to ensure the effective practical operation of the Convention in their State.[5] The aim of the questionnaire is to assist States already party to the Convention with their decision as to whether to accept an accession. Assistance to acceding States is also available in the Guide to Good Practice (in particular, Part II-Implementing measures).[6] Both the questionnaire and the Guide have been approved by the Members of the Conference.

While the questionnaire completed by acceding States does provide useful information in order to assess the accession of an acceding State to the 1980 Hague Convention, several Member States feel that this information cannot suffice in their internal decision-making procedure. They feel that information should not only be received from the acceding State itself, but should be gathered through other, independent sources such as by way of diplomatic and consular channels, evaluations and reports of non-governmental organisations, experience gathered by other States which have already accepted the accession concerned, etc.

The elements considered by Member States in proceeding to an evaluation of the accession concerned are similar to those included in the standard questionnaire for newly acceding States developed in the context of the Hague Conference. A first set of elements include general principles relating to the respect of the rule of law, including the independence of the judiciary, the respect of fundamental rights including the right to a fair trial (generally and specifically in relation to children). They further include elements specifically related to an effective application of the 1980 Convention, such as the establishment of a Central Authority under the Convention, the legislation in place to implement the Convention and the training of judges, the existing instruments for the location of children, the existing institutions for the protection of children, and more generally the system in place for the placement of endangered minors in protective custody. Further elements examined to evaluate the likelihood of a proper application of the Convention are the existence of adequate internal procedural structures to ensure procedural fairness, equal treatment of national and foreign applicants, the possibility to obtain legal aid, and an appropriate and functioning enforcement system (including, for instance, provisional enforceability of first instance decisions). Some Member States also take into consideration the availability and effective use of mediation, the concentration of jurisdiction in child abduction matters, and the overall duration of procedures on the return of children (in particular having regard to the expediency of op-

5 The questionnaire is available at <http://www.hcch.net/index_en.php?act=text.display&tid=21>.

6 The Guide to Good Practice is equally available at <http://www.hcch.net/index_en.php?act=text.display&tid=21>. Part II of the Guide to Good Practice was prepared by the Permanent Bureau and approved by the Special Commission concerning the Hague Convention of 25 October 1980 on the civil aspects of international child abduction held at The Hague from 27 September to 1 October 2002.

position or appeal proceedings). Finally, Member States take into account any possible impact of the substantive national law on the effective implementation of the Convention, for example, possible differences in the legal status of mothers and fathers in custody or contact cases.

The evaluation of the capability of the non-EU acceding State concerned to properly apply the Convention does not predominantly depend on one or the other element mentioned above. The above listed elements are only indicative and rather aim at offering a global picture allowing the States considering acceptance of the accession to assess whether to engage in mutual obligations on the basis of a sufficient level of trust. Nonetheless, one element stands out as particularly important in the evaluation, ie, the establishment of a functioning Central Authority under the Convention. In the light of the importance of the tasks of the Central Authority under the Convention, it is generally deemed that such Authority should be duly in place in the acceding State before the accession of that State may be considered. The elements taken into consideration as listed above only offer part of the picture which is considered by Member States. Political considerations may play an important part as well as other factors such as historical ties with the acceding State concerned. It should be noted that despite an apparently severe assessment process in a number of Member States, several of these States have in fact accepted a relatively high number of accessions. Therefore, while the process towards acceptance of accessions differs among Member States, the ultimate result may not always differ so much.

In the light of the above, it is clear that a way forward to process acceptances at EU level consists in the gathering of information on the elements set out above, in addition to the information already gathered by the Hague Conference itself, prior to the preparation of proposals regarding accessions of non-EU States to the Convention. This background information continues to be gathered by Member States, through the channels traditionally used for this purpose. In addition, the Union's External Action Service may equally be involved as well as any other sources of information which may be deemed useful in the case at hand.

The results of this information gathering are then discussed between the Member States and the Commission. This maximises the information available to the Commission when considering new proposals on the matter and allows the Commission to better evaluate the prospects of success of any such proposals, particularly relevant in an area where unanimity is required.

3. CONCLUSION

The future will show what the impact will be of Opinion 1/13 on the acceptance of acceding States to the 1980 Hague Child Abduction Convention. Developing a pragmatic methodology to handle accessions may be key to ensuring a positive result.

So far, the first developments post-Opinion 1/13 have been encouraging. Indeed, the Council has adopted seven of the first set of eight proposals regarding the accession of non-EU States to the Convention, in particular Andorra, Singapore, Seychelles, Russia, Albania, Morocco, and Armenia.[7] However, the absence of an established Central Authority in Gabon was considered to require further bilateral contacts with this State in order to allow any decision to be taken. As a next step, proposals on the acceptance of the accession of the Republic of Korea, Kazakhstan, and Peru were adopted on 7 June 2016.[8] Furthermore, action will be considered with respect to those non-EU States (members or not members of The Hague Conference on Private International Law) that have acceded to the 1980 Convention before the establishment of the EU's competence with the adoption of the Brussels IIa Regulation.

The first developments post-Opinion 1/13 show that it is feasible to develop a coherent and uniform Union policy with regard to international child abduction. Now that the questions on the existence and the nature of external competence have been solved, it is possible to look forward to develop such external policy. The development of a common pragmatic process to handle accessions of non-EU States is a first step in this respect. This process may be improved and fine-tuned over time and solutions may need to be found if the required unanimity were not to be found. Despite all the difficulties, however, the Union can seize this opportunity to stand stronger in its external relations towards third States. The political weight of an acceptance or non-acceptance by 27 States[9] at the same time is not to be underestimated at international level. Despite the critical reactions it received, Opinion 1/13 may therefore be considered as an important strengthening of both the Union and its Member States' external action.

---

7 Decision (EU) 2015/1023 authorising certain Member States to accept, in the interest of the European Union, the accession of Andorra to the 1980 Hague Convention on the Civil Aspects of International Child Abduction [2015] OJ L 163/29; Decision (EU) 2015/1024 authorising certain Member States to accept, in the interest of the European Union, the accession of Singapore to the 1980 Hague Convention on the Civil Aspects of International Child Abduction [2015] OJ L 163/32; Decisions (EU) 2015/2354 (Seychelles), 2015/2355 (Russia), 2015/2356 (Albania), 2015/2357 (Morocco), and 2015/2358 (Armenia) were all adopted on 10 December 2015 and published in the official journal [2015] OJ L 331. In order to avoid any possible confusion regarding the validity, under public international law, of the declarations of acceptance already made by a number of Member States the authorisations are addressed to those Member States that have not yet deposited their declaration of acceptance.

8 COM (2016) 372 (Republic of Korea); COM (2016) 368 (Kazakhstan); COM (2016) 367 (Peru).

9 Pursuant to Protocol No 22 on the position of Denmark, annexed to the Treaty on European Union and to the Treaty on the Functioning of the European Union, Denmark does not take part in the adoption of measures relating, among others, to judicial cooperation in civil matters.

INTERNATIONAL AGREEMENTS ON PRIVATE INTERNATIONAL LAW MATTERS NOT COVERED BY EU LEGISLATION – WHICH TEST SHOULD BE ADOPTED TO ASSESS THE COMPETENCE OF THE EU?

Chiara E. Tuo
University of Genova

1. THE POSITION OF THE ECJ ON THE EXTERNAL COMPETENCE OF THE EU IN THE AREA OF PRIVATE INTERNATIONAL LAW

The external competence of the EU in the field of private international law has again become topical as a result of Opinion 1/13 of the Court of Justice (ECJ), regarding the acceptance of third-State accessions to the 1980 Hague Convention on the civil aspects of international child Abduction.[1]

This paper investigates whether, and in which terms, the test applied in Opinion 1/13, as well as in the previous Opinion 1/03 concerning the revised Lugano Convention,[2] also applies to the envisaged conclusion of international agreement on matters which would not yet be paralleled, at the EU internal level, by uniform rules.

1.1. OPINION 1/13

Opinion 1/13 was rendered upon the request of the Commission. Contrary to the position taken by the Council and by several Member States[3], the Commis-

1 Opinion 1/13, EU:C:2014:2303.
2 Opinion 1/03, EU:C:2006:81.
3 More precisely, the French, Greek and Polish Governments were of the view that the matter fell

sion was of the view that the acceptance of third-State accessions to the Child Abduction Convention fell within the exclusive external competence of the EU.[4]

This view has finally been endorsed by the Court based on the following reasoning.[5] The Court asserted that the EU has an external competence to deal with cross-border family law matters in light of Article 81(3) TFEU and Regulation (EC) No 2201/2003 concerning jurisdiction and the recognition and enforcement of judgments in matrimonial matters and the matters of parental responsibility (Brussels IIa).[6] The Court relied, for this, on its own case law and on the wording of Article 216(1) TFUE, which in fact was meant to codify that case law.[7] Specifically, it found that the authority of the EU to undertake international commitments in the subject matter of the Child Abduction Convention (ie, cooperation in respect of the wrongful removal of a child from one State to another) can in fact be asserted, in spite the absence of any express Treaty or secondary law provisions to that effect, on the ground that such competence is necessary for the attainment of a specific objective pursued by the EU.[8]

The ECJ moved on to state that the EU external competence in this area is exclusive in nature. This conclusion, too, was intended to reflect the Court's case law, as codified in Article 3(2) TFEU.[9] The acceptance of non-EU countries' accessions to the Child Abduction Convention, the Court noted, falls within the EU exclusive external competence because it may adversely affect or alter the scope of the Brussels IIa Regulation. The relationship between the Convention and the Brussels IIa Regulation is one of 'overlap and close connection'.[10] Most of the Convention's provisions are in fact either mirrored or complemented and clarified by the Regulation.[11] Against this background, the meaning, scope and

outside the EU external competence, whereas Austria, Belgium, Cyprus, Czech Republic, Estonia, Finland, Germany, Ireland, Latvia, Lithuania, Portugal, Romania, Slovakia, Spain, Sweden and United Kingdom together with the Council took the position that the EU external competence could not be deemed of an exclusive nature: see para. 60 of the Opinion.

4 Of the same view were also, in addition to the Advocate general Jääskinen (see his View, EU:C:2014:2292), the EU Parliament and the Italian Government.

5 For an extensive comment on the Opinion see P Beaumont's contribution to this book.

6 [2003] OJ L 338/1.

7 Article 216(1) TFEU reads: 'The Union may conclude an agreement with one or more third countries or international organizations where the Treaties so provide or where the conclusion of an agreement is necessary in order to achieve, within the framework of the Union's policies, one of the objectives referred to in the Treaties, or is provided for in a legally binding Union act or is likely to affect common rules or alter their scope'.

8 Opinion 1/13, n 1, paras 67-68.

9 Article 3(2) TFEU reads: 'The Union shall also have exclusive competence for the conclusion of an international agreement when its conclusion is provided for in a legislative act of the Union or is necessary to enable the Union to exercise its internal competence, or in so far as its conclusion may affect common rules or alter their scope'.

10 Opinion 1/13, n 1, para. 85.

11 Ibid, paras 75-83.

effectiveness of the Regulation are at risk of being affected or altered by the Convention.[12]

The latter assertion is not contradicted by the fact that several provisions of the Regulation are consonant with those of the Convention, nor that the Brussels IIa Regulation, pursuant to its Article 60, is to be given precedence over the Convention. These circumstances do not prevent the uniform application of Brussels IIa from being adversely affected by the Convention's provisions, as it would happen if the third-State accessions to the Hague Convention were individually accepted by the Member States. Such individual acceptance would especially undermine the uniform and consistent application of the Regulation's rules 'concerning cooperation between the authorities of the Member States whenever a situation involving international child abduction involved a third State and two Member States, one of which had accepted the accession of that third State to the Convention whilst the other had not'.[13]

The ECJ thus concluded that 'the exclusive competence of the EU encompasses the acceptance of the accession of a third State to the 1980 Hague Convention'.[14]

1.2. THE *ERTA* DOCTRINE RELOADED

In Opinion 1/13 the Court widely relied on its previous case law, particularly Opinion 1/03 on the competence of the Community to conclude the revised Lugano Convention on jurisdiction and the recognition of judgments in civil and commercial matters,[15] for the purpose of verifying whether (*i*) the EU external competence covers also the acceptance of non-EU countries accessions to the Child Abduction Convention and (*ii*) whether that competence is exclusive in nature.

The Lugano Opinion provided the ECJ with the opportunity of dealing for the first time with the general principles that govern the exercise of EU external powers on matters of private international law. The following paragraphs will recall the key findings of the Court with a view to focusing on the criteria for assessing the existence and nature of the external competences of the EU in private international law matters and to understanding the scope of application of such criteria, ie, whether they may play a role in situations other than those specifically considered in Opinion 1/03.

---

12 Ibid, paras 84-85.

13 Ibid, paras 87-89.

14 Ibid, para. 90.

15 Opinion 1/03, n 2. On this Opinion, see, among others, F Pocar (ed), *The External Competence of the European Union and Private International Law* (Cedam 2007).

The Court held in Opinion 1/03 that the revised Lugano Convention falls entirely within the exclusive competence of the EU because it affected the uniform and consistent application of Regulation (EC) No 44/2001 on jurisdiction and the recognition and enforcement of judgments (Brussels I).[16] According to the Court, the Regulation sets out a 'unified and coherent system' of rules on jurisdiction and the recognition of judgments, whose uniform application and proper functioning are at risk of being affected by any international agreements which equally lay down (as the Lugano Convention does) a unified system of rules on the same matters.[17]

The Court's conclusion was based on the 'effect-on-Community-law' test elaborated in the 1971 *ERTA* judgment.[18] The Court had stated in *ERTA* that, once common rules have been adopted by the EC (now the EU), Member States have no longer the right to undertake international obligations with third countries which are liable to affect those rules.[19]

As pointed out in literature, the Court provided in Opinion 1/03 some important clarifications as to the operation of the *ERTA* doctrine.[20] To begin with, the ECJ made clear that, for the EU external competence to be exclusive, it is not necessary that the areas respectively covered by the international agreement and the EU rules coincide fully. The EU enjoys exclusive competence also when the international agreement concerns an area covered only 'to a large extent' by the EU rules, insofar as the former is found capable of altering the proper

16 [2001] OJ L 12/1. See Opinion 1/03, n 2, paras 134-173.

17 Opinion 1/03, n 2, paras 144-151 and 164-168. The arguments set out by the Court to show that the Brussels I Regulation represents a unified and coherent system were the following. As regards jurisdiction rules, the Court relied on *Owusu* (Case C-281/02, *Owusu v Jackson,* EU:C:2005:120) to state that the Brussels I Regulation applies not only to relations between Member States but also to relations between a Member State and a non-EU country; and in any case it interprets Article 4(1) of the Regulation 'as meaning that it forms part of the system implemented by the Regulation' (para. 148). As to the recognition and enforcement of judgments, the Court points out the close link between them and the provisions on jurisdiction.

18 Case 22/70, *Commission v Council* ('*ERTA*'), EU:C:1971:32.

19 Ibid, paras 15-22. The test builds on the so-called doctrine of pre-emption. It is worth remembering that *ERTA* concerned a dispute between the Commission and the Council over the negotiation of an international road transport agreement on safety rules in the absence of an express provision on external competence in the Treaty. The ECJ held that, since the adoption of a common transport policy formed a Treaty objective and common rules for the implementation thereof had already been adopted by means of a regulation (namely, Regulation (EEC) 543/69 on the harmonisation of certain social legislation relating to road transport [1969] OJ L 77/49), the relevant Treaty's provisions legitimised EU external action in that very field. In the ECJ's view, the existence of the said EU provisions prevented Member States from individually undertaking external actions in the field at hand, given that otherwise, in addition to the EU internal competence being undermined, the unity of the Common Market and the uniform application of EU law would also have been jeopardised.

20 A Malatesta, 'The Lugano Opinion and its Consequences in Family and Succession Matters', in A Malatesta, S Bariatti and F Pocar (eds), *The External Dimension of EC Private International Law in Family and Succession Matters* (Cedam 2008), 19-24; A Santini, 'The Doctrine of Implied External Powers and Private International Law Concerning Family and Succession Matters', ibid, 31.

functioning of the system resulting from EU legislation.[21] Secondly, the Court specified that when the areas covered by the envisaged international agreement and the relevant EU provisions do not perfectly overlap, the assessment as to whether the former impacts on EU law has to be carried out taking into account not only the scope of the rules in question but also their nature and content, as well as the current status of EU law in the area at issue, together with its future developments, insofar as the latter are foreseeable at the time of the analysis.[22]

More particularly, the assessment must be of such a character as to ensure that the EU constitutional principle of the conferral of powers (Article 5(2) TFEU) is complied with. Thus, the relationship between EU rules and the relevant international commitments is to be examined taking primarily into account (*i*) the areas respectively covered by the instruments in question, (*ii*) their foreseeable developments and (*iii*) the nature and content of both the EU rules and the international provisions, in order to find out whether the envisaged agreement is likely to undermine 'the uniform and consistent application of the EU rules and the proper functioning of the system which they establish'.[23]

1.3. STRETCHING THE ECJ'S TEST BEYOND ITS BORDERS

It has been submitted that the arguments developed by the ECJ in Opinion 1/03 resulted in a 'restatement of the criterion elaborated in the *ERTA* judgment', ie, the criterion of the effect of the envisaged agreement on existing EU rules.[24]

Actually, the Lugano Opinion provided for a more flexible version of the *ERTA* doctrine in that it set out that the test to be applied for the purposes of establishing whether or not the EU external competence is of an exclusive nature does not only entail the appraisal of the scope of the rules at stake, but also an assessment as to their nature, content and foreseeable development.

The position has likewise been convincingly put forward that – in light of the overall structure of the Opinion with its broad introductory part devoted to the restatement of the *ERTA* doctrine – the reasoning developed by the Court was aimed at laying down the foundation for the EU exclusive competence not only with regard to the new Lugano Convention but also in respect of other fields of private international law.[25] In this vein, it has also been held that, on the occasion of the Lugano Opinion, the *ERTA* principles have been reshaped by the Court to reflect the special features of the EU rules on jurisdiction and

21 Opinion 1/03, n 2, para. 126.

22 Ibid.

23 Opinion 1/03, n 2, para. 133.

24 A Santini, n 20, 34.

25 Ibid, 39

recognition of judgments.[26] Otherwise stated, the impact of the Lugano Opinion has not been seen as being limited to the situation with which the Court was specifically concerned.

In a way, the Court itself confirmed that this was the correct reading of the Lugano Opinion by broadly relying upon the latter with respect to a completely different area of private international law, as indeed is the area of family law with cross-border implications covered by the Child Abduction Convention.

It could even be argued that the test to be applied for the purpose of assessing whether the EU is entrusted with exclusive external competence in the field of private international law remains the test elaborated by the Court itself in its previous case law, in spite of the fact that the case law in question has been codified by the Lisbon Treaty in terms which do not exactly match those of the ECJ.

In fact, only apparently has the Court grounded the EU exclusive external competence as regards the Hague Child Abduction Convention on Articles 216(1) and 3(2) TFUE. In reality, nowhere in the said provisions are to be found the criteria on which the Court primarily based its Opinion.[27]

As a matter of fact, Opinion 1/13 falls short of clarifying 'on which basis of Article 216(1) TFEU the [EU] competence [as regards the Child Abduction Convention] arises'. So much so that, as Paul Beaumont puts it, '[t]he impression is that the Court thinks the EU has external competence whenever a matter falls within an area over which the EU has internal competence to legislate'.[28]

The above is all the more evident if one looks at the arguments which led the ECJ to regard the EU external competence as exclusive. Indeed, the Court's finding that the international agreement at stake falls within the said competence because, pursuant to Article 3(2) TFEU, it 'may affect common rules or alter their scope' rests on the application of some key concepts that originate directly from the ECJ earlier case law, as reshaped in the Lugano Opinion.[29]

In light of the foregoing, one might therefore argue that, as a result of the position taken by the ECJ in Opinion 1/13, the conditions triggering the existence of EU exclusive external competence in private international law matters have been stretched even further.

---

26 A Malatesta, n 20, 22.

27 See n 7 and 9. For a critical assessment of the way in which the ECJ case law on the EU treaty-making power has been codified by Article 216(1) TFEU see recently, among others, C Cellerino, *Soggettività internazionale e azione esterna dell'Unione europea* (Aracne 2015), 61 ff.

28 P Beaumont, n 5.

29 As pointed out by P Beaumont, n 5, the two concepts that the Court still consider relevant for the application of Article 3(2) TFEU despite their having not been codified by such Article are 'the largely covered area' and the 'foreseeable future development'. Indeed, as seen, in continuity with Opinion 1/03, n 2, the Court argued that international agreements concerned with an area largely covered by EU rules, such as the Child Abduction Convention, fall within the EU exclusive external competence if their provisions are found to affect, or alter the scope, of EU rules also in light of their foreseeable future development.

However, it bears mentioning that both the 1/03 and 1/13 Opinions were solely concerned with the issues of the existence and the nature of EU external competence as regards international agreements concerning private international law matters (at least partially) falling within the scope of application of EU rules already in force, that is to say, respectively, Regulations No 44/2001 and No 2201/2003.

Thus, the view has been expressed that if the same issues were raised with respect to an international agreement not yet mirrored by internal EU rules, the Court would not resort to the *ERTA* doctrine in that it only fits situations where the EU has already exercised its competence at the 'domestic' level. Hence, according to such view, 'in principle the impact of the Lugano Opinion should be confined to matters already covered by EU rules'.[30]

In the present author's view, this argument is not enough to exclude that the ECJ would resort to the same test as laid down in Opinions 1/03 and 1/13 for the purpose of establishing whether the EU is exclusively empowered to conclude an international agreement dealing with private international law issues that are not addressed, internally, by existing uniform rules.

A similar question could arise in relation to the Hague Convention on children intercountry adoption, should one or more of the Member States (which are all parties thereto) declare their intention to unilaterally object to the accession to the Convention by one or more non-EU countries.[31]

Based on the arguments that will be set out below, it does not seem unreasonable to expect that the ECJ would base its answer on the very same reasoning developed in Opinions 1/03 and 1/13. This position, as explained hereunder, essentially relies on the terms of such reasoning being so broad as to leave room for assessing the existence and the nature of EU external competence also in cases, such as the one referred to above, where the international commitments at stake are not yet paralleled by existing EU secondary legislation on the very same subject-matter.

30 A Santini, n 20, 39.

31 Reference is made to the Hague Convention of 29 May 1993 on protection of children and co-operation in respect of intercountry adoption, which entered into force on 1 May 1995. The Convention has been ratified by States that are members of the Conference as well as by States that are not. The updated list of the contracting States is available at <http://www.hcch.net>. According to Article 44(3), accession to the Convention by a new State 'shall have effect only as regards the relations between the acceding State and those contracting States which have not raised an objection to its accession in the six months after the receipt of the notification referred to in sub-paragraph b) of Article 48', ie, the notification of the new accession that the depositary of the Convention has to serve upon the States which are already parties to the Convention.

2. THE 'EFFECT ON EU LAW TEST' AS OPPOSED TO THE 'NECESSITY TEST' OF OPINION 1/76

As said,[32] in Opinion 1/03 the ECJ stated that the EU is vested with exclusive external competences when, on the basis of a thorough analysis of both the envisaged international agreement and the EU rules governing, to a large extent, (almost) the same area, the conclusion can be reached that such latter rules would be affected, or eventually altered in their scope of application, by the international agreement at stake.

As made clear by the Court, this analysis is to be carried out in a comprehensive and detailed manner, namely having regard not only to the EU rules already existing at the internal level, but also to their future development as foreseeable at the time of the analysis.

It has been convincingly observed that, in so doing, 'the Court strived to stick to the *ERTA* principles, which eventually were remarkably widened' up to the point of making them capable of being 'stretched still further, as far as we want'.[33]

The practice of the EU institutions with respect to international conventions concerning jurisdiction, recognition and enforcement of judgments and applicable law in areas which have been the subject matter of EU instruments has eventually confirmed that the approach followed by the ECJ in the Lugano Opinion was liable to lead to an extensive interpretation of the EU external exclusive competence. This is evidenced by Regulations (EC) Nos 662/2009 and 664/2009.[34]

The latter instruments establish the procedure to be followed for the purpose of authorising a Member State to either amend or negotiate and enter, respectively, an existent or new bilateral agreement with third countries on certain specific private international law issues considered as falling within the EU exclusive external competence (ie, on the one hand, matrimonial matters

32 See *supra*, para. 1.2.

33 A Malatesta, n 20, 28.

34 Regulation (EC) No 662/2009 establishing a procedure for the negotiation and conclusion of agreements between Member States and third countries on particular matters concerning the law applicable to contractual and non-contractual obligations [2009] OJ L 200/25; Regulation (EC) No 664/2009 establishing a procedure for the negotiation and conclusion of agreements between Member States and third countries concerning jurisdiction, recognition and enforcement of judgments and decisions in matrimonial matters, matters of parental responsibility and matters relating to maintenance obligations, and the law applicable to matters relating to maintenance obligations [2009] OJ L 200/46. On these Regulations (in addition to PA De Miguel Asensio, n 36) see M Cremona, 'Member States as Trustees of the Community Interest: Participating in International Agreements on Behalf of the European Community', *EUI Working Paper Law* 2009/17, 16-19, <http://hdl.handle.net/1814/12881>; M Niedzwiedz and P Mostowik, 'Implications of the ECJ "Lugano II" Opinion for European Union's External Actions Concerning Private International Law' (2010) 13 *Yearbook of Polish European Studies* 129, 136-142.

and the matters of parental responsibility, and, on the other, matters relating to maintenance obligations).

Despite the said Regulations having been presented as the follow-up to the Lugano Opinion,[35] it seems hardly disputable that their most restrictive scope of application as well as the exceptional character of the authorisation mechanism thereby envisaged have resulted in the EU exclusive external competence being so expanded as to cover also private international law matters not yet governed at the EU internal level, ie, for instance, the recognition and enforcement of third-country judgments.[36]

Indeed, Regulation No 664/2009 seems to be based on the assumption that when bilateral conventions with third States deal with the recognition and enforcement of judgments in a matter (other than those with which the said Regulation is expressly concerned) that is regulated by an EU instrument, the Member States cannot even be authorised to negotiate, let alone enter or amend, such conventions, as the related power now exclusively lies with the EU, regardless of the relevant EU instrument being undoubtedly not applicable to third State judgments.[37] To say it differently, the Lugano Opinion seems to have been relied upon by the EU legislator with the aim of stipulating that the EU exclusive external competence arises subject only to the condition that the envisaged international agreement deals with a private international law issue already regulated at the EU level, irrespective of the extent to which the said issue is actually governed by the relevant EU instruments.

It could therefore be argued that the terms in which the *ERTA* doctrine is referred to in the Lugano Opinion are so broad as to make one suppose that they have been used with the aim of reshaping the said doctrine to such an extent as to encompass also cases where the envisaged international agreement dealing

---

35 See Recital 5 of both Regulations.

36 See PA De Miguel Asensio, 'International Conventions and European Instruments of Private International Law: Interrelation and Codification', in PA De Miguel Asensio and JS Bergé, 'The Place of International Agreements and European Law in a European Code of Private International Law', in M Fallon, P Lagarde and P Peruzzetto (eds), *Quelle architecture pour un code européen de droit international privé?* (Peter Lang 2011), 185, 199-200. The Author is therefore of the view that bilateral agreements such as the 2003 Convention between Italy and Algeria regarding Legal Aid in Civil and Commercial Matters (entered into force on 13 December 2006) and the 2002 Convention between Italy and Kuwait regarding Judicial Cooperation and the Recognition and Enforcement of Judgments in Civil and Commercial Matters (in force since 21 December 2004) would not be authorised owing to the fact that they both lay down provisions on the recognition and enforcement of judgments in civil and commercial matters.

37 PA De Miguel Asensio, n 36, 198 and 201. As to third-country judgments, see among others, with respect to Regulation (EU) No 1215/2012 on jurisdiction and the recognition of judgments in civil and commercial matters [2012] OJ L 351/1, P Franzina, 'L'universalisation partielle du régime européen de la compétence en matière civile et commerciale dans le règlement Bruxelles I "bis": une mise en perspective', in E Guinchard (ed), *Le nouveau règlement Bruxelles I "bis": règlement n° 1215/2012 du 12 décembre 2012 concernant la compétence judiciaire, la reconnaissance et l'exécution des décisions en matière civile et commerciale* (Bruylant 2014), 39.

with private international law matters is not yet mirrored, at the EU internal level, by any specific secondary rules.

The rationale for such a choice may indeed be found – as correctly pointed out in doctrinal writings[38] – in that the ECJ regards the increasing enlargement of the EU exclusive external competences in the field of judicial cooperation in civil and commercial matters as a means for achieving the more general objective, enshrined in Article 3(2) TEU, of the establishment of an area of freedom security and justice without internal frontiers, in which the free movement of EU citizens is ensured.[39]

Hence, if – as authoritatively argued – in Opinion 1/03 the Court intended to lay down a set of criteria specifically designed to establish the existence and the nature of the EU external competence in the very field of private international law in such a way as to ensure the pursue of the more general objective envisaged by Article 3(2) TEU, it could consequently be held that the ECJ would stick to such criteria also for the purposes of establishing whether the EU is exclusively entitled to enter an international agreement on private international law issues that, despite being not yet governed by EU specific common rules, fall nonetheless in a field largely covered by Union secondary legislation. It is, in other words, submitted that the existence of the general objective enshrined in Article 3(2) TEU alongside with the EU rules already in force, or likely-to-be-adopted, for the achievement of such an objective would be deemed sufficient ground for a Court's finding that the EU is exclusively competent to undertake the relevant international commitments irrespective of the latter covering private international law issues not yet uniformly regulated at the internal level.

This means, in turn, that the ECJ would not resort to the 'necessity test' as progressively consolidated by the Court itself with the clear aim of rendering more stringent and rigorous the original version thereof as set out in Opinion 1/76.[40] The above, notwithstanding the said test being commonly put into play whenever the need arises to establish whether or not the EU has the power to enter international agreements not yet covered by secondary rules at the internal level.

It is in fact undeniable that pursuant to the terms in which such test was initially framed the competence to bind the EU in relation to third countries could

---

38 A Malatesta, n 20, 29.

39 A confirmation as to the capability of 'the list of EU objectives mentioned, for instance, in art. 3 TEU' to serve as a basis for the EU treaty-making power is eventually to be drawn from the terms in which Article 216(1) TFEU (n 7) has been couched with the aim of codifying the *ERTA* doctrine. As appropriately remarked in literature (T Konstadinies, 'EU Foreign Policy under the Doctrine of Implied Powers: Codification Drawbacks and Constitutional Limitations' (2014) 39 *European Law Review* 511, 515), the broad formulation of this article rests on 'the elusiveness characterising the doctrine of implied powers as first established in *ERTA*' and is designed to keep 'EU external action adaptable to changing needs'.

40 Opinion 1/76, EU:C:1977:63.

arise by implication from the Treaty provisions establishing internal powers in the same field as that covered by the envisaged international agreement. Accordingly, in the 1/76 Opinion the ECJ established that a treaty-making power does not even require the previous adoption of secondary legislation, provided that the conclusion of an international agreement is 'necessary' to attain a Treaty objective.

The above position has eventually been revisited on the occasion of the 1/94 Opinion, whereby the ECJ severally narrowed the circumstances in which external action to achieve EU objectives may be deemed 'necessary'.[41] Indeed, Opinion 1/94 is indicative of the ECJ's self-restraint in holding, *inter alia*, that the EU may have exclusive implied external competence to regulate a given matter only where it has adopted secondary legislation or where it has adopted provisions which concern third-country nationals.[42]

It may therefore be argued that, if put into play consistently with such latter narrow conditions, the 'necessity test' – despite being, as said, the one usually applied when the EU has not exercised its internal competence – would not serve the abovementioned purposes in which, in light of the Lugano Opinion, the EU exclusive external competence in the area of judicial cooperation in civil and commercial matters is instrumental.

Further confirmation of the above may eventually be found in that it was the Court itself that, in delivering Opinion 1/03, deliberately avoided using as a basis thereof Opinion 1/76, despite the latter having been expressly referred to in the introductory part of the decision.

Indeed, at least from a purely theoretical point of view, the opposite position could have been taken that, since Opinion 1/03 had actually to do with an international agreement (also) concerned with an area not covered by EU secondary rules of exactly the very same scope of application (ie, recognition and enforcement of non-EU States' judgments), the 'necessity test' criteria would eventually bear some relevance, thus excluding the possibility to be totally disregarded, as instead they were, by the ECJ. More particularly, the said criteria could have come into play for the purposes of establishing whether or not the EU was to be deemed exclusively competent to enter the Lugano Convention despite the latter's provisions on recognition and enforcement of third-country judgments being not even partially mirrored by the relevant Brussels I rules.

But the Court chose to follow a totally different path, ie, as seen, that of sticking exclusively to the *ERTA* doctrine with the aim of stretching the conditions for its application to such an extent as to adapt them to the special features which are inherent in the very field of private international law.

---

41 Opinion 1/94, EU:C:1994:384.

42 T Konstadinies, n 39, 516.

Therefore, by stating that the exclusive external EU competence has to be assessed in light of not only the existing EU rules but also their foreseeable future development, the ECJ appears to be in favour of an approach which, at least for the purposes of ascertaining the existence and the nature of EU external competences in the area of private international law, departs from, and actually overcomes the hurdles of, the more rigorous version of the 'necessity test' as above recalled. In this perspective, it therefore seems most appropriate the authoritatively held position whereby 'recent jurisprudence suggests that the ECJ has adopted a sectoral approach to the European Union's external competence'.[43]

To put it differently, it does not seem unreasonable to expect that, for the limited purposes of establishing whether or not the EU is exclusively entrusted to undertake international commitments on private international law matters, the Court would resort to the *ERTA* test as reshaped in the Lugano Opinion, irrespective of the international commitments at stake being concerned with an area already governed by specific EU secondary rules or not.

3. THE EU LEGAL FRAMEWORK ON FREE MOVEMENT OF CITIZENS AS THE YARDSTICK AGAINST WHICH THE EXCLUSIVE EXTERNAL COMPETENCE IN PRIVATE INTERNATIONAL LAW MATTERS SHOULD BE ASSESSED

In light of the foregoing, the conclusion may therefore be reached that the test to be carried out with the aim of verifying if the EU is exclusively endowed with treaty-making power in the very field of private international law requires the investigation as to whether the international provisions at stake are liable to affect EU rules dealing with private international law issues which, as the case may be, might be either already in force or simply likely-to-be-adopted.

Given that, according to Article 3(2) TEU, the establishment of an area of freedom, security and justice is, in turn, instrumental in the EU citizens' full and effective enjoyment of their fundamental right to free movement, the EU could be deemed exclusively entitled to enter any international agreements on private international law matters whose provisions are considered capable of affecting the achievement of such a general and wider objective, irrespective of specific EU secondary rules on the very same subject-matter as that of the relevant agreement being already in force or not.

As to the further development of the EU area of justice bearing the utmost importance for the EU citizens' full enjoyment of their right to free movement

43 T Konstadinies, n 39, 518.

suffice here to refer to the *Justice for Growth Agenda*,[44] where the EU Commission pointed out the need to remove the practical and legal obstacles that still prevent EU citizens from fully exercising the same rights they have at home in another Member State.[45]

It therefore does not come as a surprise that among the methods to be used for the purposes of enhancing EU citizens' mobility – ie, one of the three main key challenges ahead (the others being the strengthening of mutual trust and economic recovery and growth) as addressed by the Commission for the future EU justice policy – stands the adoptions of 'provisions adding to the citizenship rights referred to in the EU Treaties'.[46] Nor is it by chance that the Commission has explicitly referred to situations where citizens encounter problems, for example, related to civil status records and that, to the end of avoiding such problems, the EU legislator has expressly been recommended to assess the need for further action. Namely, the adoption of rules on family names is addressed as a priority action to be undertaken with a view to complementing 'existing proposals to facilitate the acceptance of those public documents which are of particular practical relevance when citizens or businesses make use of their free movement rights'.[47]

In line with the *Justice for Growth Agenda*, the European Council's conclusions of June 2014 once again underlined the aim of EU Justice policy to contribute to Union citizens' mobility, addressing as objectives to be prioritized 'the recognition and enforcement of judgments in family law and civil and commercial matters'.[48]

On the basis of the inextricable link existing between judicial cooperation in civil matters and the objective enshrined in Article 3(2) TEU, the EU external competence could therefore be characterised as exclusive on the grounds of the impact that the relevant international agreement on private international law matters might be deemed liable to adversely display on the existing, or likely-

44 Reference is made to the Communication of the Commission to the Parliament, the Council, the European Economic and Social Committee and the Committee of the Regions, *The EU Justice Agenda for 2020 - Strengthening Trust, Mobility and Growth within the Union*, COM (2014) 144 final.

45 Ibid, para. 3. As well known, the mobility of European citizens is facilitated by the rights attached to citizenship of the European Union: in particular the right to freedom of movement and, more generally, the right to be treated like a national in the Member State of residence. These rights are enshrined in primary EU law and implemented by means of secondary legislation. There is obviously no room here to refer to the multitude of legal sources put in place by the EU legislator with the aim of fostering Union citizens mobility; it is however worth recalling Directive 2004/38/EC of the European Parliament and of the Council of 29 April 2004 on the right of citizens of the Union and their family members to move and reside freely within the territory of the Member States [2004] OJ L 158/77.

46 *Justice for Growth Agenda*, n 44, para. 4.3.

47 Ibid.

48 European Council Conclusions of 26/27 June 2014, EUCO 79/14, 5-6.

to-be-adopted, Union rules either directly or indirectly aimed at enhancing the EU citizens' full enjoyment of free movement.

A confirmation of the above might well be drawn from the same *Justice for Growth Agenda* having made clear that EU citizens and businesses cannot be really protected in their relations with third countries without the EU itself being active in international fora and engaging with its partners. In this connection, the Commission has been straightforward in stating that the objective should be that 'what has been achieved at EU level in the justice areas for defending rights and setting standards' 'finds support and drives EU relations with third countries'. To this end, the need has also been addressed that, 'at multilateral level', focus be given to 'more efficient cooperation with the Hague Conference on Private International Law, where the EU speaks with one voice in areas of civil and commercial law'.[49]

Such statements clearly imply a shift from Member States to EU of the power to handle external relations with respect to private international law matters, at least to the extent that they involve issues which are deemed somewhat likely to affect the mobility of EU citizens. Indeed, the Commission's reasoning may be sum up as follows: (i) action in private international law matters is in itself instrumental in the free movement of persons being further implemented; (ii) the attainment of such an objective presupposes specific measures to be issued at the EU level through both the adoption of uniform internal rules and the strengthening of the EU role as a one-voice-actor on the international scene.

On the basis of the above considerations, one could therefore argue that the external competence on private international law matters in civil and commercial areas now exclusively lie with the EU, irrespective of whether or not the relevant international commitments are already paralleled, at the internal level, by secondary rules governing the very same issues as those which the said commitments are specifically concerned with. As seen, the mere likelihood that the international agreement impair the attainment of the fundamental objective as set forth by Article 3(2) TEU – and, as a consequence, affect the EU secondary rules already in force, or likely-to-be-adopted, with the aim of implementing

[49] *Justice for Growth Agenda*, n 44, para. 4.3. For the sake of completeness, it seems worth remembering that in April 2007 the (then) EC acceded to the Hague Conference on Private International Law (Council Decision 2006/719/EC on the accession of the Community to the Hague Conference on Private International Law [2006] OJ L 297/1). According to M Cremona, 'EU External Action in the JHA Domain: A Legal Perspective', *EUI Working Paper Law* 2008/24, 22, <http://hdl.handle.net/1814/9487>, the accession 'will facilitate participation in the conventions negotiated within the Hague Conference' (as indeed it has likewise been suggested by the European Council in its December 2009 legislative plan called *The Stockholm Programme – An Open and Secure Europe Serving and Protecting Citizens* [2010] OJ C 115/1). By contrast, B Audit and L D'Avout, *Droit international privé* (7th ed, Economica 2013), 55-56, are of the view that, as a result of the accession, Member States have been left with almost no residual competence in this field.

such an objective – would be deemed sufficient ground for a finding of the EU as exclusively competent to handle the international commitments at stake.

4. FROM THEORY TO PRACTICE: THE 'EFFECT ON EU LAW TEST' APPLIED TO THE INTERCOUNTRY ADOPTION CONVENTION

The above holds true, for instance, if one comes to consider international agreements in family law matters such as the Hague Convention on the intercountry adoption of children (to which, as noted earlier, all Member States are a party).[50]

No doubt as to the Convention's subject-matter as set out by its Article 1[51] being not yet governed at the EU internal level by specific rules of either a private international law or substantive law nature. Still, it seems hardly disputable that the issue of recognition of intercountry adoptions as uniformly regulated by the Convention turns out to be strictly intertwined with the exercise of a person's right to free movement. Indeed, the simpler the mechanism whereby Member States recognise adoptive status created abroad, the more EU citizens' mobility will be enhanced. Hence, the international obligations flowing from the Convention as regards the very issue of recognition of adoptions may well be addressed as capable of affecting the Article 3(2) TEU objective of the establishment of an area of freedom, security and justice as well as the secondary rules aimed at the attainment thereof.

More particularly, the Convention's provisions on the recognition of adoptions establishing permanent parent-child relationships[52] might be considered as capable of affecting the principle of mutual recognition of familial status which, in light of the consolidated ECJ case law, constitutes one of the bedrock of free movement upon which has evolved, and is indeed meant to further develop, the set of rules aimed at enhancing citizens' mobility.

As well known, the said principle has been elaborated by the ECJ as a result of the progressive enlargement of 'the State of origin' principle so as to cover also the field of free movement of persons. Initially conceived for the purposes of assessing the compatibility with the Treaty of national rules deemed capable of affecting, if not even preventing, free movement of goods among Member

50 See n 31.

51 Which reads as follows: 'The objects of the present Convention are - a) to establish safeguards to ensure that intercountry adoptions take place in the best interests of the child and with respect for his or her fundamental rights as recognised in international law; b) to establish a system of co-operation amongst Contracting States to ensure that those safeguards are respected and thereby prevent the abduction, the sale of, or traffic in children; c) to secure the recognition in Contracting States of adoptions made in accordance with the Convention'.

52 Namely, Articles 23-27 of the Convention.

States,[53] the State of origin principle as well as the mechanism of mutual recognition whereby it operates is in fact now systematically put into play by the Court also when the question arises as to whether a given domestic measure may be considered liable to impair EU citizens' mobility, irrespective of such mobility being grounded on purely economic reasons or not.[54]

The position has therefore been appropriately submitted that, as a result of the abovementioned approach, the ECJ has given rise to the principle of the EU citizen's unitary status.[55]

In this perspective, the said principle traces its origin back to the ECJ's decisions in *Dafeki* and *Garcia Avello*,[56] according to which the competent authorities of the receiving Member State have the duty to accept the civil status documents and to recognize the personal status – ie, in the abovementioned cases, the name – of the EU citizen as acquired within his or her Member State of origin. To put it differently, such decisions are to be regarded as clear evidence that, from the ECJ's standpoint, EU citizens cannot really enjoy their right to free movement without being granted full recognition of their own civil status across EU. This implies, on the one hand, that the competence to establish the EU citizen's civil status lies exclusively with his or her Member State of origin; on the other hand, that the receiving Member State is in principle precluded from putting such status into question.

As anticipated, it is, in fact, hardly disputable that a functional link exists between the effective exercise of the right of free movement and the full recognition, within the EU area of justice, of personal status created in accordance with the rules of a given Member State. An EU citizen might indeed be reluctant to leave his Member State of origin if recognition of his personal status in the receiving EU country turns out to be conditional upon so stringent requirements as to render recognition itself too difficult, if not even impossible, to be

---

53 Case C-8/74, *Dassonville*, EU:C:1974:82; Case C-120/78, *Rewe-Zentral*, EU:C:1979:42.

54 On the principle of mutual recognition see, among others, G Rossolillo, *Mutuo riconoscimento e tecniche conflittuali* (Cedam 2002).

55 R Baratta, 'Problematic Elements of an Implicit Rule Providing for Mutual Recognition of Personal and Family Status in the EC' (2007) 27 *IPRax* 4; R Baratta, 'Verso la 'comunitarizzazione' dei principi fondamentali del diritto di famiglia' (2005) 41 *Rivista di diritto internazionale privato e processuale* 573, 591-592; M Fallon, 'Constraints of Internal Market on Family Law', in J Meeusen, M Pertegás, G Straetmans and F Swennen (eds), *International Family Law for the European Union* (Intersentia 2007), 149, 163-164; L Tomasi, *La tutela degli status familiari nel diritto dell'Unione europea* (Cedam 2007), 95 and 105; M Pertegás, 'Recognition and Enforcement of Judgments in Family and Succession Matters', in A Malatesta, S Bariatti and F Pocar, n 20, 161, 179; CE Tuo, 'Riconoscimento degli effetti delle adozioni straniere e rispetto delle diversità culturali', in G Cataldi and V Grado (eds), *Diritto internazionale e pluralità delle culture* (Editoriale Scientifica 2014), 227.

56 Reference is made, respectively, to Case C-336/94, *Eftalia Dafeki*, EU:C:1997:579, and Case C-148/02, *Carlos Garcia Avello v Belgian State*, EU:C:2003:539. See also Case C-353/06, *Stefan Grunkin, Dorothee Regina Paul*, EU:C:2008:559; Case C-208/09, *Ilonka Sayn-Wittgenstein v Landeshauptmann von Wien*, EU:C:2010:806; Case C-391/09, *Malgožata Runevič-Vardyn*, EU:C:2010:784; Case C-438/14, *Nabiel Peter Bogendorff von Wolffersdorff*, EU:C:2016:401.

achieved.[57] The existence of these legal obstacles would in fact deprive the citizen of the rights that he or she would be entitled to exercise in the receiving Member State as a result of the civil status validly acquired in the EU country of origin.

It is therefore likewise hardly debatable that mutual recognition of familial and personal status validly created in a Member State has now to be regarded as a principle which, in addition to substantially contributing to the EU citizens' full and effective enjoyment of their freedom of movement, also represents a fundamental corollary thereof.[58]

Against this background, no doubt as to the recognition of intercountry adoption of children being an issue strictly interwoven with the full enjoyment of the EU citizens' freedom of movement. The mechanism whereby such adoptions are given effect in a Member State other than that of origin bears in fact the utmost relevance as a condition triggering the EU adoptive parents' and children' effective exercise of their right to freely move across EU.

As such mechanism is, as seen, actually governed, among Member States, by the common provisions established by the 1993 Hague Convention, the way it operates in practice is, under several aspects, different from one Member State to another.[59] This results in the national requirements for the recognition of intercountry adoption sometimes even remarkably lacking uniformity, which in turn means, first, that it is far from certain that adoptive status are allowed to display across EU the very same effects as those produced in the country of origin, and, second, that due to such uncertainty EU adoptive parents and children are in principle deterred from exercising their right to free movement.

In light of the above, it is therefore unsurprising that the 24 September 2014 Workshop on Upcoming issues of EU law commissioned by the Committee on Legal Affairs of the EU Parliament still addresses the issue of adoption as one of the 'systematic gaps' which currently affect the existing EU regulatory framework of private international law rules.[60] Being one of the most important

---

57 GP Romano, 'Conflicts and Coordination of Family Statuses: Towards their Recognition within the EU?', in *Adoption: Cross-border Legal Issues - Compilation of Briefing Notes*, drawn up for the Policy Department C (Citizens' Rights and Constitutional Affairs) of the European Parliament, <http://www.europarl.europa.eu/supporting-analyses>, 17.

58 L Tomasi, n 55, 109.

59 It is for each contracting State to regulate a number of issues related to recognition of intercountry adoption which are left uncovered by the Convention. See, in this regard, the Explanatory Report on the Convention drawn up by G Parra-Aranguren, available at <http://hcch.net>, paras 404 ff.

60 Reference is made to the document issued in September 2014 and co-authored by W Heusel, M Ballesteros, X Kramer, L Bently, A Radauer, A Bertolini and E Palmerini. More particularly, Xandra Kramer was the author of the chapter on *European Private International Law: the Way Forward*, at 77. This is the follow-up to an Study carried out in 2012 (*A European Framework for Private International Law: Current Gaps and Future Perspectives*) – again on request of the Committee on Legal Affairs of the European Parliament – with the purpose of identifying the

topics in the area of family law which are not yet covered by the EU legislation, adoption falls within the category of gaps that 'the primary legislative concern should focus on' due to the fact that – for the reasons briefly set out above – the 'absence of harmonised rules has an immediate effect on citizens' within the EU.

Indeed, despite the area of family law being not listed among the gaps to be tackled in the short-term,[61] (*i*) the need for 'close collaboration with the Hague Conference on Private International law' is set out 'in view of the existing Hague Conventions' (such as, for example, that on adoption) and (*ii*) status of natural persons is addressed as one of the several topics requiring 'special attention in the near future' insofar as it has 'become more pressing' 'as a result of the development of the CJEU case law'.[62]

The reference to the 'immediate effect on citizens' produced by the absence of harmonised rules on family law matters such as adoption as well as the indication that 'close cooperation with the Hague Conference' is needed to close these gaps, apparently confirm, on the one hand, that adoption – despite being not yet regulated at the EU level – is nonetheless liable to interfere with, if not even prevent, the effective exercise of the EU citizens' freedom to move; on the other hand, that – due to their being strictly intertwined with the full enjoyment of such freedom – family law topics (even if) not yet regulated at the EU level, as indeed it is the case for status of natural persons, are now to be considered as falling inside the Union competence, in both its internal and external dimensions.

The above appears to be further confirmed by the recently adopted Regulation (EU) 2016/1191 on promoting the free movement of citizens by simplifying the requirements for presenting certain public documents in the EU.[63]

---

gaps of the (then) existing framework of European private international law. Adoption was indeed included among the 'systematic gaps' affecting EU private international law already in the 2012 Study, as it undoubtedly falls 'systematically outside' the topics currently regulated by Union existing instruments.

61 Owing to the fact that, pursuant to Article 81(3) TFEU, measures in the area of family law with cross-border implications are to be established by the Council acting unanimously after consultation of the European Parliament.

62 See the 2014 Study, n 59, 99 and 102.

63 [2016] OJ L 200/1. The Commission proposal (COM (2013) 228 final) was transmitted to the European Parliament and the Council on 2 April 2013. At first reading, the proposal has been amended by the EU Parliament under a position dated 4 February 2014 (P7_TA(2014)0054) as well as by the Council, which adopted its position on 11 March 2016. The Commission's communication to the Parliament pursuant to Article 294(6) TFEU (COM (2016) 216 final) is dated 8 April 2016. Regarding the 2013 Commission's proposal, see the comments by P Callé, 'Promoting the free movement of citizens and businesses by simplifying the acceptance of certain public documents within and outside the European Union' and MP Clancy, 'Promoting the free movement of citizens and businesses by simplifying the acceptance of certain public documents in the EU and beyond', both of them published in the February 2015 Workshop for the Juri Committee on *Cross-border activities in the EU – Making life easier for citizens* (co-authored by G Rühl, J

Based on Article 21(2) (in combination with Article 114(1)) TFEU, the proposal for such Regulation has been tabled by the Commission with a view to facilitating the rights of Union citizens to move and reside freely within the territory of Member States.[64] As the exercise of free movement rights is hampered by the administrative formalities that citizens still have to undergo with the aim of proving the authenticity of public documents and getting them accepted by the receiving Member State, the proposal's objective is to remove these obstacles by simplifying the abovementioned formalities and abolishing all forms of legalisation or similar requirements.[65]

Pursuant to Article 2 of the Regulation, the public documents covered by this instrument include documents the purpose of which is to establish the status of natural persons, such as adoption. Article 3 stipulates that the expression 'public documents' refers to 'documents emanating from an authority or an official connected with the courts or tribunals of a Member State, including those emanating from a public prosecutor, a clerk of the court or a judicial officer' as well as 'notarial acts'.[66]

It is certainly true that – as set out, respectively, by Article 2(4) and Article 2(3)(a) and (b) – the Regulation does not apply (i) to the recognition in a Member State of the legal effects relating to the content of public documents issued by the authorities of another Member State nor (ii) to public documents issued by the authorities of a third country or certified copies of such documents made by the authorities of a Member State.

No doubts, however, as to this piece of legislation representing a set of rules which, in addition to further developing EU legislation aimed at fostering Union citizens' right to free movement, also stands out as the follow-up to the EU Commission recommendation that legislative measures be undertaken in relation to status of natural persons in order to 'facilitate citizens' lives' and, more particularly, 'in order to avoid situations where citizens encounter problems'.[67] The Regulation, in other words, seeks to complement the already existing legal framework on Union citizenship by adding a legislative instrument aimed at uniformly regulating a topic unequivocally related to the civil status of natural

---

von Hein, C Wendehorst, K Lechner, E Põtter, H van Loon, P Lagarde, H Schepel, P Cortés, G De Palo and G Musger) <http://www.europarl.europa.eu/RegData/etudes/STUD/2015/510003/IPOL_STU(2015)510003_EN.pdf>.

64 Explanatory Memorandum to the proposal, paras 1.2 and 3.2.

65 Ibid.

66 These definitions have been added by the Council in its first reading of the Proposal (doc. No 6812/15 ADD 1), probably on the basis of the consideration that in many Member States no specific civil status documents exist in areas such as adoption, in respect of which the relevant document could also be the court judgment or a notarial act.

67 *Justice for Growth Agenda*, n 44, 9.

persons with a view to further enhancing citizens' mobility as the ultimate objective of the construction of a EU area of freedom security and justice.

On the basis of the foregoing, the following conclusions may be drawn: (*i*) adoption is certainly not yet governed by uniform EU rules; (*ii*) recognition of adoptive parent-child status represents, nonetheless, a topic strictly intertwined with the effective exercise of free movement; (*iii*) as such, this topic may be deemed already governed at the EU level insofar as it certainly falls within the principle of mutual recognition of familial status as inferable from the well-established ECJ case law; (*iv*) moreover, natural persons' civil status has been addressed by the EU Commission's Justice for Growth Agenda as a topic on which legislative action is to be undertaken at the EU level in order to foster Union citizens' mobility; (*v*) Regulation 2016/1191 has thus been adopted with a view to simplifying formalities for the acceptance of public documents related (*inter alia*) to the civil status of natural persons, such as adoption.

Against this background, if one considers the abovementioned question as to whether EU Member States would still be entitled to individually object to the accession of new third countries to the Hague Intercountry Adoption Convention, it seems hardly disputable that the answer would be in the negative.

That EU competence now encompasses also recognition of intercountry adoption could indeed be argued on the grounds of the 'effect on EU law test' as above outlined, given that such issue – albeit not yet governed by specific EU common rules – is undoubtedly liable to adversely affect the effective exercise of the Union citizens' right to free movement as firmly anchored in primary Union law and substantially developed, or likely-to-be-developed, in secondary Union law.

Member States, in other words, could no longer be found empowered to autonomously handle new accessions to the 1993 Hague Convention, owing to the EU having acquired exclusive external competence as regards the very issue of recognition of intercountry adoption.

If the Member States rather than the EU had competence to decide whether or not to object to the accession of new third countries there would be a risk of undermining the full and effective enjoyment of free movement on the part of EU citizens. In particular this could happen in the case that accession were objected by one or more Member States.

Should such a case occur, it could result in adoptions established in the newly acceded third country being given different effects depending on the Member States requested of the recognition thereof.[68] Indeed, whilst in non-objecting Member States recognition would be fully granted in accordance with the 1993

---

[68] Indeed, as recalled above, n 31, according to Article 44(1) of the Convention accession by a new State 'shall have effect only as regards the relations between the acceding State and those contracting States which have not raised an objection to its accession'.

Hague Convention (ie, automatically or *de plein droit*), adoptions could be given only partial effects, if not even denied recognition, in those EU countries which objected to the accession. The very same adoptive parent-child relationship would, in other words, display different effects depending on the Member State in which the EU citizens thereby involved decide to move and establish their residence, which in turn would result in the freedom of movement being dramatically hampered, if not even radically prevented.

PART III

THE CHANGING FEATURES OF EU EXTERNAL RELATIONS IN THE AREA OF PRIVATE INTERNATIONAL LAW

EU EXTERNAL RELATIONS AND PRIVATE INTERNATIONAL LAW: MULTILATERALISM, PLURILATERALISM, BILATERALISM, OR UNILATERALISM?

Alex Mills *
University College London

1. INTRODUCTION

The primary focus in the development of EU private international law has thus far been on 'internal' questions and policy goals – principally, enhancing the efficient functioning of the internal market. This chapter analyses the potential 'external' dimension of EU private international law, looking at some of the roles which private international law might play in EU external relations (including potentially, in light of the recent Brexit vote, its relations with the United Kingdom).

The need to consider this question arises because the EU has, at least arguably, obtained exclusive external competence in at least most of the field of private international law. It has long been understood that exclusive external competence for the EU may arise where the (potential or actual) external rules 'are of such a kind as to affect ... Community rules',[1] even if those external rules are not directly inconsistent with Community (now EU) rules, but merely diminish their uniformity.[2] These principles have now been codified in the Treaty

* Some aspects of this chapter are further developed in A Mills, 'Private International Law and EU External Relations: Think Local Act Global, or Think Global Act Local?' (2016) 65 *International and Comparative Law Quarterly* 541.

1 Opinion 2/91, EU:C:1993:106, para. 26, developing the principle established earlier in Case 22/70, *Commission v Council* ('*ERTA*'), EU:C:1971:32. See generally G de Baere, *Constitutional Principles of EU External Relations* (Oxford University Press 2008), 43; P Eeckhout, *EU External Relations Law* (2nd ed, Oxford University Press, 2011), 70.

2 See Opinion 2/91, n 1, para. 25, noting that 'there is no contradiction between these provisions of the Convention and those of the directives mentioned'.

on the Functioning of the European Union, Article 3(2) of which provides (in relevant part) that:

> The Union shall also have exclusive competence for the conclusion of an international agreement ... in so far as its conclusion may affect common rules or alter their scope.[3]

In Opinion 1/13, directly relating to the field of private international law, the Court of Justice of the European Union held that as a consequence of this rule the EU must have exclusive competence to decide whether to accept the accession of a third state (a non-EU Member State) to the 1980 Hague Convention on the civil aspects of international child abduction, otherwise 'there would be a risk of undermining the uniform and consistent application'[4] of the Brussels IIa Regulation.[5] Pursuant to this decision, the EU has exercised this competence by authorising certain Member States to accept the accession of a number of third States to the Convention.[6]

On the basis of these authorities, there is a very strong argument that the EU must have exclusive external competence in other areas of private international law.[7] At present, for example, the main EU rules on jurisdiction and the recognition and enforcement of judgments in civil and commercial matters, set out in the Brussels I Regulations (under both the Recast Brussels I Regulation 2012[8]

3 Consolidated version of the Treaty on the Functioning of the European Union [2010] OJ C 83/47.

4 Opinion 1/13, EU:C:2014:2303, para. 89.

5 Regulation (EC) No 2201/2003 concerning jurisdiction and the recognition and enforcement of judgments in matrimonial matters and the matters of parental responsibility [2003] OJ L 338/1.

6 Decisions (EU) 2015/1023 (Andorra) and 2015/1024 (Singapore) of 15 June 2015 [2015] OJ L 163/29; Council Decisions (EU) 2015/2354 (Seychelles), 2015/2355 (Russian Federation), 2015/2356 (Albania), 2015/2357 (Morocco), and 2015/2358 (Armenia) dated 10 December 2015 [2015] OJ L 331/11. Somewhat controversially (at least in the sense that the European Commission issued a statement in objection), each decision only applies on behalf of those Member States which had not previously indicated (unilaterally) their acceptance of the third state's accession to the Convention, even though the ECJ concluded that such acts by Member States were contrary to EU law. The basis for this approach is presumably (and as suggested by Recital 12 of each Decision) a concern that such acts, even if invalid as a matter of EU law, might nevertheless have been valid as a matter of public international law, as this limitation on the competence of Member States was not 'objectively evident' prior to Opinion 1/13 – see Article 46 of the Vienna Convention on the Law of Treaties (1969), which provides that: '(1) A State may not invoke the fact that its consent to be bound by a treaty has been expressed in violation of a provision of its internal law regarding competence to conclude treaties as invalidating its consent unless that violation was manifest and concerned a rule of its internal law of fundamental importance. (2) A violation is manifest if it would be objectively evident to any State conducting itself in the matter in accordance with normal practice and in good faith.'

7 On this issue, see generally F Pocar (ed), *The External Competence of the European Union and Private International Law* (Cedam 2007).

8 Regulation (EU) No 1215/2012 on jurisdiction and the recognition and enforcement of judgments in civil and commercial matters (recast) [2012] OJ L 351/1 (henceforth, Brussels Ia Regulation), effective from 10 January 2015.

and the Brussels I Regulation 2001),[9] do not govern claims against non-Member State defendants (generally)[10] or the recognition and enforcement of non-Member State judgments. Those matters are left to national law, and so it might be thought that Member States could equally enter into international agreements which affected only these national rules.[11] However, there is a strong argument that such an exercise of external competence could have an impact on the scope of obligations under the Brussels I Regulation. For example, under the Regulation Member States are obliged to recognise and enforce judgments from other Member States, subject to limited safeguards or defences. That obligation applies irrespective of whether the Member State court which awarded the judgment took jurisdiction based on the Brussels I Regulation rules or based on its residual national rules of jurisdiction,[12] and the jurisdiction of the judgment Court may not be questioned (except for disputes concerning subject matter which attracts exclusive jurisdiction under the Regulation).[13] National rules of jurisdiction (which might be affected by international treaty arrangements) thus effectively determine the scope of the judgment enforcement obligations of other Member States under EU law.[14]

An even stronger argument can be made in relation to questions of choice of law, least insofar as these fall within the scope of existing EU Regulations including the Rome I Regulation on the law applicable to contractual obliga-

[9] Regulation (EC) No 44/2001 on jurisdiction and the recognition and enforcement of judgments in civil and commercial matters, OJ L 12/1 (henceforth, Brussels I Regulation).

[10] With the exception of the rules on exclusive jurisdiction under Articles 24 and 25. Article 26 does not clearly state whether it applies regardless of the domicile of the defendant, but (although the point is somewhat debated) its omission from mention in Article 6 (which provides that 'If the defendant is not domiciled in a Member State, the jurisdiction of the courts of each Member State shall, subject to Article 18(1), Article 21(2) and Articles 24 and 25, be determined by the law of that Member State') would suggest that it does not. See further, eg, J Fawcett and JM Carruthers, *Cheshire, North and Fawcett Private International Law* (14th ed, Oxford University Press 2008), 297.

[11] Although the ECJ already held in 2006 that the EU had exclusive competence to enter into the Lugano Convention, that might be considered a special case as that Convention was intended to extend the systemic effects of the Brussels I Regulation (see Opinion 1/03, EU:C:2006:81, paras 152 ff), which would not necessarily be the case for other private international law agreements.

[12] See further eg Fawcett and Carruthers, n 10, 224, 599.

[13] See Article 45(1)(e)(ii).

[14] Similar issues arise in relation to the rules on *lis pendens*, in two situations. First, where there are prior proceedings in other Member States, which may be based on national law jurisdictional rules – see Articles 29-30 Brussels Ia Regulation; Case C-351/89 *Overseas Union Insurance v New Hampshire Insurance*, EU:C:1991:279. Second, under the Brussels Ia Regulation, where there are prior proceedings in non-Member States. This is because the rules are conditional on the (actual or potential) enforceability of a non-Member State judgment, which is also a matter of national law – see Article 33(1)(a) and Article 34(1)(b), each of which is condition on whether 'it is expected that the court of the third State will give a judgment capable of recognition and, where applicable, of enforcement in that Member State', and Article 33(3) and Article 34(3), each of which applies if 'the proceedings in the court of the third State are concluded and have resulted in a judgment capable of recognition and, where applicable, of enforcement in that Member State'.

tions[15] and the Rome II Regulation on the law applicable to non-contractual obligations.[16] Although, as discussed further below, those Regulations were primarily motivated by internal market interests, they are universal in application – they must be applied by the courts of any Member State regardless of whether the dispute is connected with the EU, and regardless of whether the governing law is the law of any Member State.[17] Thus, for example, if an EU Member State entered into a treaty with a non-Member State which regulated choice of law questions (for contractual or non-contractual obligations), this would directly affect and potentially contradict the obligations of the Member State under the Rome I or II Regulations.

The overall conclusion follows, therefore, that the EU is likely to have exclusive external competence in private international law in civil and commercial matters, at least insofar as these are (partially or wholly) covered by EU Regulations internally. If this position is accepted, then the next question which must be asked is: what, if anything, should the EU do with this competence? This chapter identifies three potential approaches which might be pursued through 'outward facing' private international law: (*i*) multilateralism, (*ii*) plurilateralism or bilateralism, and (*iii*) unilateralism. These different approaches, which also may be associated with different traditional strands in the theory and practice of private international law,[18] are discussed in turn.

2. MULTILATERALISM

Perhaps the most obvious action which the EU might take externally in relation to private international law is to participate in efforts to reach international harmonisation or consensus concerning the rules of private international law, ideally through negotiating private international law treaties. The achievement of international harmonisation has long been an aspiration for private international law. Indeed, it was only in the nineteenth century that independent na-

15 Regulation (EC) No 593/2008 on the law applicable to contractual obligations ('Rome I'), [2008] OJ L 177/6

16 Regulation (EC) No 864/2007 on the law applicable to non-contractual obligations ('Rome II') [2007] OJ L 199/40

17 Rome I Regulation, Article 2 ('Any law specified by this Regulation shall be applied whether or not it is the law of a Member State'); and identically, Rome II Regulation, Article 3.

18 See generally eg G Rühl, 'Unilateralism', in J Basedow, K Hopt and R Zimmermann (eds), *Max Planck Encyclopedia of European Private Law* (Oxford University Press 2012); SC Symeonides, 'The American Choice of Law Revolution in the Courts: Today and Tomorrow' (2003) 298 *Recueil des cours de l'Académie de droit international de La Haye* 9, 357; SE Cox, 'Substantive, Multilateral and Unilateral Choice-of-Law Approaches' (2001) 37 *Willamette Law Review* 171; FK Juenger, 'General Course on Private International Law' (1985) 193 *Recueil des cours de l'Académie de droit international de La Haye* 119.

tional law traditions of private international law developed – the international harmonisation of private international law may be viewed as seeking reinstate an older tradition, although this would also require significant modernisation and the move should not be viewed as retrogressive for that reason.[19]

If States limit the jurisdictional overlap of their courts, apply the same choice of law rules, and recognise each other's judgments, this reduces the potential for regulatory conflict, or, in the terminology often favoured by private international lawyers, increases 'decisional harmony'. This should also reduce the incentives for forum shopping and thereby increase the efficient resolution of cross-border disputes.[20] These are all objectives which lie behind the internal harmonisation of private international law in the EU – increasing decisional harmony in the EU, leading to improvements in the efficiency of the internal market. The pursuit of equivalent objectives internationally might be viewed as a natural (international) extension of this approach. International harmonisation could also be used to pursue other less traditional policy objectives, which are arguably having an increasing influence in private international law – for example, addressing concerns of jurisdictional gaps (which may create problems of access to justice).[21]

Participation in multilateral initiatives relating to private international law would be the most obvious form of action which could be undertaken by the EU to achieve these objectives. The primary forum in which such initiatives are negotiated is the Hague Conference on Private International Law.[22] The Hague Conference is an international organisation which grew out of a series of international conferences held in the late nineteenth and early twentieth centuries, seeking to promote international harmonisation of private international law.[23] It has welcomed and facilitated the involvement of the EU by opening its membership to 'Regional Economic Integration Organisations',[24] and the EU duly

---

19 See further, eg, A Mills, 'Rediscovering the Public Dimension of Private International Law' (2012) 30 *Netherlands Journal of Private International Law* 371; A Mills, 'The Private History of International Law' (2006) 55 *International and Comparative Law Quarterly* 1.

20 See further A Mills, 'The Identities of Private International Law – Lessons from the US and EU Revolutions' (2013) 23 *Duke Journal of Comparative and International Law* 445.

21 See further A Mills, 'Rethinking Jurisdiction in International Law'(2014) 84 *British Yearbook of International Law* 187, 221.

22 See generally <http://www.hcch.net>.

23 See generally A Mills and G De Baere, 'T.M.C. Asser and Public and Private International Law: The Life and Legacy of "a Practical Legal Statesman"' (2011) 42 *Netherlands Yearbook of International Law* 3; JHA van Loon, 'The Hague Conference on Private International Law: an Introduction', in PJ van Krieken and D McKay (eds), *The Hague: Legal Capital of the World* (TMC Asser Press 2005); K Lipstein, 'One Hundred Years of Hague Conferences on Private International Law' (1993) 42 *International and Comparative Law Quarterly* 553.

24 <https://www.hcch.net/en/instruments/conventions/full-text>.

became a Member on 3 April 2007 (to date, the only Regional Economic Integration Organisation to join the Hague Conference).[25]

The direct participation of the EU in the Hague Conference has had a significant but limited practical output thus far.[26] The most prominent involvement of the EU in the work of the Hague Conference has perhaps been in relation to the Convention of 30 June 2005 on choice of court agreements. The EU signed the Convention in 2009,[27] and in December 2010 a formal decision was made to ratify the Convention;[28] the instrument of ratification was finally deposited on 11 June 2015, and the ratification became effective on 1 October 2015. This Convention governs the effectiveness of (non-consumer) jurisdiction agreements in favour of the courts of any Contracting State to the Convention, although it does not override EU rules unless at least one party to the jurisdiction agreement is resident (as defined in Article 4(2))[29] in a non-EU Contracting State.

Another potentially important area of activity is the continued work on the 'Judgments Project' at the Hague Conference.[30] This long-running project aims to achieve an international agreement providing for harmonised rules of jurisdiction in civil and commercial matters, in order to facilitate the recognition and enforcement of judgments between States. The Hague choice of court Convention was essentially a narrower 'spin-off' of the work on this project, but work on the broader project has been resumed, with the EU as a participant Member in the Working Group.[31] If successful, the Judgments Project would be likely to lead to the adoption of EU rules governing jurisdiction in the courts of Member States over non-Member State parties (now principally but not exclusively[32] regulated by national law), to reflect the terms of an international convention.

---

25 See further <https://www.hcch.net/en/instruments/conventions/status-table/notifications/?csid=992&disp=resdn> (also setting out the basis of the external competence of the EU in the field of private international law). See generally JHA van Loon and A Schulz, 'The European Community and the Hague Conference on Private International Law', in B Martenczuk and S van Thiel (eds), *Justice, Liberty, Security: New Challenges for EU External Relations* (Brussels University Press 2008).

26 For example, in 2014 the EU became a party to the Convention of 23 November 2007 on the international recovery of child support and other forms of family maintenance, and the Protocol of 23 November 2007 on the law applicable to maintenance obligations.

27 Decision 2009/397 [2009] OJ L 133/1.

28 Decision 2014/887 [2014] OJ L 353/5.

29 Article 4(2) provides that: 'For the purposes of this Convention, an entity or person other than a natural person shall be considered to be resident in the State - a) where it has its statutory seat; b) under whose law it was incorporated or formed; c) where it has its central administration; or d) where it has its principal place of business'.

30 See generally <https://www.hcch.net/en/projects/legislative-projects/judgments>.

31 See Report of the Fourth Meeting of the Working Group on the Judgments Project, 3-6 February 2015, available at <http://www.hcch.net/upload/wop/gap2015pd07b_en.pdf>.

32 Such cases are, for example, affected by Articles 24 and 25 of the Brussels Ia Regulation – see n 10.

The Hague Conference on Private International Law could offer further opportunities to participate in multilateral harmonisation efforts in the field of choice of law. The Hague Conference has, for example, recently adopted 'Principles on Choice of Law in International Commercial Contracts' (approved on 19 March 2015).[33] While these are not a formal international convention, it is possible that they may prove influential as a matter of soft law harmonisation. As discussed above, successful harmonisation efforts in the field of choice of law, even those pursued in a more flexible way through soft law techniques, are likely to decrease incentives for forum shopping and reduce the risk of conflicting judgments arising in different states.

Multilateral harmonisation of private international law has been actively pursued for more than a century, since the first Hague Conferences in the 1890s, with limited success.[34] Perhaps the single greatest difficulty of such initiatives is that they require a number of states to agree simultaneously that the goals this would pursue are valuable and politically achievable both domestically and internationally. Reaching agreement on international rules of private international law is also likely to come with a cost in terms of the content of the rules themselves. Significant compromise may be required for the sake of agreement, and this might require amendments to EU choice of law rules to bring them more closely in line with any international consensus which is reached. This means that the pursuit of international harmonisation may lead to private international law rules which the EU would not adopt were it simply to act unilaterally. A cost/benefit analysis would have to be undertaken to determine whether that would be a price worth paying for the benefits of international harmonisation.

3. PLURILATERALISM OR BILATERALISM

The achievement of a multilateral harmonisation of private international law would clearly have the greatest benefit in terms of traditional private international law goals, leading to increased efficiency in dispute resolution across the globe. A truly global approach to harmonisation is, however, also the most difficult to undertake. The pursuit of bilateral or plurilateral[35] (particularly regional) efforts at harmonisation might be considered as a more modest but also more feasible alternative.

The potential pursuit of plurilateral or bilateral harmonisation of private international law rules might be viewed as analogous to developments in the ne-

33 <http://www.hcch.net/index_en.php?act=conventions.text&cid=135>.

34 See A Mills and G De Baere, n 24.

35 The term 'plurilateral' is used to indicate arrangements which involve multiple countries but do not aspire to universal adoption, at least not in their immediate effects.

gotiation of international trade agreements. Clearly the greatest potential benefits could be achieved through multilateral negotiations such as those which gave rise to the World Trade Organisation, and indeed enormous efforts have been put into striving to achieve an international consensus on trade issues, most recently through the Doha round of trade talks.[36] The Doha round has, however, thus far proved unable to reach a global agreement. As a result, many States have fallen back to bilateral or plurilateral trade negotiations, to try to achieve more modest but obtainable benefits, such as the Comprehensive Economic and Trade Agreement (CETA) between the EU and Canada,[37] and the Transatlantic Trade and Investment Partnership (TTIP) agreement currently being negotiated by the EU and United States.[38] These (potential) agreements could be viewed as an alternative means of bargaining or negotiating towards a multilateral consensus, or as an end in themselves.

A further and similar comparison might be made with international investment law. The failure of efforts to establish multilateral consensus (such as the MAI negotiations in the 1990s) led to the adoption of a wide range of bilateral investment treaties by a range of States, including Member States of the EU.[39] The fact that (since the Treaty of Lisbon) the EU now has exclusive external competence in the field means that the EU is at least contemplating negotiating its own bilateral investment treaties,[40] including as part of CETA and TTIP, and has set up internal arrangements to manage the potentially complex issues of responsibility for their violation.[41] A close analogy might be made with private international law. If a multilateral consensus cannot be achieved on the harmonisation of private international law rules, then the achievement of agreement on the harmonisation of private international law with key trading partners may represent the best approach, either as an interim step or alternative goal. A wide range of bilateral or regional private international law treaties operated between States within the EU prior to the adoption of European Community or Union regulation,[42] and some Member States continue to be bound by bilateral

---

36 See generally <https://www.wto.org/english/tratop_e/dda_e/dda_e.htm>.

37 See further <http://ec.europa.eu/trade/policy/in-focus/ceta>.

38 See further <http://ec.europa.eu/trade/policy/in-focus/ttip>.

39 See generally A Mills, 'Antinomies of Public and Private at the Foundations of International Investment Law and Arbitration' (2011) 14 *Journal of International Economic Law* 469; M Sornarajah, *The International Law on Foreign Investment* (3rd ed, Cambridge University Press 2010).

40 See generally <http://ec.europa.eu/trade/policy/accessing-markets/investment>; 'Special Issue: The Anatomy of the (Invisible) EU Model BIT' (2014) 15(3)-(4) *Journal of World Investment and Trade*; A Dimopoulos, *EU Foreign Investment Law* (Oxford University Press 2011).

41 Regulation (EU) No 912/2014 establishing a framework for managing financial responsibility linked to investor-to-state dispute settlement tribunals established by international agreements to which the European Union is party [2014] OJ L 257, 121.

42 P Jenard, 'Report on the Convention on Jurisdiction and the Enforcement of Judgments in Civil and Commercial Matters Signed at Brussels, 27 September 1968' [1979] OJ C 59/1, 6-7; Article

agreements with non-Member States which affect their national private international law rules.[43] The EU could adopt similar initiatives, with the aim that EU actors, and potentially others, would benefit from increased harmony and efficiency in relations with the States who become parties to such agreements.

There is of course one well known example of a regional-plurilateral approach to private international law in practice – the Lugano Convention[44] – which extends the terms of the Brussels Convention to States who are not Member States of the EU but are part of the European Free Trade Area. Aside from this development, however, the EU has not (yet) attempted to negotiate bilateral or plurilateral international agreements on private international law harmonisation.[45] There is, as noted above, a strong argument that such measures should only be adopted as a fall-back if multilateral efforts prove unsuccessful, and perhaps it would be premature for the EU as a relatively new player in international harmonisation discussions to reach any such conclusion. However the possibility should not be ignored that, as in the context of trade law or investment law, bilateral or plurilateral agreements with key trading partners may at some point be viewed as a preferable alternative to the very difficult task of attempting to reach a global consensus in matters of private international law.[46]

There is, however, a significant risk associated with pursuing bilateral or regional agreements on private international law, which is that the agreements negotiated with different bilateral or regional partners might unavoidably be on different terms. This would have the consequence that private international

55 of the 1968 Brussels Convention on jurisdiction and the enforcement of judgments in civil and commercial matters, Consolidated version [1998] OJ C 27/1.

43 See further discussion in 'Study: Possibility and Terms for Applying Brussels I Regulation (Recast) to Extra-EU Disputes', Directorate General for Internal Policies, Policy Department C: Citizens' Rights and Constitutional Affairs, at the request of the European Parliament Committee on Legal Affairs, 42, <http://www.europarl.europa.eu/RegData/etudes/etudes/join/2014/493024/IPOL-JURI_ET%282014%29493024_EN.pdf>.

44 Convention on jurisdiction and the enforcement of judgments in civil and commercial matters, [1988] OJ L 391/9.

45 At least as far as this author is aware. The EU has, however, established procedures under which Member States might obtain an authorisation to negotiate such agreements individually in certain fields: Regulation (EC) No 662/2009 establishing a procedure for the negotiation and conclusion of agreements between Member States and third countries on particular matters concerning the law applicable to contractual and non-contractual obligations [2009] OJ L 200/25, and Regulation (EC) No 664/2009 establishing a procedure for the negotiation and conclusion of agreements between Member States and third countries concerning jurisdiction, recognition and enforcement of judgments and decisions in matrimonial matters, matters of parental responsibility and matters relating to maintenance obligations, and the law applicable to matters relating to maintenance obligations [2009] OJ L 200/46. Article 4(2) of each of these Regulations provides that the Commission shall take into account whether any mandate exists for the conclusion of a Community agreement with the third country, before deciding whether a Member State may be authorised to open formal negotiations – thus indirectly contemplating the EU entering into bilateral or regional private international law treaties.

46 See further discussion in 'Study', n 43.

law would become harmonised in terms of relations between particular States, but more fragmented in terms of the rules applicable within a given State. This complexity might ultimately decrease rather than increase legal certainty for EU private actors.

4. UNILATERALISM

The third major approach which could be adopted by the EU in the field of private international law is quite distinct. It considers what internal steps the EU might take with a view to their external policy effects. Because this approach involves acting internally, it does not require the use of any external competence in the field of private international law. It is, however, more broadly concerned with the ways in which the EU might use private international law rules or exceptions in its external relations.

4.1. PURSUE EXTERNAL POLICIES THROUGH PRIVATE INTERNATIONAL LAW RULES

Under the approaches outlined above – the international, plurilateral or bilateral harmonisation of private international law rules – the emphasis is on ensuring that private international law rules are the *same* in different states. This leaves unanswered the question of what the rules actually *should* be – what policy outcomes they should be designed to advance. Although most of the effects of EU private international law rules are internal, the rules may also have external effects. The possibility considered here is that EU private international law rules might be adopted in order to serve external (as well as potentially internal) policy objectives, using private international law as a means to 'project' EU values or interests outside the EU.

In the development of EU rules of private international law the focus has generally been on what kind of rules would meet the needs of the European internal market. But this does not need to be a limitation on the rules or their intended effects. As noted above, the Rome I and II Regulations, dealing with choice of law in contractual and non-contractual obligations (respectively), already apply regardless of whether the disputed events or disputing parties are inside or outside the internal market. There is, however, something of a mismatch between the scope of the rules and their objectives. The Rome I Regulation, for example, begins with a range of recitals including the following:

> (1) The Community has set itself the objective of maintaining and developing an area of freedom, security and justice. For the progressive establishment of such an area, the Community is to adopt measures relating to judicial cooperation in

> civil matters with a cross-border impact to the extent necessary for the proper functioning of the internal market. …
>
> (6) The proper functioning of the internal market creates a need, in order to improve the predictability of the outcome of litigation, certainty as to the law applicable and the free movement of judgments, for the conflict-of-law rules in the Member States to designate the same national law irrespective of the country of the court in which an action is brought.

These recitals reveal that the Regulation is focused on achieving objectives for the benefit of the internal market – leading to a focus on certainty and predictability for the parties. There are, however, no recitals which explain what the Regulation is supposed to achieve in relation to non-internal market questions. For example, if parties from Hong Kong and Singapore enter into a contract and the English courts (through choice or based on corporate presence) are seised of their dispute, the Rome I Regulation rules will still apply to determine the law governing their contract, but they cannot aim to achieve decisional harmony or improve the efficient functioning of the internal market. The external effect of the rules seems to be present here not as a matter of policy design, but almost as a matter of accident.

What this section contemplates is that EU private international rules might at least partially be developed and designed with their international impact in mind. As noted above, this would of course come with disadvantages in terms of the additional complexity which it would create (potentially requiring more than one set of rules), but it would allow private international law rules to be designed to serve a range of other policy goals. Rules governing the conduct of EU Member State companies in developing States might, for example, aim to ensure that those companies are governed by the substantive legal standards which are applicable in their home States, as a means of giving extraterritorial effect to those standards, to protect or constrain the company concerned.

Similar considerations would arise if the EU were to adopt jurisdictional rules for non-Member State defendants (as was initially proposed in the legislative process which led to the Brussels Ia Regulation,[47] and has again recently been supported by a study commissioned by the European Parliament).[48] The EU could adopt unilateral rules designed to achieve external policy goals. The rules could, for example, identify and give effect to a conception of how jurisdiction should be 'appropriately' allocated in particular cases, as well as allowing weaker parties to sue in their home court (as indeed already provided for

47 Proposal for a Regulation on jurisdiction and the recognition and enforcement of judgments in civil and commercial matters (recast), COM (2010) 748 final.

48 'Study', n 43, 42.

under the rules relating to consumers).[49] The rules might also include provision for a forum of necessity rule – again as previously proposed by the European Commission[50] – which could aim to ensure that claimants against non-Member State defendants had access to a court to pursue a remedy, if their rights have been breached in a foreign state without a functional or effective legal system.

The potential external impact of EU jurisdictional rules is, however, not limited to cases involving non-Member State defendants. Cases involving defendants from a Member State, and thus already covered by the Brussels I Regulation, may also have a potentially important external dimension. For example, if a claim is brought against a defendant domiciled in a Member State, the Regulation confers general jurisdiction on the courts of the Member State of their domicile as well as potentially other courts with subject matter connections to the dispute.[51] But the rules are silent on what significance, if any, should be attached to the connections which the dispute may have with non-Member States. It might, for example, concern immovable property in a non-Member State,[52] or matters covered by an exclusive jurisdiction agreement in favour of the courts of a non-Member State.

This is the well-known *Owusu v Jackson*[53] problem under the Regulation, which arises because the rules were designed to deal exclusively with internal market problems, but actually regulate disputes which have connections going beyond the internal market. It has been proposed that aspects of the Regulation (such as the effect given to jurisdiction agreements in favour of the courts of Member States, or the recognition of the exclusive jurisdiction of a Member State over disputes concerning title to land) may be given 'reflexive effect' to deal with these issues (applying in relation to non-Member States in a similar or identical way), thereby projecting its policies externally, but it is unclear

---

49 Pursuant to Article 18 of the Brussels Ia Regulation.

50 See n 49, Article 26, which provided: 'Where no court of a Member State has jurisdiction under this Regulation, the courts of a Member State may, on an exceptional basis, hear the case if the right to a fair trial or the right to access to justice so requires, in particular: (a) if proceedings cannot reasonably be brought or conducted or would be impossible in a third State with which the dispute is closely connected; or (b) if a judgment given on the claim in a third State would not be entitled to recognition and enforcement in the Member State of the court seised under the law of that State and such recognition and enforcement is necessary to ensure that the rights of the claimant are satisfied; and the dispute has a sufficient connection with the Member State of the court seised'.

51 Pursuant to Articles 4 and 7 of the Brussels Ia Regulation, in most cases.

52 The same argument applies in relation to any of the other matters dealt with as subject-matter exclusive jurisdiction under Article 24 of the Brussels Ia Regulation, such as disputes concerning the validity of registered intellectual property rights, or the validity of the decisions or constitution of a company.

53 Case C-281/02, *Owusu v Jackson*, EU:C:2005:120. See generally R Fentiman, 'Civil Jurisdiction and Third States: *Owusu* and After' (2006) 43 *Common Market Law Review* 705; A Briggs, 'The Death of *Harrods*: Forum Non Conveniens and the European Court' (2005) 121 *Law Quarterly Review* 535.

whether this is consistent with the Regulation.[54] The terms of the Brussels Ia Regulation arguably suggest the troubling conclusion that a reflexive effect approach is generally precluded, because they permit Member State courts to take into account certain non-Member State connections if a Member State court is seised of a dispute already before the courts of a non-Member State[55] – potentially implying that such matters could not be taken into consideration if a Member State court is first seised. If this is the case, the Regulation rules have rather strange 'external' effects. They would, for example, require Member State courts to exercise jurisdiction even if the parties have contracted to give exclusive jurisdiction to the courts of a non-Member State – thus undermining party autonomy for EU based companies, and potentially putting them at a disadvantage in international contractual negotiations. This is perhaps the clearest demonstration of how the focus on the internal market has blinded the EU to the external effects of its rules of private international law.

4.2. PURSUE EXTERNAL POLICIES THROUGH PRIVATE INTERNATIONAL LAW EXCEPTIONS

The second technique which might be pursued under the unilateral approach is to use the 'exceptions' to private international law rules to achieve policy objectives. The focus here is on the exceptions to the normal application of foreign law under choice of law rules, or the normal recognition and enforcement of foreign judgments, such as the doctrine of public policy. The use of public policy and other similar exceptions to private international law rules is generally viewed as having a negative or blocking effect – it only prevents local enforcement of the judgment, or local application of the law. But if, for example, the EU were to refuse to enforce judgments from a particular State because of a particular problem with the organisation of the judicial system in that State (such as a lack of judicial independence), that might put pressure on that State to address the problem, to increase the international effectiveness of its judgments. If EU Member States were to refuse to apply a particular foreign law because it was

---

[54] See further eg P de V Smith, B Lasserson, and R Rymkiewicz, 'Reflections on *Owusu*: The Radical Decision in *Ferrexpo*' (2012) 8 *Journal of Private International Law* 389.

[55] Pursuant to Recital 24: 'When taking into account the proper administration of justice, the court of the Member State concerned should assess all the circumstances of the case before it. Such circumstances may include connections between the facts of the case and the parties and the third State concerned, the stage to which the proceedings in the third State have progressed by the time proceedings are initiated in the court of the Member State and whether or not the court of the third State can be expected to give a judgment within a reasonable time. That assessment may also include consideration of the question whether the court of the third State has exclusive jurisdiction in the particular case in circumstances where a court of a Member State would have exclusive jurisdiction'.

identified as unjust, then that might similarly also influence the foreign State to reform the law in such a way as to increase its 'effectiveness' through its application by foreign courts.

This approach might be understood as a form of 'conditionality', a regulatory technique used by the EU in a range of circumstances to project EU policies extraterritorially.[56] For example, the EU provides enhanced access to European markets for goods which have been produced in States which have ratified and implemented certain international labour and environmental standards, as a deliberate means to incentivise developing States to comply with those standards.[57] Access to recognition of foreign laws or judgments through rules of private international law might be viewed as a further possible application of this technique. This would not require international harmonisation of private international law rules, but only an EU standardisation of private international law exceptions, such as a clearer formulation of a 'European' public policy.[58]

There is an argument that elements of this approach, intentionally or otherwise, are already present in some existing practice in relation to private international law. The European Court of Human Rights has, for example, considered the circumstances in which Convention States (including but not of course limited to Member States of the EU) must refuse recognition of a judgment from a non-Convention State which violates the standards of the ECHR.[59] In the context of criminal law, an analogous problem was considered in *Drozd and Janousek v France and Spain*.[60] The Court had to consider whether France could imprison (on behalf of Andorra) persons convicted of crimes under Andorran law, if the procedures which had been followed in Andorra (a non-Convention State) were non-compliant with the Convention. Although the court noted that state parties to the Convention are not required 'to impose its standards on third States or territories',[61] it held that Convention States 'are, however, obliged to refuse their co-operation if it emerges that the conviction is the result of a flagrant denial of justice'.[62] In a private law context, an even stricter approach was

---

56 See generally J Scott, 'Extraterritoriality and Territorial Extension in EU Law' (2014) 62 *American Journal of Comparative Law* 87.

57 Known as 'GSP+' – see further <http://ec.europa.eu/trade/policy/countries-and-regions/development/generalised-scheme-of-preferences/; http://trade.ec.europa.eu/doclib/press/index.cfm?id=1006>.

58 See further A Mills, 'The Dimensions of Public Policy in Private International Law' (2008) 4 *Journal of Private International Law* 201, 214; H Muir Watt, 'Evidence of an Emergent European Legal Culture: Public Policy Requirements of Procedural Fairness Under the Brussels and Lugano Conventions' (2001) 36 *Texas International Law Journal* 539.

59 Such judgments are, of course, not covered by the Brussels I Regulation, and thus the issue has not come before the ECJ, only the ECHR.

60 ECHR:1992:0626JUD001274787.

61 Ibid, para. 110.

62 Ibid.

following in the later decision of *Pellegrini v Italy*.[63] The ECtHR held that the Italian courts were obliged to refuse recognition of a divorce judgment from the Vatican (a non-Convention State), obtained in violation of ECHR procedural fairness standards. The effect of this decision is that Vatican divorce proceedings will have to follow ECHR standards if they are to be given effect in Italy or any other Member State, as is likely to be necessary in many cases. Under this approach, the effect of relying on an exception to EU private international law rules to block enforcement of a non-compliant foreign judgment is that the non-Convention State is (particularly if dependent on cooperation with a Convention State) likely to be pressured to comply with the Convention.

5. CONCLUSIONS

The three approaches analysed in this chapter are each distinct possibilities for an EU private international law 'foreign policy'. Each represents a different way in which private international law may be used 'externally' to effect certain policies, and each has advantages and disadvantages. The payoffs for achieving international harmonisation of private international law rules would be very significant in terms of the traditional objectives of private international law – reducing incentives for forum shopping through advancing decisional harmony, and reducing the risk of conflicting judgments. The EU is already playing a significant role in the Hague Conference on Private International Law, and it may be hoped that this will continue. Pursuing plurilateral or bilateral harmonisation (following the model of trade negotiations) would also address traditional private international law policy concerns in a potentially more achievable way, but this would risk fragmenting private international law rules and ultimately reducing legal certainty. Rules of private international law could alternatively be adopted unilaterally, to pursue external substantive policies without the need for international cooperation, but there is a great risk again that this would undermine the traditional goals and values of private international law. The use of exceptions to private international law rules to project substantive policies is also another potential option, but this would again come at a cost in terms of the traditional values and policies embodied in private international law rules, and the benefits are uncertain.

While these different techniques are in various ways in tension with one another, more than one might be pursued simultaneously in a way which compromises and balances their distinct policy concerns – it is not essential that only one technique be chosen for all EU private international law, or for a component of EU private international law (such as jurisdiction, or choice of law), or even

---

[63] ECHR:2001:0720JUD003088296.

for a single EU Regulation. The principal contention of this chapter is that it is, however, essential that the EU's approach to private international law reflects a calculated and coherent analysis of these different policy considerations, and that any exercise of external or internal competence should take into consideration not just the interests of the internal market, but also the range of ways in which private international law might advance or hinder the interests of the EU in its external relations.

EU COOPERATION IN CIVIL MATTERS AND MULTILEVEL UNIFICATION OF PRIVATE INTERNATIONAL LAW: SOME REMARKS

Alessandra ZANOBETTI
University of Bologna

1. THE MULTILEVEL UNIFICATION OF PRIVATE INTERNATIONAL LAW

The movement towards the unification of private international law, to which many European countries have participated from the outset, aspired to be conducted at a universal level.[1] The Conventions adopted in the first sessions of the Hague Conference of Private International Law in 1902 in 1905, as well as the instruments drafted under the auspices of the League of Nations and based on the work of Unidroit, were not restricted to a specific region. Also, the association established in 1929,[2] which would later be transformed into the International Commission on Civil Status, was not, in the intention of its funders, limited to European States. It is only with the adoption of the 1968 Brussels Convention and of the 1980 Rome Convention that the phenomenon of unification of private international law at a European level becomes relevant.

However, the work of unification undertaken in the mentioned fora was, at least in its first years, perceived as Eurocentric. The organizations were born in Europe or were located in European cities and had mostly, though not solely, European membership; moreover, their activity was strongly influenced by the

---

1 It is worth mentioning that, at the same time in which this movement started, an important region, i.e. Latin America, favoured the adoption of its own uniform instruments – the Montevideo Treaties of 1889 and 1940 and the Bustamante Code of 1928 – now continue this work within the Inter-American Specialised Conference on Private International Law (CIDIP).

2 Association internationale d'officiers de l'état civil, created in 1926 as a federation of national associations of civil status officers.

European legal tradition. As a result, the instruments were ratified almost exclusively by European States.

More recently, though, this state of affairs had an important enhancement and quite a few of the instruments have been ratified by numerous States of other regions of the world. Worth mentioning are some striking figures concerning instruments adopted by the Hague Conference: 112 countries are parties of the 1961 Convention abolishing the requirement of legalisation for foreign public documents (Apostille Convention); 94 States are bound by the 1980 Convention on the civil aspects of international child abduction, 96 by the 1993 Convention on protection of children and co-operation in respect of intercountry adoption, and 44 by the 1996 Convention on jurisdiction, applicable law, recognition, enforcement and co-operation in respect of parental responsibility and measures for the protection of children.

On the other hand, some instruments adopted under the auspices of the United Nations have had a significant effect on the regulation of issues of international elements: it may be sufficient to mention the 1956 Convention for the recovery of maintenance abroad, which first used the tool of creating central authorities in the contracting States to facilitate and improve the effectiveness of its operation, tool that is now considered crucial for the functioning of several private international law instruments adopted at a regional or at the EU level. The establishment of the Uncitral in 1966, which was intended also to coordinate the activities undertaken by other organisation at different levels,[3] led to other important results at a universal level, such as the 1980 Vienna Convention on contracts for the international sale of goods,[4] after the not exciting results obtained by Unidroit with the two 1964 Conventions on the sale of goods.[5]

2. THE EUROPEANISATION OF PRIVATE INTERNATIONAL LAW AND ITS IMPACT ON THE ADOPTION OF UNIFORM RULES AT REGIONAL AND UNIVERSAL LEVEL

The European Community, represented by the Commission, has taken part in the works of the Hague Conference on Private International Law since 1960, ie,

3 Uncitral was established by Resolution 2205 (XXI) of the UN General Assembly, adopted on 17 December 1966. The Resolution states in Part II, No 8, that the Commission should 'further the progressive harmonization and unification of the law of international trade', *inter alia*, by 'coordinating the work of organizations active in this field and encouraging cooperation among them'.

4 In force for 85 States.

5 Convention relating to a uniform law on the international sale of goods, and Convention relating to a uniform law on the formation of contracts for the international sale of goods, both done at The Hague on 1 July 1964.

since the first session of the Conference after the entry into force of the Treaty of Rome. An interest in the field of private international law existed already at that time.[6] At that session the Conference adopted the Apostille Convention: the simplification of the circulation of foreign documents was paramount for facilitating the development of the common market and the interest of the Community was self-evident.[7] Moreover, it was already apparent that some European legal acts should contain rules on the area; it was accordingly important that the Community (and now the Union) had direct information on the works undertaken in the field since their preliminary phase.[8] The Community was also involved in the work concerning uniform law in other regional or universal fora. An example is offered by Unidroit: the EU Commission participated as observer to the negotiation of the Conventions on international factoring and on international financial leasing (both adopted in Ottawa on 28 May 1988), and of the Convention on stolen or illegally exported cultural objects (Rome, 24 June 1995), which contains a clause referring to the specificity of the European Member States, although making use of a general formula.[9]

The Europeanisation of private international law, in particular after the entry into force of the Treaty of Amsterdam on 1 May 1999, has enhanced the participation of the European Institutions in activities aiming at unifying rules on conflict of laws and the conflict of jurisdictions. The insertion of the new competences operated by the Treaty of Amsterdam included, *inter alia*, the

6 See, among others, the pioneering contribution by R Savatier, 'Le Marché commun au regard du droit international privé' (1959) 48 *Revue critique de droit international privé* 237; U Drobnig, 'Conflict of Laws and the European Economic Community' (1967) 15 *American Journal of Comparative Law* 294; R Monaco, 'Problemi di diritto internazionale privato nell'ordinamento della Comunità europea' (1973) 56 *Rivista di diritto internazionale* 205.

7 The EC Member States adopted their own instrument – the Brussels Convention abolishing the Legalisation of Documents in the Member States of the European Communities – only in 1987, but it never entered into force, because it has not been ratified by all MS (as required by its Article 6(2)). However, six Member States have declared that it applies provisionally between them (Belgium, Denmark, France, Italy, Ireland, and Latvia). Now, many EU acts provide for the abolition of the requirements of legalisation for documents falling within their scope. See now Regulation (EU) 2016/1191 on promoting the free movement of citizens by simplifying the requirements for presenting certain public documents in the EU [2016] OJ L 200/1, which, however, does not abolish the requirement of apostille for all documents, on the assumption that apostille may, in some circumstances, be a useful tool for avoiding fraud.

8 J Basedow, 'Worldwide Harmonisation of Private Law and Regional Economic Integration – General Report' (2003) 8 *Uniform Law Review* 40; H Duintjer Tebbens, 'Les règles de conflit contenues dans les instruments de droit dérivé', in A Fuchs, H Muir Watt and E Pataut (eds), *Les conflits de lois et le système juridique communautaire* (Dalloz 2004), 101.

9 In the latter instrument, with a view of ensuring that its ratification by the Member States would have not conflicted with European rules on the same subject, a specific provision was adopted which permitted 'Contracting States which are Members of organisations of economic integration or regional bodies' to declare that 'they will apply the internal rules of these organisations or bodies and will not therefore apply as between these States the provisions of this Convention the scope of application of which coincides with that of those rules' (Article 13(3)).

promotion of 'the compatibility of the rules applicable in the Member States concerning the conflict of laws and of jurisdiction', 'insofar as necessary for the proper functioning of the internal market'. Article 2 of the Treaty of Lisbon has modified this last sentence, replacing 'insofar as necessary' by 'particularly when necessary' and accordingly enlarging the possibility of intervention of European law in this domain.

The adoption of several instruments in different matters has supplied the European institutions with the legal basis for the exercise of external competences in the same domains, as stated now by Article 3(2) TFEU. The Court of Justice had already pointed out in Opinion 1/03, relying on previous rulings concerning other fields of EU law, that these competences exist when 'a specific analysis of the relationship between the agreement envisaged and the Community law in force' renders clear that 'the conclusion of such an agreement is capable of affecting the Community rules'; moreover, 'it is not necessary for the areas covered by the international agreement and the Community legislation to coincide fully'.[10] The Court added that this assessment 'must be based not only on the scope of the rules in question but also on their nature and content', and it must take into account 'not only the current state of Community law in the area in question, but also its future development, insofar as that is foreseeable at the time of that analysis'.[11] Opinion 1/13 adds that this exclusive competence exists even when 'there would be a risk of undermining the uniform and consistent application' of a Regulation in the Member States.[12]

The intensification of the participation of the Union to the adoption of uniform rules of private international law at different levels has followed different paths. The first has entailed concertation procedures of the participation of EU Member States to the negotiations underway at the regional or universal level. The second consists of enabling the Union to accede to the new instruments. The third involves the membership of the Union itself in international organisations active in the field of private international law, which, as is well known, has so far resulted in its accession to the Hague Conference.[13]

The results seem, however, far from being encouraging.

---

10 Opinion 1/03, EU:C:2006:81, paras 124-126.

11 Ibid, para. 126.

12 Opinion 1/13, EU:C:2014:2303, para. 89.

13 On this accession, see A Schulz, 'The Accession of the European Community to the Hague Conference on Private International Law' (2007) 56 *International and Comparative Law Quarterly* 939. This accession required a modification of the Statute of the Conference, whose Article 3(1) now allows the accession of any Regional Economic Integration Organisation, defined in Article 3(9) as 'an international organisation that is constituted solely by sovereign States, and to which its Member States have transferred competence over a range of matters, including the authority to make decisions binding on its Member States in respect of those matters'. This definition is modelled on the definition drafted at the occasion of the accession of the Community to FAO.

The Hague Convention of 30 June 2005 on choice of court agreements has recently entered into force, upon ratification by Mexico and by the European Union on behalf of its Member States (with the exception of Denmark). As is well known, this text is a by-product of a more ambitious project whose abandonment has to be directly linked to the conversion of the 1968 Brussels Convention into a regulation, shortly after the entry into force of the Treaty of Amsterdam.[14] In 2007, the same year of the EC accession, the Conference adopted two new texts: the Convention of 23 November 2007 on the international recovery of child support and other forms of family maintenance, which is now in force in 32 States (*ie*, all the EU Member States, with the exception of Denmark) and a few other European countries (Albania, Bosnia Herzegovina, Montenegro Norway, and Ukraine), and the Protocol of 23 November 2007 on the law applicable to maintenance obligations, in force in all EU Member States (with the exception of Denmark and the United Kingdom) and Serbia. Although it is possible, and desirable, that more States accede to these instruments, for the time being the impression is that mainly the Union and its close neighbours are interested in their entry into force.

After the adoption of these agreements, eight years have passed without any new text being adopted; this is the longest period without achievements in the recent history of the Conference. The last instrument finalised – the Principles on choice of law in international commercial contracts, approved on 19 March 2015 – will not be submitted for ratification as it is a non-binding text. It will thus be difficult to have an exact measure of its success.[15]

---

14 A Special Commission of the Hague Conference adopted, in October 1999, the text of a Preliminary draft Convention on jurisdiction and foreign judgments in civil and commercial matters, intending to submit it to the Conference at its next session. The text of the Preliminary draft and a Report by the Special Commission is available at <http://www.hcch.net/upload/wop/jdgmpd11.pdf>. The Conference decided to abandon the project, because several of its Member States considered that there was not sufficient consensus to continue the negotiations. The position of the US is illustrated in a letter, dated 22 February 2000, by JD Kovar, Assistant Legal Advisor for Private International Law at the US State Department, to the Secretary General of the Hague Conference, which details the reasons for which the US delegation considers that the project should be abandoned. The letter indicates that, in the view of the US delegation, 'there is not enough common ground demonstrated in the current preliminary draft text to warrant scheduling and moving forward to a diplomatic conference', and that there is not 'a strong enough interest in the creation of a worldwide convention for a controlling majority of delegations to depart substantially from the approach of Brussels-Lugano': <http://www.cptech.org/ecom/hague/kovar2loon22022000.pdf>. It is worth mentioning that a project with the same scope, referred to as the 'Judgments Project, is now again in the agenda of the Conference.

15 So far, one country – Paraguay – has explicitly implemented the Principles adopting the *Ley No 5393/2015 sobre el derecho aplicable a los contratos internacionales*. It should be added that the Principles have been adopted with a specific procedure, different from the one generally followed for the Conventions: the draft is the result of the work of a Working Group set up by the Permanent Bureau of the Conference upon mandate of its Council for General Affairs and Politics, and the text was approved by the members of the Conference on 15 March 2015.

Although it is perhaps early for openly speaking of a crisis at The Hague – and, in truth, many of the Hague's instruments have not resulted in attracting a high number of parties even in the past – the least that can be said is that the EU accession has not given a boost to its activities. Moreover, it is to be feared that the adoption of instruments at the European level can render more difficult, or even impede, the attainment of a consensus at a different level.[16]

Also in other contexts, the influence of the Union appears to be detrimental. An example is the International Commission on Civil Status (ICCS). This independent intergovernmental organisation based in Strasbourg has adopted, since its creation in 1950, several conventions that provide rules aiming at the mutual recognition of civil status documents or creating uniform documents – as, for instance, multilingual certificates. Accordingly, these rules may be valuable devices in overcoming obstacles to the free circulation of persons. An agreement between the Commission and the European Community was signed in 1983, but the cooperation between the two organisations was never effective. In spite of the good quality of the instruments adopted under the auspices of the ICCS and of their practical usefulness,[17] many EU Member States have decided to quit the organisation. Austria has exercised its right of retreat in 2007; since then, Croatia, Hungary, the United Kingdom, Italy, Portugal, and Germany have followed, and the exodus might continue. An official presentation of the organisation's activities affirms that presumably these decisions are linked to the creeping influence of the EU in the domains pertaining to the Commission's core business;[18] the authors do hope that this will not produce the disappearance of the only entity which is specialised in matters of civil status, precisely at the moment in which this specialisation becomes more and more necessary.[19] It seems, however, difficult to predict a rosy future for ICCS.

---

16 On this point see below, § 7. The title of an article by A Struycken, published shortly after the entry into force of the Treaty of Amsterdam, may appear premonitory: 'Brussels Shadows over The Hague' ('Het verdrag van Amsterdam en de Haagse Conferentie voor internationaal privaatrecht – Brusselse schaduwen over Den Haag' (2000) 131 *Weekblad voor privaatrecht, notariaat en registratie* 735.

17 A document published in 2010, upon the request of the Committee on Legal Affairs of the European Parliament (Recognition and Registration of Civil Status Documents in Cross-Border Cases, PE 425.653, at <http://www.europarl.europa.eu/studies>), underlines the good quality of the conventions adopted by the ICCS and the interest that their ratification could represent for EU Member States to their ratification; it has to be pointed out that the document's author is Paul Lagarde, Secretary General of the ICCS and, accordingly, favourably inclined towards its instruments.

18 As a matter of fact, for the time being no legislation has been adopted on the same matters covered by the ICCS activities. See, however, the Proposal quoted above, n 8.

19 See J Massip, F Hondius and C Nast, *Commission Internationale de l'État Civil (CIEC)*, 2014, 7-8, <http://www.ciec1.org>, and, in English, 'International Commission on Civil Status (ICCS)', in *International Encyclopaedia of Laws, Encyclopaedia of Intergovernmental Organizations*, Suppl. 52, 2014, 14.

3. THE INTERACTION BETWEEN EU PRIVATE INTERNATIONAL LAW AND OTHER PRIVATE INTERNATIONAL LAW INSTRUMENTS

An interesting aspect that can be analysed is the influence of the Europeanisation of private international law on the methods adopted by uniform instruments.

The regulations enacted so far, and those under preparation, make use of the classical methods and tools of private international law. As for the applicable law, the provisions mostly consist of bilateral, conflict-of-law rules; the general provisions concern public policy, *renvoi*, overriding mandatory provisions, and include specific rules for States with more than one legal system; recourse is made, when appropriate, to substantive rules of private international law.[20] It is thus difficult to see differences of methodology among the EU regulations and the Hague conventions, or the instruments adopted under the auspices of other organisations, or even among the regulations and many of the domestic conflict-of-laws systems. The same can be said for rules on jurisdiction; the EU regimes adopted so far include grounds for jurisdiction, often both general and special, rules on *lis pendens*, and related actions.

The fact that EU private international law makes recourse to the same techniques as other uniform instruments may permit their interaction. An example is offered by the Brussels IIa Regulation,[21] which 'complements and clarifies'[22] some rules of the 1980 Hague Convention on the civil aspects of international child abduction. Another example is offered by Regulation (EC) No 4/2009 on jurisdiction, applicable law, recognition and enforcement of decisions and cooperation in matters relating to maintenance obligations,[23] whose Article 15 makes reference for the 'Determination of the applicable law' to the 2007 Hague Protocol on the law applicable to maintenance obligations. Regulation (EU) No 650/2012 on successions is yet another case: its Articles 27 and 75 achieve a uniform solution for the form of dispositions upon death for all the Member States, whether or not they are parties to the 1961 Hague Convention on the conflicts of laws relating to the form of testamentary dispositions.

---

20 As, for instance, in Articles 31, 32, and 33 of Regulation (EU) No 650/2012 on jurisdiction, applicable law, recognition and enforcement of decisions and acceptance and enforcement of authentic instruments in matters of succession and on the creation of a European Certificate of Succession [2012] OJ L 201/107, concerning, respectively, adaptation of rights *in rem*, *commorientes* and estates without a claimant.

21 Regulation (EC) No 2201/2003, concerning jurisdiction and the recognition and enforcement of judgments in matrimonial matters and the matters of parental responsibility [2003] OJ L 338/1.

22 The words are those of the Court of Justice in Opinion 1/13, n 13, para. 77.

23 [2009] OJ L 7/1.

This coincidence of techniques also permits to the European legislator to benefit from the longest experience that the Hague Conference has acquired in this area of law: many provisions of Regulation No 650/2012 that we just mentioned follow the model offered by the Hague Convention of 1 August 1989 on the Law Applicable to Succession to the Estates of Deceased Persons.

4. EU PRIVATE INTERNATIONAL LAW AS A TOOL FOR THE ESTABLISHMENT OF AN AREA OF FREEDOM, SECURITY AND JUSTICE

Notwithstanding this similarity of ingredients, EU private international law possesses a different flavour. This was noticeable since its first appearance under the form of international instruments, such as the 1968 Brussels Convention and the 1980 Rome Convention.[24] This difference depends by the fact that the adoption of uniform rules is functional and instrumental to the attainment of the objectives of the treaties. The harmonisation of international solutions, which is the sole purpose of the international movement towards unified rules on private international law, is of course one of the objectives, as it provides a legal environment that favours the legal security and the continuity of interpersonal relations; but it is accompanied by other objectives such as, first and foremost, the proper functioning of the internal market, and, now, the establishment of an 'area of freedom, security and justice', as stated in Recital 1 of all the regulations adopted so far.[25]

There are clear illustrations of the coexistence of these two objectives in the EU conflict-of-laws rules. A striking example is offered by the main connecting factors adopted by Regulation No 1259/2010,[26] ie, the choice of the parties (although restricted to the law of a country which presents a connection with at least one of the spouses, but with the possibility of choosing also the law of the forum) and, in the absence of such choice, the law of the habitual residence of the spouses, 'provided that the period of residence did not end more than 1 year before the court was seized, in so far as one of the spouses still resides in that State at the time the court is seized'. As it has been clear-sightedly pointed

[24] H Rasmussen, 'A New Generation of Community Law? Reflections on the handling by the Court of Justice of the Protocol of 1971 relating to the Interpretation of the Brussels Convention on Jurisdiction and Enforcement of Judgments' (1978) 15 *Common Market Law Review* 249.

[25] The only exception is Regulation (EU) 2015/848 on insolvency proceedings (recast), OJ L 141/19, which refers in general terms to the area of freedom, security and justice in its Recital 2, but links the adoption of the Regulation in Recital 3 to the 'proper functioning of the internal market'.

[26] Regulation (EU) No 1259/2010 implementing enhanced cooperation in the area of the law applicable to divorce and legal separation [2010] OJ L 343/10, which applies in Austria, Belgium, Bulgaria, France, Germany, Greece, Hungary, Italy, Latvia, Lithuania, Luxembourg, Malta, Portugal, Romania, Spain, and Slovenia.

out, these rules appear as a compromise between two contrasting objectives. First, the purpose, normally inherent in any work of codification of conflicts of law undertaken at an international or supranational level, to establish within the circle of the participating States a legal environment capable of ensuring the legal security and the predictability of law and harmony decisions. Second, the objective, connected to the development of the integration strategy between the Member States of the Union, to promote the freedom of circulation of the European citizens, by the possibility conferred by these rules to take advantage of the freedom of movement for the application of a law favourable to their interests or to escape disadvantageous legislation.[27] It seems, in this case, that when the reconciliation of these two different objectives cannot be attained, the typical purposes of uniform rules of private international law – predictability, legal security, and harmony of decisions – surrender to the needs of the EU integration.

The attainment of these different results by recourse to the same techniques and tools is favoured by a number of circumstances that differentiate EU private international law from the rules created in other fora. The first, and probably the most important, is the fact that EU private international law rules belong to the European legal order, which has its own principles and values. The requirement of a uniform interpretation, typical of all instruments of uniform law, is consequently accompanied by the duty of a construction in the light of those principles and values and of the objectives that they pursue. This duty falls primarily upon the Member States authorities; should a doubt arise, a judicial body may (or must) request for a preliminary ruling from the European Court of Justice, giving the Court the possibility of expressing its authoritative interpretation of the provisions at issue. The driving role played by the Court in building a European legal system functional to the development of the integration is well known.[28]

Secondly, the EU lawmaker can often go further in some subject matters in which harmonisation at a different level is hindered by the fact that the divergences of the different legal systems – which generally exist also within the EU Member States – are not compensated by the strong political will that may form

---

27 A Davì, 'Le renvoi en droit international privé contemporain' (2010) 352 *Recueil des cours de l'Académie de droit international de La Haye* 9, 329 ff; see also P Franzina, 'The Law Applicable to Divorce and Legal Separation under Regulation (EU) No 1259/2010 of 20 December 2010' (2011) 3 *Cuadernos de derecho transnacional* 85, 96 ff, who underlines that the connecting factors adopted by the Regulation aim at balancing the needs of integration, one 'of the core concerns of the Union in this area', with the preservation of cultural identity, by permitting spouses to choose to submit their separation or divorce to their national law, with the further consequence, in case of spouses national of third countries, of facilitating the recognition of decisions rendered by EU courts in their countries of origin.

28 A-L Calvo Caravaca and J Carrascosa González, *Derecho internacional privado* (13th ed, Comares 2012), 187.

within the European Institutions. An example can be drawn from the system of recognition and enforcement of foreign decisions put in place by the Brussels I Regulation, and reinforced at the occasion of its recast by Regulation (EU) No 1215/2012, which is now considered as an essential tool for the Member States; its extension to a broader circle of parties is, however, difficult to envisage, by reason of the mutual trust among the interested States that it presupposes.

This is not to say that the EU legal system cannot seek recourse to methods that are different from those classically employed by uniform instruments adopted at different levels. Recourse to the *méthode de la reconnaissance*[29] and the reference to the country of origin complement the pertinent rules on private international law by ensuring that the application of the latter in a specific case does not result in hindering the attainment of the fundamental principles of the EU treaties, in particular the free circulation of physical and legal persons.[30] They do not, however, and at least for the time being, eliminate the need for uniform rules applicable in relations both within the Member States and among the Member States and third countries.

The Europeanisation of private international law has influenced also the phase of negotiations of instruments adopted at different levels. The participation of the EU Commission as an observer in the various fora where uniform rules have been drafted has resulted in drawing attention to the inadequacy of the classical modalities of negotiating an international text – such as the possibility for an observer to speak only when all the delegations have already exercised their right of intervention, and not participating in the vote – to the new situation. This has brought the Hague Conference to modify its practice and to switch to less formal rules that involve the adoption of a provision by consensus, as is codified in the new Article 8(2) of its Statute, amended in 2007: 'The Sessions, Council and Special Commissions shall, to the furthest extent possible, operate on the basis of consensus.'

The texts of the instruments have seen the appearance of new clauses, in particular those concerning the possibility of accession by REIO's[31] and the

29 This *méthode* is not employed solely within the EU legal system, although the Court of Justice has made reference to it in some of its decisions. See P Lagarde, 'La méthode de la reconnaissance est-elle l'avenir du droit international privé?' (2015) 371 *Recueil des cours de l'Académie de droit international de La Haye* 9.

30 A Davì, n 27, 442.

31 As for the former clause, it was during the negotiations, in 2001, of the Cape Town Convention and its Aircraft Protocol that the question of the accession of the European Community first arose in connection with a uniform law convention. Practice connected with the so called 'mixed' agreements had already developed in other areas, and had brought a solution specifically targeting the Community, or to the insertion of a more general formula. The Cape Town Diplomatic Conference adopted a text which subsequently provided the example for many other uniform law texts, sometimes with some drafting adjustments. The clause allows for accession by any 'regional economic integration organization'. The term, which had already been used on other occasions, contains a reference to integration and allows the exclusion of a number of organizations that

so-called disconnection – or compatibility – clauses,[32] and new modalities of ratification.[33]

5. EU AND UNIFORM INSTRUMENTS IN THE FIELD OF INTERNATIONAL TRADE

The adoption of uniform instruments of private international law has always proved to be a difficult task. In view of the establishment of the area of justice security and freedom, the EU Member States are obtaining important results also in areas that were so far considered too complex to be harmonized, or in domains in which the efforts at a wider level were unsuccessful. There are, however, sectors pertaining to the wide area of international trade, which includes contract law, transports, international payments, banking, and the financial sector, towards whose instruments the position of the Union appears different. This domain has its own instruments, mostly originating in the private practice, often – but not always – codified in binding instruments.

The Union shows generally a certain deference to these rules. An example is offered by the proposal concerning the Common European Sales Law, which

> may be used only if the seller of goods or the supplier of digital content is a trader. Where all the parties to a contract are traders, the Common European Sales Law may be used if at least one of those parties is a small or medium-sized enterprise ('SME').[34]

The proposed regulation does not want to interfere with the standards of international trade, in particular with the application of the 1980 Vienna Convention on the International Sale of Goods. Rather, the proposed regulation aims at offering a unified and sound regime for contracts with consumers or

---

remain in single phase of cooperation. It is also necessary that this organization is equipped for 'competence over certain matters' governed by the instrument to which the clause pertains.

32 These clauses have been defined by the Court of Justice in Opinion 1/03, n 11, as mechanisms 'seeking to prevent any conflict in the enforcement of the agreement' and 'providing that the agreement does not affect the application by the Member States of the relevant provisions of Community law' (para. 130), 'the purpose of which is to prevent conflicts in the application of the two legal instruments' (para. 154).

33 The practice shows a progressively increasing role of the Union; the last instruments adopted at The Hague have been ratified only by the Union, but are binding upon all Member States, as explained in a specific declaration made at the time of the ratification, For example, in the case of the 2007 Convention on the international recovery of child support and other forms of family maintenance, the declaration stated: 'The European Union declares that it exercises competence over all the matters governed by the Convention. The Member States shall be bound by the Convention by virtue of its approval by the European Union'.

34 Article 7.

weak professional parties, characterized by international elements that are not included in the scope of the instrument adopted at the universal level, or are not its main target.

Another example is arbitration. As is well known, arbitration is excluded from the scope of the Brussels I Regulation; the Court of Justice has been requested in quite a few occasions to evaluate the impact of this exclusion on connected issues, such as court proceedings ancillary to arbitration proceeding or asset-freezing orders.[35] The proposal of the Commission in view of the Recast of the Regulation included a new article aimed at clarifying the relationship between arbitration and jurisdiction of Member States.[36] However, following the concerns expressed by some arbitration centres,[37] not only has the proposed addition not been adopted, but the new text contains a specific provision on the prevalence of the New York Convention over the Regulation[38] and a complex recital which reaffirms the precedence of the Convention.[39]

---

35 For an account of the decisions issued by the Court on the relationship between the Brussels I instruments and the New York Convention, see TC Hartley, 'The Brussels I Regulation and Arbitration' (2014) 63 *International and Comparative Law Quarterly* 843, 847 ff.

36 Proposal for a Regulation of the European Parliament and of the Council on Jurisdiction and the recognition and enforcement of judgments in civil and commercial matters (Recast), Brussels, 17 December 2010, Article 29.4: 'Where the agreed or designated seat of an arbitration is in a Member State, the courts of another Member State whose jurisdiction is contested on the basis of an arbitration agreement shall stay proceedings once the courts of the Member State where the seat of the arbitration is located or the arbitral tribunal have been seised of proceedings to determine, as their main object or as an incidental question, the existence, validity or effects of that arbitration agreement. This paragraph does not prevent the court whose jurisdiction is contested from declining jurisdiction in the situation referred to above if its national law so prescribes. Where the existence, validity or effects of the arbitration agreement are established, the court seised shall decline jurisdiction. This paragraph does not apply in disputes concerning matters referred to in Sections 3, 4, and 5 of Chapter II.'

37 Proposal, No 3, Consultation and impact assessment: 'several arbitrators' associations expressed concern on the impact of any regulation on the leading role of European arbitration centres at world-wide level. Views diverged on whether the best way forward, i.e., either to actively promote arbitration agreements by avoiding parallel proceedings and abusive litigation tactics, or to exclude arbitration more broadly from the scope of the Regulation. In any event, most stakeholders expressed general satisfaction with the operation of the 1958 New York Convention, which should not be undermined by any Union action on the matter'.

38 See Article 73.2: 'This Regulation shall not affect the application of the 1958 New York Convention'; cf A Leandro, 'Towards a New Interface Between Brussels I and Arbitration?' (2015) 6 *Journal of International Dispute Settlement* 2; TC Hartley, n 36, 843; P Bertoli, *Diritto europeo dell'arbitrato internazionale* (Giuffrè 2015), 9 ff.

39 Recital 12.

6. PERSPECTIVES ON THE UNIFICATION OF PRIVATE INTERNATIONAL LAW

The more important effect of the Europeanisation of private international law on the work aiming at adopting uniform rules at different levels seems to be its influence on the subject matter of unification itself. Suffice to recall, after the impasse of the negotiation of the judiciary convention at The Hague in 2000,[40] the adoption by the Conference of instruments that, as we have already mentioned, States from regions different from Europe are not willing, at least for the time being, to ratify, and the difficulty encountered in choosing new matters for its agenda. The reason is twofold. On the one side, the European States have always been the central nucleus of any instrument adopted so far by the Conference, both in the phase of negotiation and in the phase of ratification. If they do not need to negotiate under the auspices of an organisation, the organisation itself may become superfluous, as is happening with the ICCS. On the other side, once a European instrument has been adopted, it seems difficult to reach a result on the same subject matter at a different level.[41] This would require the other States to agree on the provisions adopted by the EU lawmaker, or the European Member States to depart from the result attained, often after a long procedure and not without efforts, within their circle, in view of a wider harmonisation. Though of course possible – as was the case, for instance, with the Lugano Convention, albeit within a small circle of States, and in the frame of the establishment of the European Economic Space – none of these scenarios seems likely to occur in a near future.

---

40 See above, § 2, and n 15.

41 The item 'jurisdiction, and recognition and enforcement of decisions in matters of succession upon death' was deleted from the agenda of the Hague Conference in 2013, ie, at the first meeting of the Council on General Affairs following the adoption of Regulation (EU) No 650/2012; Council on General Affairs and Policy of the Conference (9-11 April 2013), <http://www.hcch.net/upload/wop/gap2013concl_e.pdf>.

THE LUGANO MODEL – COOPERATIVE ENHANCEMENT OVER ENHANCED COOPERATION

Chris THOMALE *
University of Heidelberg

1. INTRODUCTION

In September 2010, during the legislative process leading to the recast of Regulation (EC) No 44/2001 on jurisdiction and the recognition and enforcement of judgments in civil and commercial matters (Brussels I), the European Parliament was faced with a proposal by the Commission, which suggested far-reaching inclusions of non-Member States bordering to a *loi uniforme*. The European Parliament responded that,

> in view of the existence of large numbers of bilateral agreements between Member States and third countries, questions of reciprocity and international comity, *the problem is a global one* and a solution should also be sought in parallel in the Hague Conference through the resumption of negotiations on an *international judgments convention*',

and accordingly mandated the Commission

> to use its best endeavours to revive this project, the Holy Grail of private international law' and urged the Commission to explore the extent to which *the 2007 Lugano Convention could serve as a model and inspiration* for such an international judgments convention.[1]

---

* I would like to thank Paul Beaumont, Pietro Franzina, Brooke Marshall and Marta Pertegás for their comments. Further thanks go to Christoph Lukas for his editorial support. All mistakes and inaccuracies remain entirely mine.

1 Resolution of 7 September 2010, 2009/2140(INI), para. 15 (emphasis added).

This resolution, to which the Committee of Legal affairs adhered,[2] sheds some light on the modern internal European perspective on the Lugano Convention: Lugano is the inter-governmental version of the Brussels I Regulation. Where Brussels I can thrive upon the primacy of the European 'new legal order'[3] and hence follow the maxim *lex iubeat, non disputet*,[4] Lugano must seek refuge in permanent consultation between the Convention States[5] as laid out in its Protocol 2. While for the purpose of European integration, Lugano has delivered, harmonised regulation already having been reached, it is allegedly that very weakness which might be turned into a strength when looked at from an international political perspective. In the following, this apparent claim shall be assessed in four steps. *First*, some background on Lugano, its content and its historical development will be given. We will arrive at the conclusion that originally Lugano was planned as a soft vehicle for European integration. *Second*, the article will then sketch out a taxonomy of European integrative techniques spanning from simple bilateral treaties to quasi-federal, full integration in the European Union. It will be shown that in this spectrum Lugano is most aptly described as a multilateral treaty with a qualified institutional connection to the European Union and notably the ECJ. This will set the stage for a *third* point: Lugano once was an apt tool by which to transform large parts of the EFTA into an integrated EC and EU. By now, this process is almost completed. With only Switzerland, which opposed accession to the EEA in the first place,[6] Norway and Iceland being non EU-Convention States, Lugano has lost this initial rationale. It, moreover, might even have evolved to constitute a disincentive to further integration, giving away a free semi-clone[7] of Brussels I without insisting on full EU-Membership as a prerequisite. Being useless on a European Union level, however, does not preclude the possibility that the Lugano mod-

---

2 Report on the Proposal for a Regulation of the European Parliament and of the Council on jurisdiction and the recognition and enforcement of judgments in civil and commercial matters (recast), A7-0320/2012, 139.

3 Case C-26/62, *van Gend & Loos*, EU:C:1963:1; Case C-6/64, *Flaminio Costa v ENEL*, EU:C:1964:66.

4 'The law does not dispute, it commands': Seneca, *Epistulae morales ad Lucilium*, lib. XV, ep. XCIV, 38.

5 The term is somewhat misleading in the light of the fact that the European Union, formerly: European Community, as a legal person is a party to the Lugano Convention, whereas it is *inter alia* its Member States that are bound by it: cf F Dasser, 'Art. 1', in F Dasser and P Oberhammer (eds), *Übereinkommen über die gerichtliche Zuständigkeit und die Anerkennung und Vollstreckung von Entscheidungen in Zivil- und Handelssachen vom 30. Oktober 2007 - Kommentar* (2nd edition, Stämpfli 2011) 107. The expression 'Convention state', as used in this contribution, shall signify the latter. On further implications of this discrepancy see C Kohler, 'La Convention de Lugano devant la Cour Internationale de Justice: l'affaire *Belgique c. Suisse*' (2012) 22 *Schweizerische Zeitschrift fur Internationales und Europaisches Recht* 441; see also below, n 32.

6 Swiss references: *Bull. EG* 12-1992, 1.4.3; *Bull. EG* 3-1993, 1.3.2; Anpassungsprotokoll zum Abkommen über den Europäischen Wirtschaftsraum v 17.3.1993, BGBl. 1993 II, 1294.

7 See A von Mehren, 'The Hague Jurisdiction and Enforcement Convention Faces an Impasse - A Diagnosis and Guidelines for a Cure' (2000) 20 *IPRax* 465, 466.

el might survive internationally, facing the challenge of a global international judgments convention. This is what the European Parliament seems to be pondering in the resolution quoted above. Indeed: there have been changes on the international legal landscape nourishing the courage to launch yet another attempt in order to arrive at an international agreement on at least recognition and enforcement of judgments. However, as will be shown, there is little reason to believe that Lugano, of all possible options, should be the way to go. Rather, and *finally*, Lugano can sensibly provide a model for further vertical integration within the EEA and Switzerland: service of documents and taking of evidence are fields in which EU Regulations have made significant progress as compared to the relevant Hague Conventions, which should be made a part of the upcoming revision of the Lugano Convention.

2. THE LUGANO CONVENTION: COOPERATIVE ENHANCEMENT TOWARDS AN INTEGRATED EUROPEAN ECONOMIC AREA

In an incremental process, starting 16 September 1988, the Lugano Convention entered into force between the European – as it then was – Community, comprising 12 Member States as well as the EFTA States Austria, Finland, Iceland, Norway, Sweden and Switzerland.[8] Its main purpose was to extend the Brussels Convention of 27 September 1968 to the European Free Trade Association in order to build a more integrated European Economic Area, in modern terms: a common market. The parties were convinced that harmonized rules on jurisdiction, recognition and enforcement would foster legal certainty and hence 'strengthen legal and economic cooperation in Europe.'[9] Consistent with this general thrust, the Lugano Convention mirrored the Brussels Convention down to its numeration. Despite certain deviations,[10] the label *convention parallèle*[11] overall seems justified. But Lugano did not simply copy Brussels. Reception was no one way street. Rather, Lugano went on to codify existing case-law and adapted the Convention's wording in accordance with the experience that had been gained from the application of the Brussels Convention. In response to

8 This excludes Liechtenstein, which acceded EFTA on 1 September 1991, see Paragraph 3 of the Preamble of the Convention establishing the European Free Trade Association, consolidated version, last amended on 1 July 2013.

9 Paragraph 3 of the Preamble of the Lugano Convention (1988). See also: S Auer, in R Geimer and R Schütze, *Internationaler Rechtsverkehr in Zivil- und Handelssachen*, BI 1e EuGVÜ und LugÜ (606), Einleitung, para. 42 (updated as of EL 19; November 2015).

10 T Schmidt-Parzefall, *Die Auslegung des Parallelübereinkommens von Lugano* (Mohr Siebeck 1995), 15.

11 On the use of this term, starting in 1985, see T Schmidt-Parzefall, n 10, 14, fn 66.

these adjustments, the Brussels Convention itself was amended in 1989, in order conform with the Lugano progress. This mutually influential parallelism between Brussels and Lugano could be witnessed again, when after the conversion of the Brussels Convention into the Brussels I Regulation of 22 December 2000, the Lugano Convention was adapted to the changes made in 2007.[12]

Now, after the recast of the Brussels I Regulation brought about by Regulation (EU) No 1215/2012 (Brussels Ia), this parallelism has been broken somewhat or, shall we say, awaits a Lugano III drawing level with those recent changes. There is neither reason nor time to rehearse the whole Convention here. Suffice it to point out the key differences between the Lugano Convention of 2007 and the Brussels Ia Regulation as they stand today. These differences each fall into one of two categories, of which more in the following.

2.1. CRACKS IN THE BRUSSELS/LUGANO REGIME DUE TO THE RECAST BRUSSELS I REGULATION

First, the deviation between the Lugano Convention of 2007 and the recast Brussels I Regulation can be seen as a diachronic one, essentially stemming from the changes made to Regulation No 44/2001 in its 2012 amendment.

Among those changes, the abolition of *exequatur* procedure clearly stands out.[13] It coincides with the defendant's right to apply for a refusal of recognition and enforcement according to Article 45 of the Brussels Ia Regulation. The

12 Convention on jurisdiction and the recognition and enforcement of judgments in civil and commercial matters, signed in Lugano on 30 October 2007 - Explanatory report by Professor Fausto Pocar [2009] OJ C 319/1, 12. See also Opinion 1/03, EU:C:2006:81, para. 136.

13 'Following the political mandate by the European Council in the Tampere (1999) and The Hague (2004) programs, the main objective of the revision of the Regulation should be the abolition of the *exequatur* procedure in all matters covered by the Regulation', Report from the Commission to the European Parliament, the Council and the European Economic and Social Committee of 21 April 2009 on the application of Council Regulation (EC) No 44/2001 on jurisdiction and the recognition and enforcement of judgements in civil and commercial matters, COM (2009) 174 final, 4; S Giroud, N Meier and R Rodriguez, 'Le règlement Bruxelles I bis, un modèle pour une nouvelle Convention de Lugano?', in Guinchard (ed), *Le nouveau règlement Bruxelles I bis* (Bruylant 2014), 419, 435; G Cuniberti, 'Some Remarks on the Efficiency of *Exequatur*', in *Grenzen überwinden - Prinzipien bewahren – Festschrift für Bernd von Hoffmann zum 70. Geburtstag* (Gieseking 2011), 568; P Oberhammer, 'The Abolition of *Exequatur*' (2010) 30 *IPRax* 197, 202 ('no need for specific *exequatur* proceedings'); pointing out probable important impacts of abolishing *exequatur*: P Schlosser, The Abolition of *Exequatur* Proceedings – Including Public Policy Review?, ibid, 101; and P Beaumont, E Johnston, 'Abolition of the *Exequatur* in Brussels I: Is a Public Policy Necessary for the Protection of Human Rights?', ibid, 105. Subdued support by T Domej, 'Die Neufassung der EuGVVO – Quantensprünge im europäischen Zivilprozessrecht' (2014) 78 *Rabels Zeitschrift für ausländisches und internationales Privatrecht* 508, 517 ff, expressing doubts on the validity of the impact assessment provided by the Centre for Strategy & Evaluation Services in their final report of 17 December 2010, 34, <http://ec.europa.eu/justice/civil/files/study_cses_brussels_i_final_17_12_10_en.pdf>.

recast provides for a consolidated procedure, in which, according to its recital 30, 'a party challenging the enforcement [is] able to invoke, in the same procedure, in addition for the grounds for refusal provided for in this Regulation, the grounds for refusal available under national law and within the time-limits laid down in that law.'[14] This enforcement regime, according to the amended Article 2(a), explicitly excludes provisional measures *ex parte*.[15]

Furthermore, the limited inclusion of non-Member States should be noted.[16] Although the European Parliament, as quoted above, rejected the Commission's proposal of a *loi uniforme* in matters of international jurisdiction, protective venues favouring consumers and workers as contained in Articles 18 and 21 of the Brussels Ia Regulation have been 'bilateralised'. Also, according to Article 33 of the recast, *lis pendens* in a non Member State can justify a Member State's court to stay its proceedings subject to an assessment of 'all the circumstances of the case', installing a 'flexible mechanism' that comes very close to the infamous common law doctrine of *forum non conveniens*.[17]

Equally noteworthy is Article 25(1) of the Brussels Ia Regulation, which, consistently with Article 5 of the Hague Convention on Choice of Court Agreements of 30 June 2005, now calls upon the law of the chosen court's Member State to assess the substantive validity of the agreement of the parties.[18] The old rule was to apply the *lex fori* of whatever court seised.[19] Choice of court agreements are privileged even further by Article 31(2) of the recast Regulation,

---

14 This is a deliberate refutation of Case C-139/10, *Prism Investments BV v Jaap Anne van der Meer*, EU:C:2011:653, which, applying Regulation No 44/2001, held to the contrary, that specific objections against international *exequatur* on the one and general defences against enforcement of a judgment on the other hand should be kept strictly separate.

15 See also Recitals 25, 33.

16 On the applicability to Extra-EU disputes see L Mari and I Pretelli, 'Possibility and Terms for Applying the Brussels I Regulation (Recast) to Extra-EU Disputes Law' (2013/2014) 15 *Yearbook of Private International Law* 211.

17 See Recitals 23 f. On *forum non conveniens* see also: Article 15 of the Brussels IIa Regulation 2201/2003 and Article 6(a) of Regulation 650/2012 on successions [2012] OJ L 201/107; F Marongiu Buonaiuti, '*Lis Alibi Pendens* and Related Actions in the Relationships with the Courts of Third Countries in the Recast of the Brussels I Regulation' (2013/2014) 15 *Yearbook of Private International Law* 87. The emerging European recognition of a quasi *forum non conveniens* is highlighted by T Domej, n 13, 540; C Thomale,'The Forgotten Discipline of Private International Law: Lessons from *Kiobel* v. *Royal Dutch Petroleum*', *Transnational Legal Theory*, forthcoming, at II(2)(a)(cc). This convergence weakens the classical position, according to which the *lis pendens / forum non conveniens* divide between the European continent and the anglo-american world were insurmountable, see F Juenger, 'Eine Haager Konvention über die Urteilsanerkennung?', in H Schack (ed), *Gedächtnisschrift für Alexander Lüderitz* (CH Beck 2000), 329, 341 ff.

18 According to Recital 20, this includes the prorogated Member State's conflict-of-law rules. See T Domej, n 13, 526 f.

19 See C-269/95, *Benincasa v Dentalkit*, EU:C:1997:337, para. 25; U Magnus, 'Gerichtsstandsvereinbarungen im Vorschlag zur Reform der EuGVVO', in *Grenzen überwinden - Prinzipien bewahren*, n 13, 667 f, with further references; U Magnus, 'Article 23', in U Magnus and P Mankowski (eds), *Brussels I Regulation* (2nd ed, Sellier 2012), 436, 476, fn 81.

ordering 'any court of another Member State [to] stay the proceedings until such time as the court seised on the basis of the agreement declares that it has no jurisdiction under the agreement.'[20]

For the time being, all these recent amendments to the Brussels regime have not been received by the Lugano Convention.

2.2. THE SPECIFIC INTERGOVERNMENTAL, COOPERATIVE AND EXPANSIONIST DESIGN OF LUGANO

A *second* category of differences between Brussels and Lugano is more deeply rooted in the heterogeneous structure and nature of both acts: the Brussels I Regulation marks a definitive and exclusive, directly applicable regime on free movement of judgments in a fully integrated EU market, backed up by mutual trust. Conversely, the Lugano Convention, while regarding itself as being 'part of Community rules',[21] has stayed in essence an international treaty. Whereas Brussels stands for trans-governmental enhanced cooperation (in a non-technical sense), Lugano relies on inter-governmental cooperative enhancement. This is why, in Articles 64(3) and 67(4), the Lugano Convention of 2007 offers additional grounds for refusal of enforcement, on top of those already recognized under the Brussels regime: Convention states may close *one* eye on each other's judiciary's mistakes, but they will not recognize foreign decisions blindly.[22]

The hybrid, Janus-faced nature of the Lugano regime between public international form and European content becomes most apparent when looking at its interpretation. According to Protocol 2 to the Lugano Convention of 2007, an 'interpretation as uniform as possible' both of the Lugano Convention itself in its various Member States and of the Lugano Convention together with the Brussels regime is intended.[23] In order to achieve such uniformity, however, whereas the Brussels regime can rely on preliminary rulings of the ECJ under Article 267 TFEU,[24] the Lugano regime lacks such an integrated judiciary. For

---

20 On the pleading standard of stating a plausible choice of court agreement see T Domej, n 13, 535 f, with further references. This arrangement does not cover arbitration: see Recital 12.

21 Protocol 2, Preamble; Pocar Report, n 12, 197. But see still, on Lugano (1988), Convention on jurisdiction and the enforcement of judgments in civil and commercial matters done at Lugano on 16 September 1988 - Report by Mr P. Jenard and Mr G Möller, [1990] OJ C 189/57, 110: 'not a source of Community Law.' Cf C Kohler, 'Balancing the judicial dialogue in Europe: some remarks on the interpretation of the 2007 Lugano Convention on jurisdiction and judgments', in J Forner Delaygua, C González Beilfuss and R Viñas Farré (eds), *Entre Bruselas y La Haya. Estudios sobre la unificación internacional y regional del Derecho internacional privado - Liber Amicorum Alegría Borrás* (Marcial Pons 2013), 565, 567: 'change of parameters'.

22 Cf Jenard and Möller Report, n 21, 14-17, 67, 79-84; Pocar Report, n 12, 139.

23 Protocol 2, Preamble.

24 This is not to deny the shortcomings of the preliminary ruling approach, especially when facing the case-specific intricacies of civil procedure, see K Lipstein, 'Enforcement of Judgments under

want of an EEA adjudicative body, which was deemed illegal by the ECJ,[25] Lugano has to rely on a 'principle of consultation and not on judicial hierarchy.'[26] This procedure asks

> any court applying and interpreting [the Lugano Convention to] pay due account to the principles laid down by any relevant decision concerning the provision(s) concerned ... rendered by the courts of the States bound by this Convention and by the Court of Justice.[27]

In this context, the prevalent importance, the successively 'broader role'[28] of ECJ case-law is underscored by Article 2 of Protocol 2, giving non-EU Convention States an *amicus curiae* standing before the ECJ in its preliminary rulings according to Article 23(3) and (4) of the ECJ Statute.[29] Furthermore, the consultation procedure is backed up by a 'system of exchange of information concerning relevant judgments' which is also led and managed by the Registrar of the ECJ.[30] Thus, an attenuated version of *acquis communautaire*, an 'acquis conventionnel',[31] is supposed to be built up incrementally. It is only as a residual means that the neutral Standing Committee of the Lugano Convention is called upon to consider *inter alia* amendments to the Convention under Article 4(2) of Protocol 2.

With the Standing Committee, a further structural difference between the Brussels and Lugano regimes is connected. The Committee is competent to administer the accession of new States to the Convention. After its 2007 amendment, according to Articles 70(1)(b) and (c), 72, this includes non-European territories of EU Members as well as any other State.[32] In other words, while the

---

the Jurisdiction and Judgments Convention: Safeguards' (1987) 36 *International and Comparative Law Quarterly* 873, 877 f. However, it is certainly superior to having no common adjudicatory body after all. See eg Høyesterett, Judgment of 20 December 2012, *Trico Subsea AS* v *Raffles Shipping Projects Pte Ltd*, HR-2012-2393-A, *Norsk Retstidende* (Rt) 2012, 1951 and the incisive review provided by C Kohler, 'Homogeneity or Renationalisation in the European Judicial Area? Comments on a Recent Judgment of the Norwegian Supreme Court', in *The EEA and the EFTA Court: Decentred Integration* (Hart Publishing 2014), 237.

25 Opinion 1/91, EU:C:1991:490. Cf C Kohler, n 21, 570, arguing for an EFTA court, competent to decide on the interpretation of the Lugano Convention in all EFTA States.

26 Jenard and Möller Report, n 21, p. 111. See also T Schmidt-Parzefall, n 10, 57.

27 Article 1(1) Protocol 2.

28 Pocar Report, n 12, 196.

29 Protocol (No 3) on the Statute of the Court of Justice of the European Union. See Pocar Report, n 12, 198.

30 Article 3 Protocol 2.

31 C Bernasconi and A Gerber, 'Der räumlich-persönliche Anwendungsbereich des LugÜ' (1993) 3 *Schweizerische Zeitschrift für internationales und europäisches Recht* 39, 41.

32 Pocar Report, n 12, 187. The exclusive competence of the EU to accept new States flows directly, first, from its status as a Contracting Party and, second, from the EU provenience of the Lugano Convention after its 2007 amendment, see supra n 21. These facts thus supersede the two-tiered

Brussels regime, by its very nature, is a closed entity confined to EU Member States, Lugano strives to be an open legal instrument. This open or expansionist momentum of the Lugano regimes pervades the whole Convention. It is the reason why, eg Article 64(2) of the Lugano Convention of 2007 uses the general term of 'a State' in which Lugano but not Brussels applies, despite the fact that when the Convention was enacted, only Norway fulfilled that double condition. Likewise, in the Lugano Convention of 2007, superseded bilateral and multilateral conventions of the various Convention States are listed not as a part of the Convention,[33] but in a separate Annex VII.[34] The political rationale is obvious: as Annexes can be changed more easily than usual Convention content, namely, in compliance with Article 77, through simple notification of the Depositary, the Lugano regime is preparing for future accessions.[35] This also holds true for the Lugano's intertemporal regime: being geared towards expansion, Article 63(1) of the Convention of 2007 provides for an explicit rule on how cases should be managed where proceedings are commenced in a Convention State at a time where the State of enforcement has not acceded the Convention:

> [t]his Convention shall apply only to legal proceedings instituted and to documents formally drawn up or registered as authentic instruments after its entry into force in the State of origin and, where recognition or enforcement of a judgment or authentic instruments is sought, in the State addressed.[36]

On closer inspection, the Brussels regime lacks such a provision as it addresses all Member States simultaneously, without having to account for a successive coming into force, at least not in the Regulation itself.[37] It was thus disturbing, to say the least, that in *Wolf Naturprodukte*[38] the ECJ would base its ruling on Article 66 of Regulation No 44/2001, which only envisages the Regulation's

assessment performed by the ECJ in Opinion 1/13, n 50, paras 74 ff on the 1980 Hague Convention on child abduction; S Giroud, N Meier, R Rodriguez, n 13, 441, call the Lugano Convention an 'instrument ouvert à des États tiers'.

33 Compare Article 69 of Regulation No 44/2001. In the meantime, supposedly for the sake of convenience, Article 69 of Regulation No 1215/2012 has also adopted an Annex-like solution. This provides another formidable example of how Lugano can influence the evolution of the Brussels regime as well. See supra, n 12.

34 Pocar Report, n 12, 178.

35 Cf R Wagner, U Janzen, 'Das Lugano-Übereinkommen vom 30.10.2007', (2010) 30 *IPRax* 298, 307, fn 115.

36 See generally: Pocar Report, n 12, 176; T Domej, 'Art. 63', in F Dasser and P Oberhammer (eds), n 5, 929.

37 On the accession of Denmark, Ireland, Great Britain and Northern Ireland 9 October 1978, see eg Article 34 of the Accession Treaty and the Schlosser Report, [1979] OJ C 59/71, 137.

38 Case C-514/10, *Wolf Naturprodukte GmbH v SEWAR*, EU:C:2012:367.

applicability to proceedings and documents instituted or drawn up *before the Brussels regime entered into force in the State of origin.*[39]

We can thus observe a comparatively expansionist momentum in the Lugano as opposed to the Brussels regime. Building on this momentum, as a European integrating measure, Lugano has been an overwhelming success: Until 1992, all EFTA States apart from Iceland[40] and Liechtenstein had *applied* for a Membership in the European Community. To be sure, some of these applications were later withdrawn, notably due to negative referenda.[41] However, it seems safe to say that the convergence, brought about by Lugano and the EEA it supported, was a driving factor convincing the States to at least make accession become an issue and bring membership in the EC onto their domestic and international agenda.[42]

3. DIFFERENTIATED INTEGRATION IN EUROPE: THE LUGANO CONVENTION AS A MULTILATERAL INTERNATIONAL TREATY WITH A QUALIFIED CONNECTION TO EU LAW

Inside geographic Europe, we behold a large variety of instruments, striving to reconcile European diversity with some form of unity.

The most integrated, unity-focussed legal framework is full EU membership and the partial cession of national sovereignty that goes with it. However, below this maximum, discrete levels of limited integration can be found.

---

[39] After thus having confused the problem of pending proceedings in the State of origin with the real question of successive entry into force, the ECJ went on to clearly misstate the decisive moment at which the Regulation must be applicable in both the State of Origin and the State addressed: While it should have referred, just like Article 63(1) Lugano, to the moment when proceedings are instituted in the State of origin, probably by accident it chose the time when the decision is rendered in that State. See C Thomale, 'Brüssel I und die EU-Osterweiterung - zum raumzeitlichen Anwendungsbereich der EuGVVO' (2014) 34 *IPRax* 239, 240.

[40] Iceland applied to join the EU 16 July 2009 and, after acceding Lugano in 2011, suspended its application for EU membership 13 September 2013. See 4.1, below.

[41] Norway's application for admission was accepted by the Commission of the European Communities on 19 April 1994 (94/C 241/01), by the European Parliament on 4 May 1994 (94/C 241/02) and by the Council of the European Union on 16 May 1994 (94/C 241/06). However, the result of a referendum on Norwegian EU membership held 28 November 1994 was 52.18% against and 47.82% for joining the EU. The result reflected that of the referendum on EC membership in 1972 when the Norwegian electorate rejected membership by 54% to 46%. See *European election database on the Norwegian Social Science Data Services*, <http://www.nsd.uib.no/european_election_database/election_types/eu_related_referendums.html>.

[42] For Austria's point of view G Reichelt, "Lugano' und Österreich – Österreich vor der Ratifikation des Parallelübereinkommens zum EuGVÜ', in E Jayme (ed), *Ein internationales Zivilverfahrensrecht für Gesamteuropa. EuGVÜ, Lugano-Übereinkommen und die Rechtsentwicklungen in Mittel- und Osteuropa* (Müller 1992), 273, 281.

To start with – according to Protocols 21 and 22 of the Lisbon Treaty – the UK, Ireland and Denmark are generally exempt from the ambit of judicial co-operation in civil matters according to Article 81 TFEU, with the option to *opt in* at will.[43] This differentiation *ratione personae* in certain ways is mirrored by another instrument, which *ratione materiae* allows regulative diversity inside the EU: the competence of enhanced cooperation. According to Article 20 TEU and Articles 326 to 334 TFEU, nine Member States or more, following a certain procedure whose conditions I have assessed in more detail elsewhere[44], can obtain the power to pass EU legislation applicable only amongst them. Such legislation does not form part of the *acquis communautaire* (Article 20(4) TEU), but it is still valid EU law. The Rome III Regulation on the law applicable to divorce and legal separation[45] provides an excellent example in the field of private international law. First entering into force on 30 December 2010 in Belgium, Bulgaria, Germany, France, Italy, Latvia, Luxembourg, Hungary, Malta, Austria, Portugal, Romania and Slovenia, until now, Lithuania[46] and Greece[47] joined the Regulation on 21 November 2012 and 27 January 2014 respectively. This leaves geographic Europe with a deeply split international family law, *European Union* family law being only one of many solutions in the field.

Going beyond EU law in a technical sense, we find differentiated integration achieved by the EEA, focussing on an extension of the common market, which also extends to basic freedoms and their private international implications. To give just one example: as far as freedom of establishment commands the private international theory of incorporation, at least in inbound situations with regard to the host State, this encompasses all EEA states, be they EU Member States or not.[48]

It would seem, at first sight, as if anything beyond the EEA were plain Public International Law, ie multilateral and even bilateral treaties. But this is a picture

---

43 Since the Treaty of Lisbon, Denmark has the possibility of opting-in when a 'proposal or initiative has been presented to the council pursuant to title IV of part Three of the Treaty on the Functioning of the European Union', cf Protocol No 22 on the position of Denmark, annexed to the Treaty on European Union and the Treaty on the Functioning of the European Union.

44 C Thomale, 'Verstärkte Zusammenarbeit als Einigungsersatz? Eine Gegenrede am Beispiel des Europäischen Privat- und Gesellschaftsrechts', (2014) 23 *Zeitschrift für europäisches Privatrecht*, 517.

45 Regulation (EU) No 1259/2010 implementing enhanced cooperation in the area of separation 2010 the law applicable to divorce and legal separation.

46 [2012] OJ L 323/18.

47 [2014] OJ L 23/41.

48 On inbound situations inside the EU see Case C-212/97, *Centros*, EU:C:1999:126; Case C-208/00, *Überseering*, EU:C:2002:632; Case C-167/01, *Inspire Art*, EU:C:2003:512. On the repercussions regarding the EEA: MP Weller, 'Niederlassungsfreiheit via völkerrechtlicher EG-Assoziierungsabkommen', (2006) 35 *Zeitschrift für Unternehmens- und Gesellschaftsrecht*, 748; C Thomale, MP Weller, 'Freedom of Establishment', in J Basedow, F Ferrari, P de Miguel Asensio and G Rühl (eds), *Encyclopedia of Private International Law*, forthcoming.

too rough and ready to uphold. Rather, we find subtle shades, one might say: integrative tuning, among the international treaties applicable in Europe. One way is to integrate or transform international conventions into EU law such as happened in Regulation (EC) No 4/2009 on maintenance obligations being virtually parasitic on the 2007 Hague Protocol in the field.[49] In a more attenuated form, this is also what the Brussels IIa Regulation 2201/2003 does with the 1980 Hague Convention on the civil aspects of international child abduction. It 'complements and clarifies'[50] and, in fact, *is being* complemented and clarified[51] by the Convention. It is submitted that in a procedural way, Lugano falls into the same category: Lugano and Brussels are collaborate regimes. We have been able to observe that link with regard to their texts, which have constantly been adapted to each other. What is more, an overarching procedural framework of mutual consultation – if not mutual trust – has been established in order to ensure uniform interpretation and application under the leadership of the ECJ. It is in this sense that the Lugano Convention can be labelled a multilateral international treaty with a qualified connection to EU law.

4. LUGANO OUTDATED: WHY LUGANO IN ITS *STATUS QUO* IS NO VIABLE MODEL OF EUROPEAN OR GLOBAL INTEGRATION

4.1. EU INTEGRATION OF EFTA STATES AT A DEAD END

As shown in the foregoing, Lugano once not only was designed to foster European integration through a *convention double* on jurisdiction as well as recognition and enforcement, but arguably was also considerably successful in doing so. It is questionable, however, to what extent this old rationale still persists.[52] On a European level, only Iceland, Norway and Switzerland are left to be integrated further, ie induced to accede the European Union. None of these States

[49] The Hague Protocol of 23 November 2007 on the law applicable to maintenance obligations. See generally P Beaumont, 'International Family Law in Europe – The Maintenance Project, the Hague Conference and the EC: A Triumph of Reverse Subsidiarity' (2009) 73 *Rabels Zeitschrift für ausländisches und internationales Privatrecht* 509, 525; M Andrae, in T Rauscher (ed), *Europäisches Zivilprozess- und Kollisionsrecht* (4th ed, Sellier 2015), Article 15 EC Maintenance Regulation; B Hess and S Spancken, 'Setting the Scene – The EU Maintenance Regulation', in P Beaumont, B Hess, L Walker and S Spancken (eds), *The Recovery of Maintenance in the EU and Worldwide* (Hart Publishing 2014), 331, 334.

[50] Opinion 1/13, EU:C:2014:2303, para. 77.

[51] Ibid, para. 79, referring to Article 21 of the 1980 Hague Convention.

[52] T Schmidt-Parzefall, n 10, 110: 'Mit jedem EU-Betritt verliert das LugÜ an eigenständiger Bedeutung.'

has indicated any substantiated interest in acceding the EU in any near future. To the contrary, several referenda evidenced a public opinion explicitly opposing EU accession.[53] Not only does the rather technical Lugano Convention seem powerless to overcome such an anti-EU resentment, but the Convention might even strengthen this impulse on an utilitarian, game-theoretical level: It may precisely be the ready availability of the strikingly attractive Brussels/ Lugano regime *outside* the EU that takes away an important incentive to become a Member State.[54] Iceland should provide a good example: Initially, once accession negotiations had commenced on 16 July 2009, Iceland deliberately postponed joining the Lugano agreement under the auspices of adopting the Brussels/Lugano regime as a future Member State.[55] Its ratification of Lugano 1 May 2011 could therefore at hindsight be interpreted as a bad omen, leading to the suspension of its application for membership in the EU 13 September 2013. Latest news has it, that Iceland is even formally going to withdraw from its EU candidacy.[56]

Consequently, Lugano must be abandoned as a vehicle for integration into the European Union. In this institutional sense, the Lugano regime – using the words of the early Ludwig Wittgenstein – is a ladder one must throw away once one has climbed up on it.[57]

4.2. LUGANO AS AN UNPROMISING MODEL FOR GLOBAL FREE MOVEMENT OF JUDGMENTS

Whatever the merits of the old EFTA-rationale, the Lugano regime's latest inaptitude in terms of European integration does not, in itself, prejudice the Convention to be used on a global level, which seems to be exactly the path the European Parliament would like to follow.

This takes us to the ongoing Hague project on an international judgments convention.[58] The question is, whether Lugano could provide, if not a blueprint,

53 On Switzerland, see generally the adoption of proposal No 580 'Against mass immigration' by referendum on 9 February 2014, (2014) *Official Compilation of Federal Legislation*, 1391.

54 See on the similar strategic objection against the inclusion of Third States into the Brussels/Lugano regime: H Schack, 'Perspektiven eines weltweiten Anerkennungs- und Vollstreckungsübereinkommens' (1993) 1 *Zeitschrift für Europäisches Privatrecht* 306, 309, with further references in fn 19, 331; T Domej, n 13, 522.

55 R Wagner, U Janzen, 'Das Lugano-Übereinkommen vom 30.10.2007' (2010) 30 *IPRax* 298, 310.

56 For one example of the ample press coverage, see <http://www.dw.de/iceland-withdraws-eu-accession-bid/a-18313183>.

57 L Wittgenstein, *Tractatus logico-philosophicus* (Kegan Paul, Trench, Treubner & Co. 1922), 6.54.

58 HCCH Judgments Project (Recognition and Enforcement of Foreign Judgments): Report of the fourth Meeting of the Working Group on the Judgments Project (3-6 February 2015) and Preliminary Draft Text resulting from the Meeting: <http://www.hcch.net/upload/wop/gap2015pd07b_en.pdf>.

maybe at least a framework for such a convention. Anecdotal evidence from the ongoing negotiations seems to suggest that negotiators are unhappy with such an approach.[59] Indeed, severe doubts should be harbored as to whether the quoted resolution of the European Parliament is anything more than wishful thinking. One should, however resist the temptation to base this hesitation on the various unsuccessful attempts *per se*, which the Hague Conference has been making since 1925 in promoting a judgments convention. Since the last meaningful try in 1971,[60] the political landscape has changed. Many important procedurally focused Conventions such as the 1965 and 1970 Hague Conventions on the service of documents and the taking of evidence have acquired significant support,[61] exorbitant jurisdiction is in strong decline internationally speaking[62] and even a transatlantic common market is being negotiated.[63] So there has been enough convergence in international procedure to justify giving

---

59 I am indebted to Marta Pertegás and Paul Beaumont for sharing their invaluable front-line insights into the subject with me. Earlier scepticism waged specifically against extending Lugano to the US is expressed, eg, by H Schack, n 54, 310, 313; F Juenger, n 17, 329; A von Mehren, 'Recognition of United States judgments abroad and foreign judgments in the United States. Would an international be Useful?' (1993) 57 *Rabels Zeitschrift für ausländisches und internationales Privatrecht* 449; Id, n 7, 465; SP Baumgartner, *The Proposed Hague Convention on Jurisdiction and Foreign Judgments* (Mohr Siebeck 2003). More enthusiasm is shared in this respect by ECY Lau, 'Update on the Hague Convention on the Recognition & Enforcement of Foreign Judgments', (2000) 6 *Annual Survey of International and Comparative Law* 13. Still considering the Lugano and Brussels Conventions as potentially useful 'source d'inspiration': A Bucher, 'Vers une convention mondiale sur la compétence et les jugements étrangers' (2000) *La Semaine judiciaire*, II, Doctrine, 77, 78.

60 The Hague Convention of 1 February 1971 on the recognition and enforcement of foreign judgments in civil and commercial matters came into force between Cyprus, the Netherlands and Portugal only, enlarged by accessions of Kuwait on 1 February 2002 and of Albania on 1 November 2010 and depending on successive bilateral confirmation via supplementary agreements (Article 21 ff). The ensuing 1997 initiative did not even make it that far, formulating only a 2000 Preliminary Draft Convention on Jurisdiction and Foreign Judgments in Civil and Commercial Matters, procured by Peter Nygh and Fausto Pocar, <http://www.hcch.net/upload/wop/jdgmpd11.pdf>. It was abandoned, leading to the Hague Choice of Court Convention of 30 June 2005.

61 Convention of 15 November 1965 on the service abroad of judicial and extrajudicial documents in civil or commercial matters; Convention of 18 March 1970 on the taking of evidence abroad in civil or commercial matters.

62 C Thomale, n 17, *inter alia*, on the US Alien Torts Statute. This decline, among other reasons, seems to result from an more comprehensive view on the public international limits to the domestic exercise of private international jurisdiction, see: A Mills, *The Confluence of Public and Private International Law* (Cambridge University Press 2009), 228; A von Mehren, 'The Case for a Convention-mixte Approach to Jurisdiction to Adjudicate and Recognition and Enforcement of Foreign Judgments' (1997) 61 *Rabels Zeitschrift für ausländisches und internationales Privatrecht* 86, 90 stating 'a world-wide convention with a strict duality approach[, as followed by Brussels and Lugano,] would lead to complications and confusion' and therefore proposes a *convention mixte*, to which H Schack, 'Entscheidungszuständigkeiten in einem weltweiten Gerichtsstands- und Vollstreckungsübereinkommen', (1998) 5 *Zeitschrift für Europäisches Privatrecht* 951 agrees.

63 See the negotiations on a Transatlantic Trade and Investment Partnership (TTIP). This was different in 2000, when US 'union' and the European 'common market' were two entirely distinct and discrete areas still. Cf A von Mehren, n 59, 467.

a global or at least transatlantic judgments convention another shot.[64] From a global governance perspective, this even seems a pressing need. If as early as 1958[65] States were already able to overwhelmingly agree on the international enforcement of arbitral awards, loosely regulated at best, what light does it cast upon the international community that public courts, usually endowed with true independence, monetary disinterest and far-reaching procedural guarantees, should be trusted less? Therefore, the international community has to act and it should act multilaterally through the Hague Conference.

However, the Hague Conference would be well advised not to fall into overhasty actionism. After all, what counts is not the agreement on a text in itself, but its actual adoption through ratification by the States. In this respect, Hague Conventions have been less successful than its impeccable reputation and the ubiquitous lip service to multilateralism would suggest: Most Hague Conventions never made it to any meaningful ratification record, leaving the Hague Conference, grimly speaking, with a 'cemetery of nascituri'.[66] It is hence of utmost importance both for the judgments project in particular and for the Hague Conference in general, to confirm diligently that the next proposal for a judgments convention be mutually agreeable by key players such as notably the US and the UK.

Given this high pressure, this condemnation to success, the intellectual starting point for a Hague judgments convention must be chosen in anticipation of prospects for worldwide ratification. I am convinced that the Lugano model is the wrong approach to achieve international integration outside EFTA. This is, among other reasons well rehearsed in the debates ensuing the abandonment of the 2000 Preliminary Draft Convention,[67] mainly because the world will not live under the quasi-aegis of the ECJ as do Lugano Convention States. Lugano offers a EU- and ECJ-centered 'unbalanced structure'[68] for judicial dialogue, bearing understandably little attraction for non-Member States of the EU.

This does not mean, of course, that the Lugano Convention should be disregarded across the board. *Some* designs and formulations of it may well provide a sound basis for negotiations just as invaluable experiences made with its application in European case-law should be taken into account. However, this input should feed into a larger, global assessment, also considering other existing judgment conventions such as, *inter alia*, the 1889 and 1940 Montevideo

64 For updated Draft Articles of the ongoing Hague Judgments project, please consult <http://www.hcch.net/index_en.php?>.

65 Convention on the recognition and enforcement of foreign arbitral awards (New York, 10 June 1958) (hereinafter referred to as the 'New York Convention').

66 Such was the expression used by Alfonso Luis Calvo Caravaca in an oral conversation.

67 Supra n 59, 63.

68 C Kohler, n 21, 568.

Conventions[69] in South America as well as the 1952 Convention of the Arab League on the Enforcement of Judgments and Arbitral Awards and the 1983 Riyadh Arab Agreement for Judicial Cooperation in the Middle East.[70] It may also be especially promising to consider 'home' recognition schemes of possible objectors to a Hague judgments convention, such as the US 'full faith and credit' system of recognition inside the Union.[71]

In any event, the Hague Conference in its very own best interest should strike off its European preconceptions, biases and path-dependencies and, instead, embrace a truly global approach to a global judgments convention. It is at this point where the Lugano model, as could be shown, ceases to fit in. Thus, European Parliament crusaders may be justifiedly searching for the Holy Grail of global free movement of judgments. However, using the Lugano model in order to achieve that goal, they are riding a dead horse that will never take them to Jerusalem, let alone The Hague.

5. LUGANO RELOADED: FURTHER POTENTIAL IN SERVICE OF DOCUMENTS AND TAKING OF EVIDENCE

As could be shown, the Lugano model has no convincing 'business case' in either European or global integration – that is, within the material scope of jurisdiction, recognition and enforcement of judgments. However, considering ancillary issues such as service of documents and the taking of evidence, the Lugano concept might be extended to those areas, increasing vertical integration inside EFTA.[72]

---

69 Tratado de derecho commercial terrestre internacional de Montevideo. See W Goldschmidt and M Perugini Zanetti, *Derecho Internacional Privado* (10th ed, Abeledo Perrot 2011), 887, with further references.

70 For further references see R Michaels, 'Recognition and enforcement of foreign judgments', in R Wolfrum (ed), *Max Planck Encyclopedia of Public International Law* (Oxford University Press 2009), C.4.b.

71 US Constitution, Art. IV, § 1. See A von Mehren, n 61, 87: '[The full faith and credit clause] can be seen as analogous to a recognition and enforcement convention.'

72 Legal aid shall not be considered here, despite the fact that the 1980 Hague Convention on international access to justice leaves a lot of room for refinement and improvement. The problem is that on a EU level only Directive 2002/8/EC of 27 January 2003 is in place, setting minimum standards but leaving it to the Member States to provide 'more favorable arrangements' (Recital 31) as well as to decide on the inclusion of the opponent's cost imposed on the recipient of legal aid (Recital 12) and the threshold of indigence in order to qualify for legal aid (Recital 14). This leaves too wide a range of regulatory pluralism for the Lugano model to generate legal certainty through coordinated interpretation.

5.1. SERVICE OF DOCUMENTS

The service of documents has always been regarded as a necessary adjunct to the Brussels regime. Therefore, the Brussels Convention of 1968, in Article IV of its Protocol, already provided for certain minimum recognition standards with regard to foreign judicial and extrajudicial documents. In the meantime, these standards have been specified successively, leading to Regulation (EC) No 1393/2007 of 13 November 2007 on the service in the Member States of judicial and extrajudicial documents in civil or commercial Matters. This instrument is considerably advanced as compared to the Hague Service Convention of 1965 in terms of procedural efficiency. Not only does it limit the rights of the addressee for refusal to accept the document to be served (Article 8), but it also specifies the date of service (Article 9; Recital 15), which is of paramount importance not only to the procedural conduct of a case but also to substantive questions like prescription and the award of interest.[73] The question arises, whether this enhanced integration should be limited to EU Member States. Quite revealingly, in 1988, the Lugano Convention also mirrored the Brussels Convention with regard to the service of documents, containing in Article IV of its Protocol 1, a provision similar to Article IV of the Brussels Protocol.[74] The initial parallelism has been broken, however, in the 2007 amendment. Now, Article 26 of the Lugano Convention of 2007 and Article I of Protocol 1 thereto explicitly differentiate between EU Member States amongst which the Regulation applies and other Convention States. This divide makes no sense. If EFTA integration is sufficient to warrant an extension of EU rules on jurisdiction, recognition and enforcement through the Brussels/Lugano regime, so it should allow harmonized rules on the far less intricate issue of the service of documents.

5.2. TAKING OF EVIDENCE

European Union integration of civil procedure soon revealed that not only jurisdiction, recognition and enforcement but also service of documents require harmonisation. Therefore, Regulation 1206/2001 of 28 May 2001 on coopera-

73 In many legal systems, even specific liability rules attach to the service of process. See eg on German law, § 292, 987 ff of the German Civil Code.

74 Cf Jenard and Möller Report, n 21, 104: 'This Article reproduces Article IV of the Protocol annexed to the Brussels Convention.'

tion between the courts of the Member States in the taking of evidence in civil or commercial matters, states in Recital 7 that

> [a]s it is often essential for a decision in a civil or commercial matter pending before a court in a Member State to take evidence in another Member State, the Community's activity cannot be limited to the field of transmission of judicial an extrajudicial documents. … It is therefore necessary to continue the improvement of cooperation between courts of Member States in the field of taking of evidence.

This Regulation, as between the Member States, takes priority over the 1970 Hague Convention on the taking of evidence in the field (Article 21(1)). Again, as is the case with the EU Regulation on the service of documents in comparison with the corresponding Hague Convention, the Regulation comes out superior to the older Convention in terms of efficiency. While the Convention in its Article 12 confers a broad right onto a requested court to refuse execution whenever the addressed State's 'sovereignty or security would be prejudiced', it is only a very limited and clearly defined set of exceptional cases in which such can be done under Article 14 of the Regulation.[75] This facilitates transnational litigation and increases legal certainty as to the availability of evidence located in Member States.[76] One may wonder whether this progress inside the European Union should not be extended to EFTA States. Once again, the discrepancy with Brussels/Lugano seems odd. While foreign judgments based on foreign evidence procedures generally have to be recognised, the availability of domestic evidence procedures to foreign litigation is very limited. In other words: States will rather recognise and enforce a judgment whose evidence procedures they cannot influence than lend their very own procedures to the court rendering the judgment. The untenability of this position becomes most apparent when one considers that the necessity to take evidence in a foreign state oftentimes indicates that enforcement will later be sought in the same state, too. Hence, an extension of EU rules on taking of evidence to EFTA states is indicated.

---

75 Cf Recital 11: 'To secure the effectiveness of this Regulation, the possibility of refusing to execute the request for the performance of taking of evidence should be confined to strictly limited exceptional situations.'

76 Having said that, of course, the Regulation in itself at some point will have to be further developed. On some recent shortcomings see F Niggemann, 'Ausländische Beweissicherungsmaßnahmen im Rahmen der EuGVVO: Neue Ansätze, aber noch immer keine überzeugende Lösung' (2015) 35 *IPRax* 75.

5.3. THE VERTICAL EXTENSION OF LUGANO

The foregoing elucidates that the Lugano model still has a future in the integration process of civil procedure. However, this future does not lie in a horizontal extension of its territorial scope towards a global judgments convention. Rather, Lugano should stick to its guns, namely the increasing integration of the EEA and Switzerland short of EU membership. There, the procedural issues of the service of documents and the taking of evidence show what one may call an unjustified deficit of integration. It is upon international policymakers to even out this imbalance. One possible framework would be an amendment to the Lugano Convention of 2007, a 'Lugano III'.[77] Such amendment suggests itself anyway, in order to catch up with the Brussels I Regulation, as recast in 2012.[78] It is submitted that the incorporation of Regulations Nos 1393/2007 and 1206/2001 should also be brought to the table in these negotiations. If it were, this would tie in with the long-standing tradition of regulatory cooperation between EU and EFTA and, at the same time, would answer to the new maxim of consolidation as declared in the post-Stockholm program.[79]

---

77 Cf S Giroud, N Meier, R Rodriguez, n 13, 419 ff, arguing for an adapted parallelism with the intention to sever and transform the plain enhancements made in the Brussels (2012) amendment while discarding specifically Union-based elements such as *inter alia* external effects of protective fora; F Pocar, 'A Partial Recast: Has the Lugano Convention Been Forgotten?', in F Pocar, I Viarengo and FC Villata (eds), *Recasting Brussels I* (Cedam 2011), 117, 120: '[Lugano countries'] acceptance of harmonized external rules of jurisdiction would imply their adhesion to an approach towards a tighter connection with the European Union, including to its general policy of protecting the internal market by common rules applicable in the relations of its Member States with third countries. There is no sign of the Lugano countries moving in this direction.'

78 Pocar, n 79, 121, calls the Lugano/Brussels parallelism a 'cornerstone of the success of the European judicial cooperation in civil and commercial matters.'

79 Cf R Wagner, 'Justizielle Zusammenarbeit in Zivilsachen – Quo vadis?' (2015) 23 *Zeitschrift für Europäisches Privatrecht* 1, 2.

REGULATIONS (EC) NOS 662/2009 AND 664/2009: CAN EXCLUSIVITY BE SUCCESSFULLY RECONCILED WITH FLEXIBILITY?

Jan-Jaap Kuipers
Senior Associate with De Brauw Blackstone Westbroek, Amsterdam

1. INTRODUCTION

In the past two decades, the Union has made a significant contribution to the area of judicial cooperation in civil matters having cross-border implications.[1] The idea of international cooperation in cross-border civil matters is certainly not new. Already in 1893, the first steps towards such cooperation were taken in the framework of what would later become the Hague Conference on Private International Law. The Hague Conference became a permanent international organisation in 1955. Its objective is to strengthen legal certainty by striving for the progressive harmonisation of the rules of private international law.[2] Besides the Hague Conference, Member States have concluded a web of bilateral agreements to facilitate cooperation in cross-border civil matters.

---

1 C Kohler, 'Interrogations sur les sources du droit international privé européen après le traité d'Amsterdam' (1999) 88 *Revue critique de droit international privé* 1; J Basedow, 'The Communitarisation of the Conflict of laws under the Treaty of Amsterdam' (2000) 37 *Common Market Law Review* 687; H Jessurun d'Oliveria, 'The EU and a Metamorphosis of Private International Law', in J Fawcett (ed), *Reform and Development of Private International Law: Essays in honours of Sir Peter North* (Oxford University Press 2002), 111; P Lagarde, 'Développement futurs du droit international privé dans une Europe en voie d'unification: quelques conjectures' (2004) 68 *Rabels Zeitschrift für ausländisches und internationales Privatrecht* 225; M Bogdan, *Concise Introduction to EU Private International Law* (Europa Law Publishing 2006), 6-14.

2 H van Loon, 'The Hague Conference on Private International Law: Asser's Vision and an Evolving Mission', (2011) 24 *Hague Yearbook of International Law* 3; F Pocar and H van Loon, 'The 120th anniversary of the Hague Conference on Private International Law' (2014) 50 *Rivista di diritto internazionale privato e processuale* 517; P Trooboff and F Stikkelbroeck, 'Reflections on the Hague Conference on Private International Law at 140 – 20 Years Forward' (2012) 25 *Hague Yearbook of International Law* 59.

Until well in the 1990's, the Hague Conference was mainly composed of European states. In the absence of any clear competences of the Union with regard to private international law, it appeared that judicial cooperation in civil matters would take place mainly via the Hague Conference.[3] This changed with the entry into force of the Treaty of Amsterdam. Following the Treaty of Amsterdam, the Union progressively adopted measures aimed at the harmonisation of private international law, while at the same time, the Hague Conference gradually evolved into a truly international organisation. The membership of the Hague Conference has doubled in size since 1997 and its members now include important emerging economies such as Brazil, India, the Russian Federation and South Africa.[4] Moreover, the European Community became, on behalf of the Union,[5] a member of the Hague Conference in 2007.[6] Although the emergence of the Union as an important actor in the area of private international law should be welcomed in principle, it may come at the expense of the ability of the Member States to participate in traditional fora and enter into bilateral agreements with third countries. The risk is that the pursuit of wider international cooperation in cross-border civil matters is substituted for cooperation amongst Member States.[7] This risk has become more real in the light of the broad understanding by the Court of Justice of the European Union (CJEU) of the Union's external competence in private international law.

Most recently, in Opinion 1/13 the CJEU decided that the exclusive competence of the Union encompasses the acceptance of the accession of a third state to the 1980 Hague Convention on child abduction (1980).[8] After Opinion 1/13, it strongly appears that the exclusive external competence encompasses all policy areas covered by the EU private international law Regulations. In or-

---

3 P North, 'Is European Harmonisation of Private International Law a Myth or Reality?', in T de Boer (ed), *Forty Years on: the Evolution of Postwar Private International Law in Europe* (Kluwer 1990), 29.

4 J Kuipers, 'The European Union and the Hague Conference on Private International Law – Forced Marriage or Fortunate Partnership', in H de Waele and J Kuipers (eds), *The European Union's Emerging International Identity: Views From the Global Arena* (Brill 2013), 159.

5 Prior to the entry into force of the Lisbon Treaty, only the European Community enjoyed international legal personality under Article 281 EC Treaty.

6 A Schulz, 'The Accession of the European Community to the Hague Conference on Private International Law' (2006) 56 *International and Comparative Law Quarterly* 939; H van Loon and A Schulz, 'The European Community and the Hague Conference on Private International Law', in B Martenczuk and S van Thiel (eds), *Justice, Liberty, Security: New Challenges for the External Relations of the European Union* (Brussels University Press 2007), 257; R von Wagner, 'Die Haager Konferenz für Internationales Privatrecht zehn Jahre nach der Vergemeinschaftung der Gesetzgebungskompetenz in der justiziellen Zusammenarbeit in Zivilsachen' (2009) 73 *Rabels Zeitschrift für ausländisches und internationales Privatrecht* 215; M Traest, 'Over de Haagse Conferentie en het Europese IPR' (2010) *SEW – Tijdschrift voor Europees en Economisch Recht* 94.

7 See with further references: R Plender and M Wilderspin, *The European Private International Law of Obligations* (Sweet & Maxwell 2009), 16-17.

8 Opinion 1/13, EU:C20142303.

der to balance such broad understanding of the Union's powers with the need for Member States for some flexibility to shape their individual relations with third countries in accordance with the applicable economic, cultural and political ties, two regulations were already adopted in 2009. Regulation (EC) No 662/2009 establishes a procedure for the negotiation and conclusion of agreements between Member States and third states on particular matters concerning the law applicable to contractual and non-contractual obligations[9] and Regulation (EC) No 664/2009 establishes a procedure for the negotiation and conclusion of agreements between Member States and third states concerning jurisdiction, recognition and enforcement of judgments and decisions in matrimonial matters, matters of parental responsibility and matters relating to maintenance obligations, and the law applicable to matters relating to maintenance obligations.[10]

This paper attempts to analyse whether Regulation No 662/2009 and Regulation No 664/2009 have successfully reconciled the exclusivity of the Union's external competence in the area of private international law with the need of the Member States for flexibility. For that purpose, a concise overview of the Union's evolving competences in private international law is provided in paragraph 2. In paragraph 3, the external dimension of the most important EU private international law instruments is analysed. Regulations Nos 662/2009 and 664/2009 are addressed in paragraph 4. Finally, the author assesses whether these instruments are a successful template for guaranteeing the continuance of international cooperation in civil matters having a cross-border implication.

2. EVOLVING UNION COMPETENCES IN PRIVATE INTERNATIONAL LAW

Until the 1990's, it appeared that the influence of the Union on private international law would be only fairly limited.[11] The original EEC Treaty contained only one reference to private international law. Article 293 EEC stipulated that Member States would enter into negotiations with each other concerning the simplification of the recognition and enforcement of judicial decisions which resulted in the Brussels Convention (1968). It was striking that the Rome Convention on the Law Applicable to Contractual Obligations (1980) lacked any specific legal basis in the Treaty, but was based upon the desire to continue the harmonisation of private international law, as commenced by the Brussels Convention, in the area of applicable law. Formally speaking, the Brussels and

9 [2009] OJ L 200/25.

10 [2009] OJ L 20/46.

11 P North, n 3, 29-48.

Rome Conventions were not instruments of Community law, but international conventions, albeit negotiated under the auspices of the Community.[12]

The Treaty of Maastricht (1991) formalised existing practices and incorporated in Title IV of the EU Treaty two articles on judicial cooperation in civil matters providing for the legal basis for the negotiation and adoption of private international law conventions by the Member States. The next step was taken in the Treaty of Amsterdam: Article 65 EC empowered the Community to take measures in the field of private international law when necessary for the functioning of the internal market. The Treaty of Amsterdam thus transformed the role of the Union from that of being a facilitator for the conclusion of international conventions to that of an autonomous legislator.[13] The trend of enlarging EU competences in private international law was continued in the Lisbon Treaty: Article 81 TFEU empowers the Union to take legislative measures *in particular* when necessary for the internal market. Legislative measures thus no longer strictly depend on the internal market criterion.[14]

The Union has made wide use of its private international law competence. Most notably, the Brussels Convention was replaced by the Regulation (EC) No 44/2001 on jurisdiction and the recognition and enforcement of judgments in civil and commercial matters (Brussels I)[15] and the Rome Convention into Regulation (EC) No 593/2008 on the law applicable to contractual obligations (Rome I). Moreover, Regulation (EC) No 2201/2003 concerning jurisdiction and the recognition and enforcement of judgments in matrimonial matters and the matters of parental responsibility (Brussels IIa) and Regulation (EC) No 864/2007 on the law applicable to non-contractual obligations (Rome II) were adopted. In Europe, the Union has replaced the Hague Conference on Private International Law as the principal forum for the convergence of private international law.

---

12 R Plender and M Wilderspin, n 7, 3-15.

13 C Kohler, n 1, 3-30; K Boele-Woelki, 'Unification and Harmonization of Private International Law in Europe', in J Basedow et al (eds), *Private Law in the International Arena: Liber Amicorum Kurt Siehr* (TMC Asser Press 2000), 61; J Basedow, n 1, 687 ff; J Israel, 'Conflicts of Law and the EC after Amsterdam: A Change for the Worse?' (2000) 7 *Maastricht Journal of European and Comparative Law* 81; H Jessurun d'Oliveria, n 1, 111 ff.

14 G de Groot and J Kuipers, 'The New Provisions on Private International Law in the Treaty of Lisbon', (2008) 15 *Maastricht Journal of European and Comparative Law* 109; H Mansel, K Thorn and R Wagner, 'Europäisches Kollisionsrecht 2009: Hoffnungen durch den Vertrag von Lissabon', (2010) 30 *IPRax* 1; I Barrière Brousse, 'Le Traité de Lisbonne et le droit international privé' (2010) 137 *Journal du droit international* 3.

15 Which in its turn has been replaced by Regulation (EU) No 1215/2012 on jurisdiction and the recognition and enforcement of judgments in civil and commercial matters (Brussels Ia).

3. THE EXTERNAL DIMENSION OF THE EU PRIVATE INTERNATIONAL LAW REGULATIONS

The effect of each of the EU private international law Regulations on situations involving a link with a third country differs per instrument.[16] Private international law is traditionally subdivided in three different branches. The first branch determines the jurisdiction of national courts over international disputes, the second is concerned with the determination of the applicable law, while the third branch contains rules as to the recognition and enforcement of foreign judicial decisions. The fact that a court assumes jurisdiction does therefore not mean that it will apply its own law, nor will the fact that a foreign court did not have jurisdiction to settle a dispute according to the rules of the forum necessarily prevent recognition and enforcement of that decision. The separate branches fulfil their functions according to their own logic and differ in their effect on foreign powers, which makes a separate treatment in the context of the Union's external competence necessary.[17]

3.1. THE BRUSSELS Ia AND BRUSSELS IIa REGULATION

The Brussels Convention was a double convention. It contained not only rules on jurisdiction, but rules concerning the recognition and enforcement of judgments as well. The reason for this is that the harmonisation of the rules on jurisdiction was deemed necessary in order to achieve the required degree of mutual trust between the courts of the Member States to allow for the free movement of judgments. The Brussels Convention therefore aimed to create rules which were highly predictable. The main rule is that a person should be sued in the courts of the state where he is domiciled. In its turn, the high degree of mutual trust between the courts of the Member States justifies a system where there are only limited possibilities to refuse or prevent the recognition and enforcement of a judgment from another Member State. The Brussels Convention has been highly successful and was after the Treaty of Amsterdam with minor modifications converted into the Brussels I Regulation. In its turn, Brussels I has been replaced by the Brussels Ia Regulation with effect from 10 January 2015. Under the Brussels Ia Regulation, the free movement of judgments is even further facilitated.[18]

---

16 A Borrás, 'The Effect of the Adoption of Brussels I and Rome I on the External Competences of the EC and the Member States', in J Meeusen, M Pertegas and G Straetmans (eds), *Enforcement of International Contracts in the European Union* (Intersentia 2004), 1107.

17 M Traest, *De Europese Gemeenschap en de Haagse Conferentie voor het Interntionaal Privaatrecht* (Maklu 2003), 269-275.

18 X Kramer, 'Abolition of Exequatur Under the Brussels I Regulation: Effecting and Protecting

The effects of the Brussels instruments are primarily limited to the territory of the Member States.[19] As regards jurisdiction, Brussels Ia puts in place a system for the distribution of international jurisdiction amongst the courts of the Member States. The Regulation can only confer jurisdiction on the courts established in one of the Member States. The Brussels Ia Regulation follows a doctrine dominant on the European Continent: jurisdiction is a matter of public law and a regulation cannot confer jurisdiction on a foreign court. The conditions on the basis of which a foreign court assumes jurisdiction should in principle be left to that foreign court to decide. Nevertheless, the Brussels Ia Regulation may apply in situations where one of the parties is domiciled in a third country, for example when a third country domiciled plaintiff brings proceedings in a Member State against a defendant domiciled in the Union.

The limitation of jurisdiction to the territory of the Member States is mirrored in the recognition of judgments. The free movement of judgments only applies to decisions taken by the courts in a Member State. The Brussels Ia Regulation does not provide for any rules on the recognition and enforcement of a decision stemming from a third country. Consequently, it remains for a Member State to determine under which conditions these decisions will be recognised or enforced. The decision to recognise or enforce only produces effects in the Member State where the *exequatur* is obtained.[20] *Exequatur sur exequatur ne vaut*; it is not possible to obtain the recognition and enforcement of a decision to recognise a foreign judgment. This means that, for example, if the enforcement of an Indian judgment is sought in England, the English decision to recognise and enforce the Indian judgment would not benefit from the free movement of judgments, and thus not bind a court in Italy.[21] The recognition and enforcement of a judgment thus differs significantly from the admission of goods and services into the Community in the framework of a common commercial policy. Whereas once a good has entered the Community it can freely circulate between the Member States, a judgment cannot.

The Brussels Ia Regulation may nevertheless impact relationships affecting a third country. In *Owusu*, the CJEU was confronted with a tort allegedly committed in Jamaica. The plaintiff had rented a holiday house with a private beach

Rights in the European Judicial Area' (2011) *Nederlands Internationaal Privaatrecht* 633; P Beaumont and E Johnston, 'Can Exequatur be Abolished in Brussels I whilst Retaining a Public Policy Defence?' (2012) 6 *Journal of Private International Law* 249.

19 T Kruger, *Civil Jurisdiction rules of the EU and their Impact on Third States* (Oxford University Press 2008).

20 It is a generally accepted principle of private international law that '*exequatur sur exequatur ne vaut*.' See G Kegel, '*Exequatur sur exequatur ne vaut*', in A Dieckmann (ed), *Festschrift für Wolfram Müller-Freienfels* (Nomos 1986), 377.

21 E Pataut, 'L'exécution des jugements nationaux et la Convention de Bruxelles', in *Les effets des jugements nationaux dans les autres Etat membres de l'Union européenne* (Bruylant 2001), 31.

in Jamaica from a defendant established in the United Kingdom.[22] The plaintiff dove onto an obstacle submerged in the sea and suffered personal injury. He brought proceedings against both the company leasing the holiday house as well the Jamaican company that owned the private beach. The English court sought to declare itself a *forum non conveniens* on the grounds that all the evidence relating to the tort was situated in Jamaica and that Jamaican courts were therefore in a better position to adjudicate the case. The doctrine of *forum non conveniens* is, however, not known in every Member State and was not laid down in the Brussels Convention. The CJEU held that the doctrine

> would be likely to affect the uniform application of the rules of jurisdiction contained therein in so far as that doctrine is recognised only in a limited number of Contracting States, whereas the objective of the Brussels Convention is precisely to lay down common rules to the exclusion of derogating national rules.[23]

The fact that the dispute concerned one Member State exclusively and a third country did not matter. The CJEU held that the common rules were not intended to apply only to situations in which there would be a real and sufficient link with the working of the internal market, which would by definition involve a number of Member States. The common rules were thus also applicable to a situation involving only one Member State and a third country. Regardless of any other links, Member States are bound to accept jurisdiction when it is conferred on them by the Brussels Ia Regulation.

The Brussels IIa Regulation on matrimonial matters and parental responsibility follows a similar logic. The Regulation provides rules for the distribution of concurrent jurisdiction between the courts of the Member States. These rules may also govern situations which do not have a real and sufficient link with the working of the internal market. As is the case with the Brussels Ia Regulation, the free movement of judgments under the Brussels IIa Regulation leaves the recognition and enforcement of decisions in matrimonial matters and the matters of parental responsibility stemming from a court in a third country to the national laws of the Member States.

3.2. THE ROME I AND ROME II REGULATIONS

Whereas the Brussels Regulations in principle govern the relations between the courts of the Member States, a different principle underpins the Rome I and Rome II Regulations. Article 2 of the Rome I Regulation and Article 3 of the

22 Case C-281/02, *Owusu v Jackson*, EU:C:2005:120.

23 Ibid, para. 43.

Rome II Regulation provide: 'Any law specified by this Regulation shall be applied whether or not it is the law of a Member State.' Rome I and Rome II thus have a universal scope of application.[24] It does not matter whether their provisions lead to the application of the law of a Member State or the laws of a third country.

The Rome Regulations follow the conflict of laws traditions that existed previously in the Member States. The overarching aim of this conflict of laws tradition was to promote the international harmony of decisions. Within a circle of civilised nations, the outcome of a dispute would be similar regardless of where the proceedings were brought. In contracts, the international harmony of decisions was pursued by locating the centre of gravity of the legal relationship. A contract was most closely connected to the jurisdiction in which the party that had to render the most characteristic performance was situated, irrespective of in which jurisdiction that place was located.

The differences underlying the structures of the Brussels and Rome Regulations become particularly important in the context of external relations. Since the Brussels Regulations govern the relations between the courts of the Member States, they may not be adequately equipped to deal with situations when one of the parties is domiciled in a third country. Moreover, the Brussels Regulations leave a gap with regard to the recognition of decisions rendered in third countries. Bi- or multilateral conventions are needed to fill this legislative void. On the other hand, Rome has a universal scope of application. No gaps occur in the legal areas that are covered by both regulations. The Rome Regulations can lead to the application of any law, even the law of a third country. International conventions might be needed to strive towards an international harmony of decisions, for example by aligning the EU conflict of laws rules with those of third countries, but not to fill any legislative voids left open by the Rome I and Rome II Regulations.

3.3. EXTERNAL POWERS

The Union enjoys international legal personality under Article 47 of the TEU,[25] but in contrast with states does not enjoy unrestricted external powers.[26] The Union may not go beyond the powers assigned to it. Neither Article 81 TFEU, nor any of its predecessors, explicitly addresses the issue of the Union's external

24 R Plender and M. Wilderspin, n 7, 98.

25 A Metz, *Die Außenbeziehungen der Europäischen Union nach dem Vertrag über eine Verfassung für Europa* (Ducker & Humblot 2007); M Cremona, 'Defining Competence in EU External Relations: Lessons from the Treaty reform Process', in A Dashwood and M Maresceau (eds), *Law and Practice of EU External Relations* (Cambridge University Press 2008), 34.

26 Ibid.

competences in the area of private international law. It is established case law, however, that an external power can not only arise from an explicit conferment, but also follow indirectly from the powers conferred on the Community to act internally. The CJEU held that the system of internal Community measures could not be separated from that of external relations. The adoption of internal measures by the Community could thus give rise, by implication, to a power to act externally in the area covered by that measure. In Opinion 1/76 the CJEU went one step further: whenever Community law created powers for institutions within its internal system for the purpose of attaining a specific objective, the Community had authority to undertake international commitments necessary for the attainment of that objective even in the absence of an express provision to that effect.[27] An implied external competence could thus even arise even if no secondary Community law existed.

It is also established case law that the adoption of internal measures may not only give rise to an external power, but that that power may also be exclusive.[28] If the external power is exclusive, Member States are no longer allowed to act. The CJEU held in *AETR* that when the Community implements a common policy envisaged by the Treaty, by adopting provisions laying down common rules, Member States no longer have the right to undertake obligations with third countries that affect those rules.[29] A detailed analysis of the envisaged agreement is required, but what matters is that the agreement may potentially prejudice the common rules. An actual conflict is not necessary. Exclusive competence could also arise when the internal competence could only be exercised at the same time as the external competence.[30] The conclusion of an international agreement would in such circumstances be necessary for the realisation of an internal goal and preclude the adoption of autonomous rules by the Member States.

With regard to private international law, it was already noted that the Brussels and Rome Conventions were formally international conventions negotiated under the auspices of the Community, but not instruments of Community law. It seemed unlikely that the Brussels or Rome Convention triggered any implied external competences in favour of the Community. To the contrary, the Brussels and Rome Conventions explicitly confirmed the ability of the Member States to

---

27 Opinion 1/76, EU:C:1977:63, para. 3. See also Opinion 2/91, EU:C:1993:106, para. 7.

28 P Eeckhout, 'Exclusive External Competences: Constructing the EU as an International Actor', in A Rosas, E Levits and Y Bot, *The Court of Justice and the Construction of Europe* (TMC Asser Press 2013), 613; A Rosas, 'Exclusive Shared and National Competence in the Context of EU External Relations: Do Such Distinctions Matter?' in *The European Union in the World: Essays in Honour of Professor Marc Maresceau* (Martinus Nijhoff Publishers 2014), 17.

29 Case 22/70, *AETR*, EU:C:1971:32,

30 Opinion 1/76, n 27, paras 4 and 7; Case C-466/98, *Commission v United Kingdom (Open Skies)*, EU:C:2002:624, paras 82-84.

enter into new international agreements in the areas covered by those Conventions. Article 57(1) of the Brussels Convention provided that the Convention shall not affect 'any conventions to which the Contracting States are or will be parties and which in relation to particular matters, govern jurisdiction or the recognition or enforcement of judgments.' The same situation existed under the Rome Convention. Article 21 stipulated that the Rome Convention would not prejudice the application of international conventions to which a Contract State becomes party. Article 23 specifically reserved the right to become a party to a multilateral convention whose principal aim is to lay down rules of private international law concerning any of the matters governed by the Rome Convention. A Contracting Party could accede to a multilateral convention, and hence unilaterally modify the common rules, even if this was opposed by all other Contracting States.[31] Such a possibility is hard to reconcile with the specific nature of Community law. In the process of transforming the Brussels and Rome Convention into the Brussels I and Rome I Regulation, these provisions were therefore deleted.[32] Both instruments left the division of external competence between the Union and the Member States open.

As was discussed above, the Brussels and Rome Conventions were transformed into Community instruments on the basis of Article 65 EC. This provision empowered the Community to act 'when necessary for the proper functioning of the internal market'. A literal reading of Article 65 would suggest that the power of the Community was limited to situations having a clear link with the internal market and that Member States remained free to enter into bi- and multilateral agreements with third states.[33] The practice of several Member States indeed suggested that they were, instead of the Union, competent to enter into bilateral agreements with third countries. For instance, Italy concluded the Convention regarding legal aid in civil and commercial matters (2003) with Algeria. Articles 15-20 contain provisions on the recognition and enforcement of judgments. Italy also concluded the Convention regarding judicial cooperation and the recognition and enforcement of judgments in civil and commercial

---

31 Article 22 in combination with Article 23 of the Rome Convention. See as well C Brière, 'Le droit international privé européen des contrats et la coordination des sources' (2009) 136 *Journal du droit international* 791, 799.

32 M Traest, n 17, 257.

33 On this discussion see: B Hess, 'Les compétences externes de la Communauté européenne dans le cadre de l'article 65 CE', in A Fuchs, H Muir Watt and E Pataut (eds), *Les conflits de lois et le système juridique communautaire* (Dalloz 2004), 81; M Wilderspin and A Rouchaud, 'La compétence externe de la Communauté européenne en droit international privé' (2004) 93 *Revue critique de droit international privé*, 1; F Pocar, 'The "Communitarization" of Private International Law and its Impact upon the External Relations of the European Union', in A Malatesta, S Bariatti and F Pocar (eds), *The External Dimension of EC Private International Law in Family and Succession Matters* (Cedam 2008), 3; P de Vareilles-Sommières, 'La compétence internationale de l'espace judiciaire européen', in *Vers de nouveaux équilibres entre ordres juridiques: Liber amicorum Hélène Gaudemet-Tallon* (Dalloz 2008), 397.

matters with Kuwait. Furthermore, Spain concluded the Convention on judicial aid in civil and commercial matters (2005) with Algeria. Articles 16-21 provide rules on the recognition and enforcement of judgments. Finally, Spain concluded the Convention on judicial aid in civil and commercial matters (2006) with Mauritania. Also this Convention contains a section dealing with the recognition and enforcement of judgments.[34]

Italy and Spain concluded these bilateral agreements only very shortly after the decision of the CJEU in *Owusu*. As was discussed above, the CJEU in *Owusu* held that the common rules on jurisdiction were not only intended to apply to situations involving a real and sufficient link with the internal market. Brussels I would thus also apply to matters involving a link with one Member State exclusively and a third country. The applicability of the common rules to international situations strongly suggested that, at least with regard to jurisdiction, the Community enjoyed exclusive external competence in the areas covered by Brussels I. It could therefore be argued that Italy and Spain had lost their competence to enter into a bilateral agreement with third countries.

3.4. THE LUGANO OPINION

The issue of external competence was finally settled by the CJEU in the Lugano Opinion.[35] The Lugano Convention (1988) aimed to establish in the relations between a state which is a party to the Brussels Convention and an EFTA Member State which is a party to the Lugano Convention, and in relations between the EFTA Member States which are parties to the Lugano Convention *inter se*, a system which is, although with some exceptions, the same as the regime under the Brussels Convention. When the Brussels Convention was transformed into the Brussels I Regulation, the modifications required the Lugano Convention be updated. The question was whether that new convention should be signed by the Community or by the Member States, or both, in other words: whether the area of jurisdiction and recognition and enforcement of judgment in civil matters had become an exclusive implied Community competence.

The CJEU repeated its findings in *Owusu* and stated that the common rules on jurisdiction were not meant to apply only to situations involving a link with

---

34 P De Miguel Asensio and J Bergé, 'The Place of International Agreements and European Law in a European Code of Private International Law', in M Fallon, P Lagarde and S Poillot Peruzetto (eds), *Quelle architecture pour un code européen de droit international privé?* (Peter Lang 2011), 185, 200-201.

35 Opinion 1/03, EU:C:2006:81. See M Fallon, 'L'applicabilité du règlement "Bruxelles I" aux situations externes après l'avis 1/03', in *Vers de nouveaux équilibres entre ordres juridiques*, n 33, 241; P Kuijper, 'The Opinion on the Lugano Convention and Implied External Relations Powers', in B Martenczuk and S van Thiel (eds), n 6, 187.

the internal market. The CJEU reiterated that Brussels Ia aimed to lay down a unified and coherent system as regards jurisdiction and the recognition and enforcement of judgments in civil matters. Any international agreement also establishing a unified system of rules on conflict of jurisdiction such as that established by Brussels Ia is capable of affecting the common rules. As an example the CJEU described the circumstance where a choice of court clause would confer exclusive jurisdiction upon a court established in one of the EFTA Member States. Under the Brussels I Regulation, exclusive jurisdiction due to a choice of court agreement can only be conferred on a court established in one of the Member States.[36] The extension of Brussels I by means of the Lugano Convention would mean that exclusive jurisdiction by a choice of court agreement could also arise in favour of the courts established in one the EFTA Member States. This would prejudice the application of the common rules because, in the case of a valid choice of court agreement in favour of a court in an EFTA Member State, the courts of the Member States would have to decline jurisdiction, whereas under the Brussels I Regulation, they would be obliged to accept it. The CJEU therefore held that the Lugano Convention could affect the application of common rules on jurisdiction.[37] Since the rules on recognition and enforcement were indissociably linked from those on the jurisdiction of courts, the Community enjoyed in the area of Brussels I an implied exclusive competence.[38]

The CJEU adopted in the Lugano Opinion a very broad view of the Community's external competences in private international law.[39] As was discussed above, Brussels I does not attempt to harmonise the rules of the Member States as regards the recognition and enforcement of judgments stemming from a court in a third country. The implications of the Lugano Opinion were much wider than Brussels I. If Brussels I gave by implication rise to an external exclusive competence of the Union, the same would *a fortiori* apply to the areas covered by the Rome I and Rome II Regulations. Member States realised that the pending transformation of the Rome Convention into the Rome I Regulation and the Rome II Regulation would give rise to an implied exclusive external competence and were concerned that this would deprive them of the flexibility required in the cooperation in cross-border civil cases. The preambles to Rome I and Rome II therefore announced that the Commission would make a proposal for a separate instrument concerning 'the procedures and conditions according to which Member States would be entitled to negotiate and conclude,

---

36 M Fallon, n 35, 252. Against: A Briggs, *Agreements on Jurisdiction and Choice of Law* (Oxford University Press 2008), 291.

37 Opinion 1/03, n 35, para. 161.

38 Ibid, para. 172.

39 R Brand, 'Evolving Competence for Private International Law in Europe: the External Effect of Internal Developments', in G Venturini and S Bariatti (eds), *Liber Fausto Pocar* (Giuffrè 2009), 163.

on their own behalf, agreements with third countries in individual and exceptional cases, concerning sectoral matters and containing provisions on the law applicable to [non]contractual obligations'. The regulation adopted following this announcement in the preambles to the Rome I and Rome II Regulations are discussed below.

3.5. OPINION 1/13

Whereas the external exclusive competence of the Union seemed with regard to the subject areas covered by the Rome I and Rome II Regulations firmly settled, the image was clear for the area of jurisdiction and recognition and enforcement. In the Lugano Opinion, the CJEU based the exclusive competence of the Community on the fact the Lugano Convention could affect the scope of common rules by taking away, at least in some cases, the mandatory jurisdiction of a court in a Member State under Brussels I. The implied exclusive competence also extended to the area of recognition and enforcement because of the 'indissociable' link between the rules on jurisdiction and those on recognition and enforcement. The question remained whether exclusive external competence existed if the international convention were to only relate to the area of recognition and enforcement and only produce legal effects in the relations between a specific Member State and a third country.

This situation occurred with regard to the Hague Convention on Child Abduction. The Hague Convention is a procedural instrument which seeks to restore the *status quo* that existed prior to the wrongful removal of a child.[40] The Hague Convention on Child Abduction has been ratified by all Member States. At the same time, the issue of the removal or retention of a child is also covered by the Brussels IIa Regulation. The latter Regulation takes precedence over the Hague Convention, but does not replace it.[41] The Brussels IIa Regulation complements the Hague Convention by providing the courts of the Member State of origin with an additional (and very effective) possibility to secure the return of the child, even though the return of the child has been refused by the Member State of refuge in accordance with the Hague Convention.[42]

---

40 See in general: K Trimmings, *Child abduction within the European Union* (Hart Publishing 2013); R Schulz, *The Hague Child Abduction Convention: a Critical Analysis* (Hart Publishing 2013).

41 P McEleavy, 'The New Child Abduction Regime in the European Union: Symbiotic Relationship or Forced Partnership?' (2005) 1 *Journal of Private International Law* 5.

42 L Walker and P Beaumont, 'Shifting the Balance Achieved by the Abduction Convention: the Contrasting Approaches of the European Court of Human Rights and the European Court of Justice' (2011) 7 *Journal of Private International Law* 231; J Kuipers, 'The (Non) Application of the Charter of Fundamental Rights to a Certificate for the Return of a Child' (2012) 17 *European Human Rights Law Review* 397; K Lenaerts, 'The Best Interests of the Child Always Come First: the Brussels II bis Regulation and the European Court of Justice' (2013) *Jurisprudence* 1302, <http://

The Hague Convention is a multilateral convention to which any state may accede. The Hague Convention is built on the premise of a high degree of mutual trust in the executing institutions of each Contracting Party. In order for the Hague Convention to take effect, the ratification by the new Contracting Party has to be accepted by the existing Contracting Party. Until the ratification is accepted, the Hague Convention does not enter into force in the bilateral relations between those countries. From the perspective of the Union, the entry into force of the Hague Convention between a Member State and a third country cannot affect the common rules on jurisdiction. After all, the Hague Convention is a procedural instrument which does not govern the issue of jurisdiction. Moreover, the acceptance by a Member State of the ratification of a third country only produces the effect of extending the mechanism of the Hague Conference to the bilateral relations between those countries. Between 2007 and 2011, hence after the Lugano Opinion, Armenia, Albania, the Seychelles, Morocco, Gabon, Singapore, Andorra and the Russian Federation deposited the instrument of accession to the Hague Convention. The Commission adopted a proposal with respect to each Contracting Party which provided that the Member States were to deposit in the interest of the Union a standard declaration of acceptance.[43] The proposals were never adopted by the Council, however. There was a widely held belief amongst the Member States that they, instead of the Union, were competent to accept the ratification by third countries of the Hague Convention. Save for Austria, Luxembourg, Portugal and the United Kingdom,[44] all Member States accepted the accession of at least one of the eight aforementioned Contracting Parties.[45]

www.mruni.eu>.

43 Gabon (COM(2011) 904 final), Andorra (COM(2011) 908 final), the Seychelles (COM(2011) 909 final), the Russian Federation (COM(2011) 911 final), Albania (COM(2011) 912 final), Singapore (COM(2011) 915 final), Morocco (COM(2011) 916 final) and Armenia (COM(2011) 917 final).

44 It should be noted that also Denmark did not accept any of the accessions of the new Contracting Parties, but due to the special position of this Member State with regard to the Area of Freedom, Security and Justice, the external competence of the Union would in any case not affect the position of Denmark.

45 The accession of the new Contracting Parties was approved by the following Member States: Armenia: Slovakia, Latvia, Ireland, Czech Republic, Poland, Sweden, France, Lithuania, Finland, Spain, Slovenia, Germany, Malta, Cyprus, Hungary, Belgium, Estonia and Italy; Albania: Latvia, Germany, the Netherlands, Poland, Greece, Slovakia, Czech Republic, Ireland, Sweden, Lithuania, Finland, Spain, Slovenia, France, Cyprus, Malta, Hungary, Belgium, Estonia and Italy; Morocco: the Netherlands, France, Czech Republic, Latvia, Finland, Greece, Slovakia, Germany, Cyprus, Sweden, Hungary, Spain, Belgium, Estonia, Malta, Romania, Lithuania, Italy and Ireland; Gabon: the Netherlands, Greece, Czech Republic, Latvia, Sweden, Estonia, Slovakia, France, Malta, Lithuania and Ireland; Singapore: Germany, Greece, Czech Republic, Latvia, Sweden, Belgium, Estonia, Slovakia, France, Spain, Malta, Italy and Ireland; Andorra: Germany, Finland, Latvia, Belgium, Estonia, Slovakia, France, Czech Republic, Italy, Spain, Lithuania and Ireland; the Russian Federation: Estonia, France, Greece, Croatia, Czech Republic, Finland, Slovenia, Spain, Slovakia, Romania, Lithuania and Ireland.

The Commission therefore requested the CJEU to clarify whether the external competence of the Union encompassed the acceptance of the accession of a third state to the Hague Convention on Child Abduction. In Opinion 1/13, the CJEU answered this question in the affirmative. The legal merits of this decision are addressed elsewhere in this book.[46] In short, the CJEU held that despite the precedence of the Brussels IIa Regulation over the Hague Convention, the scope and effectiveness of the common rules laid down by the regulation were likely to be affected when the Member States individually made separate declarations accepting third country accessions to the Hague Convention. According to the CJEU the risk of undermining the Brussels IIa Regulation would arise in particular with regard to the rules concerning cooperation between the authorities of the Member States, whenever a situation involving international child abduction involved a third country and two Member States, one of which had accepted the accession of that third state to the Convention whilst the other had not.

The risk identified by the CJEU seems exaggerated, if real at all. The CJEU appears not to have been guided by a strict legal analysis of whether the individual acceptance by a Member State of the accession of a third state would produce legal effects which could undermine the rules of the Brussels IIa Regulation, but by a broader approach, including the need to protect and strengthen the Union's external policy regarding international child abduction. In his views, AG Jääskinen appealed to this broader policy perspective. According to AG Jääskinen, it was essential that the reliability of any acceding third state, in so far as concerns judicial and administrative cooperation, should be assessed jointly under the coordination of the Council pursuant to a proposal from the Commission. AG Jääskinen moreover explicitly invoked the coherency of the Union's external policy to justify the exclusive external competence:[47]

> Finally, it must be observed that, even though the 1980 Hague Convention may be regarded as operating on the basis of a series of bilateral relations between contracting States, any amendment of the wording of the convention would require the unanimous consent of all those States. Therefore, any new accession to the convention would increase the number of parties with which the Member States of the European Union would need to negotiate and reach a consensus in the event that the EU should wish to alter the content of the convention. Since the acceptance of the accession of a third State creates a new political situation and alters the parameters of the interplay between the Brussels IIa Regulation and the convention, it is, to my mind, essential that there be joint scrutiny within the European Union of the matter of accepting third States which accede to

46 See the contribution of P Beaumont to this volume. See also I Govaere, 'Setting the International Scene: EU External Competence and Procedures Post-Lisbon Revisited in the Light of ECJ Opinion 1/13' (2015) 52 *Common Market Law Review* 1277.

47 View of AG Jääskinen on Opinion 1/13, EU:C:2014:2292, para. 102.

the convention, in particular with reference to the ability of those States to fulfil the obligations laid down by the convention and their political will to cooperate genuinely with the European Union.

Although the argument of AG Jääskinen may in this particular context not be very convincing,[48] the message is clear. In policy areas covered by the common rules, Member States are to act with one voice. Although this may certainly lead to a loss of sovereignty and flexibility in the area of private international law, the Member States are to an extent shedding crocodile tears. Member States have repeatedly called upon the Union to develop an external policy with regard to private international law. The European Council, whose members are the heads of state or government of the Member States, already underlined in the Tampere Conclusions (1999) that all competences and instruments at the disposal of the Union, and in particular, in external relations must be used in an integrated and consistent way to build the area of freedom, security and justice.[49] In The Hague Programme (2004), the European Council furthermore urged the Commission and the Council to ensure coherence between the EU and the international legal order and continue to engage in closer relations and cooperation with the Hague Conference to coordinate initiatives and to maximise synergies between the activities and instruments of the Hague Conference and the EU instruments.[50] The Hague Programme considered the development of a coherent external dimension of the Union policy of freedom, security and justice a growing priority. The existence of internal policies was explicitly identified as the major parameter justifying external action.[51] Finally, the Stockholm Pro-

48 An important distinction should be drawn between membership of the Conference and being bound by a Hague Convention. The Hague Conference offers a framework for the negotiation of Hague Conventions, but membership of the Hague Conference does not mean that a state is automatically party to a Hague Convention. The question which states and/or entities may accede to the Hague Convention is determined by the respective Convention itself. Should a member of the Conference decide to accede to a Convention, a separate act of ratification is required. Conversely, the ratification of a Hague Convention by a state who is not a member of the Hague Conference, does not give that state the right to participate in the negotiations of a new instrument in the same subject area. The negations in the Hague Conference are rather informal, however. A state or entity which is not party to the Hague Conference may participate in the deliberations as observer. The statement that any new accession to the Hague Convention on Child Abduction would increase the number of parties with which the Member States of the European Union would need to negotiate and reach a consensus in the event that the Union should wish to alter the content of the convention is therefore not correct. See on the workings of the Hague Conference: A Schulz, n 4; R Wagner, 'Principle of Consensus and European Union Legislative Competence in Relation to Judicial Cooperation in Civil Matters: Challenges Facing The Hague Conference on Private International Law', in *A Commitment to Private International Law: Essays in Honour of Hans van Loon* (Intersentia 2013), 643.

49 Tampere Presidency Conclusions, point 59.

50 *The Hague Programme: strengthening freedom, security and justice in the European Union* [2005] OJ C 53/1, para. 3.4.5.

51 Ibid, para. 4.

gramme (2010) identified the promotion of civil cooperation with third states as policy objective of the Union. According to the Stockholm programme:

> The Union should use its membership of The Hague Conference on Private International Law to actively promote the widest possible accession to the most relevant Conventions and to offer as much assistance as possible to other States with a view to the proper implementation of these instruments. The European Council invites the Council, the Commission and the Member States to encourage all partner countries to accede to those Conventions which are of particular interest to the Union ...
>
> The European Council invites the Council and the Commission to:
> — define a strategy in the area of civil matters for the coming years which is coherent with overall Union external action.[52]

The Union has implemented the Stockholm Programme by, for example, in its bilateral relations with Russia striving for Russia's ratification of the Hague Convention on Child Abduction. In the proposal for a decision on the declaration of acceptance in the interests of the Union by the Member States of the accession of Russia to the Convention it is explained that:

> As the prevention of child abduction is an essential part of the EU policy to promote the rights of the child, the European Union is active at international level to improve the application of the 1980 Convention and encourages third States to accede it. In particular, the Commission has always stressed the need for the Russian Federation to accede to the 1980 Hague Convention in order to rely on a common legal framework EU-Russia to deal with cases of child abduction.[53]
>
> The issue was discussed for several years at different levels, namely in the context of the EU-Russia Permanent Partnership Council on Justice, Freedom and Security, and finally Russia decided to deposit the accession instrument to the 1980 Convention on 28 July 2011. The Convention entered into force in Russia on 1 October 2011.

If the Union is charged with the promotion of the widest possible accession of the most relevant Hague Conventions, it should also be given the instruments to do so. The pursuit of this objective would certainly be undermined if the Union could indeed push for Russia's accession to the Hague Convention, but not

---

52 *The Stockholm Programme – An open and secure Europe serving and protecting citizens* [2010] OJ C 115/1, para. 3.5.1.

53 Proposal for a Council Decision on the declaration of acceptance by the Member States, in the interest of the European Union, of the accession of Russian Federation to the 1980 Hague Convention on the Civil Aspects of International Child Abduction, COM (2011)911 final.

ensure that Russia's accession will ultimately be accepted by the Member States. From this point of view, it certainly makes sense that the external competence of the Union encompasses the acceptance of the accession of a third state to the Hague Convention on Child Abduction.

The loss of flexibility for a Member State to decide, based on its own reasons and interests, whether to accept the accession of a new Contracting Party is inherent in the concept of exclusive external competence. It remains to be seen whether this loss of flexibility will come at the expense of wider international cooperation in this area. On the one hand, the policy pursued by the Union seems at least to have contributed to Russia's decision to accede to the Hague Convention. This can only be seen as a positive development. Moreover, the Commission adopted a proposal with regard to each of the new Contracting Parties which provided that the Member States were required to deposit a standard declaration of acceptance in the interest of the Union. If the proposals had been adopted, all Member States would have been obliged to accept the accession of the new Contracting Parties. This would only have contributed to a wider application of the Hague Convention. On the other hand, the decision-making process in the Council in the area of private international law relating to family matters is governed by unanimity.[54] This means that a single Member State could block the adoption of a decision which would require all Member States to accept the accession. As a consequence of the external exclusive competence of the Union, and in the absence of decision by the Council, none of the Member States would then be able to accept the accession. It is very difficult to predict whether this new dynamic of 'all or nothing' will enhance or strain the international cooperation in cross-border civil matters.

Whether or not a deadlock arises in the Council very much seems to depend on the reasons why a Member State does not want to accept the accession of a new Contracting Party to the Hague Convention. A Member State could have doubt about the quality of the institutions in the acceding state. The ratification by Russia of the Hague Convention may again serve as an example. Although Russia did ratify the Hague Convention, it failed to designate a Central Authority, which is essential for the effective application of the Convention. In the proposal for a Council Decision, the Commission therefore observed that:

> [i]t is crucial for the practical application of the 1980 Convention that a Contracting Party designates a Central Authority required by its Article 6 to discharge the duties which are imposed by the Convention upon such authorities. All Member States have designated Central Authorities under the 1980 Convention. To date, the Russian Federation has not yet designated the Central Authority that is needed to assist the European citizens in cases of wrongful removal of

54 Article 81(3) TFEU.

> children to Russia. Therefore, it is desirable that the declaration of acceptance of the accession of the Russian Federation to the 1980 Convention takes effect upon the designation of the Central Authority by the Russian Federation.

If the reason for a Member State's hesitation to accept the accession of a third country to the Hague Convention relates to the ability of the new Contracting Party to duly execute the responsibilities stemming from the Hague Convention, the Union may, acting as a block, seek the adoption of measures by that third country to remedy the situation via formal and informal routes. This does not appear to unduly strain civil cooperation in the area of private international law. The requirement to act as a block could more problematic in cases where a Member State objects for purely political reasons to the acceptance of the accession of a new Contracting Party to the Hague Convention. For example, Cyprus has never accepted the accession of Turkey. If Turkey had acceded to the Hague Convention after Opinion 1/13, Cyprus would have had in the Council the choice between (*i*) being legally obliged to accept Turkey's accession to the Hague Convention, or (*ii*) blocking the adoption of the Commission's proposal altogether. In cases where the political stakes are so high, one cannot exclude that a Member State would choose the second option. Unfortunately, that would mean that none of the Member States could accept the accession.

Outside the context of a political deadlock, one can imagine that a Member State has a particular interest in a bilateral agreement with a third country. For instance, Suriname gained its independence from the Netherlands in 1975. Due to this historical reason, there are significant economic, cultural and political ties between these two countries. The Netherlands therefore has a significant interest in the facilitation of the recognition of decisions on matrimonial matters and parental responsibility rendered in Suriname, while other Member States will rarely be confronted with decisions originating in this small country in Latin America. Given the absence of the relevance for the other Member States, the Netherlands may fail to convince the Union to start the negotiations of a bilateral agreement with Suriname. In that case, the agreement would never be concluded at all.

4. THE REGULATIONS

A possible solution for this constitutional straightjacket could be found in the instrument announced in the preambles of Rome I and Rome II concerning 'the procedures and conditions according to which Member States would be entitled to negotiate and conclude, on their own behalf, agreements with third countries in individual and exceptional cases'. Two regulations were finally adopted. Regulation No 662/2009 establishes a procedure for the negotiation and conclusion of agreements between Member States and third states on particular matters concerning the areas covered by the Rome I and Rome II Regulations[55] and Regulation 664/2009 establishes a procedure for the negotiation and conclusion of agreements between Member States and third states concerning the areas covered by the Brussels IIa Regulation and Regulation (EC) No 4/2009 on jurisdiction, applicable law, recognition and enforcement of decisions and cooperation in matters relating to maintenance obligations (the Maintenance Regulation).[56]

Regulations Nos 662/2009 and 664/2009 recognise that judicial cooperation in civil matters is traditionally governed by agreements between Member States and third countries. These agreements reflect the special ties between a Member State and a certain third country. Whereas Regulations Nos 662/2009 and 664/2009 confirm the Union's exclusive external competence in the areas covered by those regulations, they nevertheless establish a procedure whereby Member States may be allowed to negotiate and conclude international agreements with third countries. Under the special procedure, a Member State must notify the Commission of its intention to open negotiations with a third country. The Commission will then ascertain whether there is an agreement envisioned between the Community and the third country concerned within the next 24 months. If not, the Commission will assess whether the following conditions are met: (*i*) the Member State concerned has demonstrated a specific interest in concluding the agreement due to economic, geographic, cultural, historical, social or political ties between that Member State and the third country concerned; (*ii*) the envisaged agreement does not appear to render Community law ineffective nor undermine the proper functioning of the system established by that law; and (*iii*) the envisaged agreement would not undermine the object and purpose of the Community's external relations policy.[57] The envisaged agreement must also contain a clause leading to denunciation or replacement of that agreement in the case of a subsequent agreement between the Community and the third country.[58] If the proposed agreement satisfies these criteria, the Commission must produce a reasoned decision within a period of 90 days after the notification authorising or refusing the Member State opening formal negotiations. The Member State must present the result of the negotiations to the Commission. The Commission will authorise the signing if the result of the negotiations still meets the aforementioned criteria.[59]

Regulations Nos 662/2009 and 664/2009 should be distinguished from situations in which the Community delegates a competence back to the Member

55 [2009] OJ L 200/25.

56 [2009] OJ L 7/1.

57 Article 4(2) Regulation 662/2009 and Article 4(2) 664/2009.

58 Article 5(2) Regulation 662/2009 and Article 5(2) 664/2009.

59 Article 8(2) Regulation 662/2009 and Article 8(2) 664/2009.

States. In those circumstances, Member States act on behalf of the Community.[60] Re-delegation of competences can be feasible when the Community is confronted with a large number of pre-existing international agreements and it cannot deal with those all at once. The Community therefore allows Member States to (re)negotiate these agreements and bring them in line with Community law.[61] Whereas in re-delegation cases the aim is gradual replacement of the bilateral agreement between Member States and third countries by Community agreements, with regard to Regulations Nos 662/2009 and 664/2009, Member States act on their own behalf and it is possible that the international agreement will never be replaced by a Community agreement. The Regulations appear to be a novelty in EU external relations. Whether they can be used to preserve the flexibility required by the Member State in the area of private international law will depend on how the Commission will apply them in practice. Since the entry into force of the Regulations, the Commission has authorised the opening of formal negotiations on two occasions. The Regulations, and the two Commission decisions, are discussed below.

4.1. APPLICABLE LAW (REGULATION No 662/2009)

As discussed above, Regulation No 662/2009 establishes a procedure with regard to the areas covered by Rome I and Rome II for initiating and concluding bilateral agreements or a regional agreement between a limited number of Member States and of third countries neighbouring Member States which is intended to address local situations.[62] The potential application of Regulation No 662/2009 seems very restricted. Both Rome I and Rome II underlie the principle of universal application. The regulations can thus lead to the application of the laws of a third country. The rationale of universal application is to prevent a fragmentation of legal sources. Departure from the main rule is possible with regard to specific type of conflicts, but not with regard to specific countries. Any bilateral agreement would risk undermining that principle since it would create a special regime between a specific Member State and a third country. A risk of fragmentation therefore arises and this will most likely make the Commission reluctant to authorise the opening formal negotiations.

---

60 M Cremona, 'Member States as Trustees of the Community Interest: Participating in International Agreements on behalf of the European Community', *EUI Working Paper Law* 2009/17, <http://hdl.handle.net/1814/12881>.

61 M Cremona, 'Defending the Community Interest: the Duties of Cooperation and Compliance', in M Cremona and B de Witte (eds), *EU Foreign Relations Law: Constitutional Fundamentals* (Hart Publishing 2008), 125, 140.

62 Article 2 Regulation No 662/2009.

The only practical application of Regulation No 662/2009 seems to be reserved for micro-treaties. Regional circumstances might oblige Member States to cooperate with third countries on a micro-level. For example, France requested under Regulation No 662/2009 the authorisation to enter into an international agreement with Switzerland regarding the European Organization for Nuclear Research (CERN)[63] and into a tripartite agreement with Switzerland and CERN.[64] CERN was initially established in Switzerland, but its facilities were extended to the French side of the border in the 1960's. The Convention between France and Switzerland relating to the extension of the Organization's site into French territory (1965) contains a clause regarding the applicable law: activities performed in France are governed by French law, whereas activities performed in Switzerland are governed by Swiss law. The arrangement proved to be unworkable in practice because - under the same agreement – services were sometimes interchangeably provided in France and in Switzerland. Under a strict application of the Convention, the provision of these services would be governed by a different law. In order to resolve the associated difficulties, the tripartite agreement requires CERN to identify in advance in which country the works will most likely predominantly take place. The service contract between CERN and the service provider will be governed by the law of that country. The agreement also envisages an additional conflict of laws rule relating to labour law: any enterprise which concludes a contract for services with CERN must apply to its employees the legal provisions applicable to posted workers in the host country on whose territory the major part of the services are to be performed.

In its decision authorising France to conclude both agreements, the Commission emphasised the specific nature of the situation. The agreements sought to regulate the law applicable to a contract concluded between a service provider and CERN and did not envisage the participation of other Member States. Moreover, the agreements applied to a well-defined area of labour law. The agreements could therefore undermine neither the proper functioning of Rome I nor the object and purpose of the Community's external relations policy as decided by the Community.[65]

If this first decision is indicative of the Commission's decisional practice under Regulation No 662/2009, the Commission seems to apply a very pragmatic

---

[63] Protocole d'amendement de la convention entre le gouvernement de la République française et le Conseil Fédéral suisse relative à l'extension en territoire français du domaine de l'Organisation européenne pour la recherche nucléaire, conclue le 13 septembre 1965, *Journal officiel* 2013-583.

[64] Accord entre le gouvernement de la République française, le conseil fédéral suisse, et l'organisation européenne pour la recherche nucléaire sur le droit applicable aux entreprises intervenant sur le domaine de l'organisation afin d'y réaliser des prestations de services revêtant un caractère transnational, *Journal officiel* 2014-141.

[65] Commission Decision of 19 March 2010 on an authorisation addressed by the European Commission to France in application of the transitional provisions of Article 12(2) of Regulation EC No 662/2009, COM (2010)1714.

test to the requirement that the envisaged agreement may not render Community law ineffective or undermine the proper functioning of the system established by that law. Although the scope of the CERN agreements may be very confined, Rome I and the CERN agreements do have a different connecting factor. Under Article 4(1)(b), in the absence of a choice of law, a contract for the provision of services shall be governed by the law of the country where the service provider has his habitual residence (principle of closest connection). The agreements, on the other hand, operate on the basis of territoriality: the law applicable to service contract is the law of the place where the service will be predominantly performed. This may give rise to some practical difficulties. The agreements only bind CERN, France and Switzerland and not other Member States. A court in a Member State other than France will therefore not apply the CERN agreements, but the Rome I Regulation, to determine the law applicable to a contract between CERN and a service provider. CERN is located not far from the Italian border. Imagine an Italian undertaking which provides services to CERN predominantly in France but incidentally also in Switzerland. If the law applicable to the service contract were to be established by an Italian court in accordance with Rome I, the service contract would be governed by Italian law. If the applicable law were to be established by a French court on the basis of the CERN agreements, the service contract would be governed by French law. The determination of the law applicable to a contract would then depend on the place where the proceedings are brought, which is exactly the situation which Rome I seeks to avoid. This problem cannot be fully remedied in the service contract by a choice of law clause in favour of the law of the place where the contract will be predominantly performed. For instance, the agreements also determine the law applicable to the employment contract between the service provider and the employee. In their restricted scope of application, the agreements do therefore appear to undermine the objectives of Rome I. The Commission did not engage in an in-depth analysis of the substantive rules of the agreements, however. After the Commission established that (i) the CERN agreements purport to serve a specific interest between France and Switzerland; (ii) have a very limited and specific scope of application; and (iii) did not thwart a foreign policy pursued by the Union, the authorisation was granted.

The Commission, moreover, adopted a very pragmatic interpretation of the other conditions laid down by Regulation No 662/2009. For instance, Member States can under the Regulation only apply for the authorisation to conclude a bilateral agreement with a 'third country' or regional agreement between a limited number of Member States and of 'third countries neighbouring Member States'. Although CERN is not a country, France nevertheless obtained the authorisation. It was according to the Commission also not necessary to include a clause leading to the denunciation or replacement of the CERN agreements in the case of a subsequent agreement between the Community and Switzerland. In light of the specificity of the situation, the requirement laid down in Article 5(2) of Regulation No 662/2009 did therefore not have to be observed by France.[66]

4.2. JURISDICTION AND RECOGNITION AND ENFORCEMENT OF JUDGMENTS (REGULATION No 664/2009)

The practical application of Regulation No 664/2009 may be wider. The Brussels IIa Regulation and the Maintenance Regulation distribute in their respective spheres of application the jurisdiction amongst the courts of the Member States and provide for the facilitated recognition and enforcement of decisions stemming from a court in another Member State. Unlike the Rome I and Rome II Regulations, the Brussels IIa Regulation and the Maintenance Regulation do not have a universal scope of application and leave the enforcement and recognition of decisions stemming from a court in a third country completely to the Member States. International coordination is therefore necessary. Political, cultural and historical ties in these areas indeed largely determine with which countries bilateral agreements exist.

The systematic conclusion of bilateral agreements between Member States and third countries does not appear to have the possibility to undermine the common rules. A distinction must be drawn between jurisdiction on the one hand and recognition and enforcement on the other. As regards jurisdiction it must be noted that also bilateral conventions may take away jurisdiction of a court established in one of the Member States, where that court would under the Brussels IIa Regulation or the Maintenance Regulation have jurisdiction. In that sense, the bilateral agreement could render Community law ineffective, or undermine the system established by the Brussels IIa Regulation or the Maintenance Regulation. Since the recognition and enforcement of decisions stemming from third countries is left to the national laws of the Member States, there appears to be only a remote risk that a bilateral agreement would undermine or render the common rules ineffective.

The Commission appears to have taken a pragmatic approach towards Regulation No 664/2009 as well. In 2010, France requested authorisation to start negotiations with the Russian Federation in order to conclude an agreement on the wrongful removal of children and the facilitation of cross-border rights of access for the parent not having custody of the child. The first part of the proposed agreement, as envisaged by France, should cover mainly provisions concerning jurisdiction, recognition and enforcement in matrimonial matters and matters of parental responsibility and contribute to solving issues relating to the

66 Ibid, Recital 16.

wrongful removal of children between France and Russia. The second part of the proposed agreement sought the establishment of mutual judicial assistance between France and Russia in matters of rights of custody and rights of access. The mutual judicial assistance would take place through the designated central authorities of each state.

The first part of the agreement was inspired by the same principles that also underpin the Brussel IIa Regulation. Like the Brussels IIa Regulation, the proposed agreement largely followed the rules of the Hague Convention on Child Abduction and the Hague Convention of 19 October 1996 on jurisdiction, applicable law, recognition, enforcement and cooperation in respect of parental responsibility and measures for the protection of children. These Conventions were at the time not ratified by Russia. In its decision, the Commission recalled that the policy of the European Union, as laid down in the Stockholm Programme, is to encourage third countries to accede to these two Hague Conventions. The primary issue therefore did not appear to be whether the proposed private international law rules would undermine the common rules, but whether the negotiation of a bilateral agreement with Russia would thwart the policy of the Union to encourage third countries to accede to Hague Conventions on family law. Although the Commission hinted that this could be the case, it did recognise that the accession to the Hague Conventions can for cultural, legal or political reasons take time. Whereas the exercise of the exclusive external competence by the Union should be the rule, priority should still be given to the protection of the best interests of the child. The Commission emphasised that the protection of the rights of the child should not be made subordinate to strategic considerations to promote the realisation of the Union's external policy objectives. Moreover, the Commission observed that the proposed agreement followed the fundamental principles of the two Hague Conventions. The implementation of the proposed agreement, if adopted, would compel Russia to establish a central authority with functions similar to those of the central authorities provided for by the Hague Conventions. The proposed agreement could therefore be an important step towards Russia's accession to these instruments. From that point of view, the proposed agreement would actually promote the implementation of the Union's external policy. Finally, France had explicitly acknowledged that the proposed bilateral agreement would cease to apply as soon as the European Union and the Russian Federation concluded an agreement in the same area. The Commission therefore authorised the opening of negotiations. In order to avoid undermining the Union's strategy on judicial cooperation in civil matters at the international level, by reducing the incentives for Russia to accede to the Hague Conventions on family law, the proposed agreement should be concluded for a limited period of five years.[67]

---

[67] Commission Decision of 7 December 2010 on an authorisation addressed by the European

The agreement between France and the Russian Federation was ultimately not adopted in its proposed form. Instead, Russia acceded to the Hague Convention on Child Abduction on 28 July 2011 and France and Russia signed a much more restricted bilateral agreement; the Agreement regarding the establishment of a commission on the protection of the rights of the child within the framework of family disputes (2011).[68] The commission established under this agreement may advise on issues such the exercise of parental rights by the parent who does not live with the child or return of a child taken by one of his parents from Russia to France, or the other way around. The commission cannot make any binding decisions. Since the final agreement does not contain any rules of private international law, France did not apply to the European Commission for authorisation to conclude the bilateral agreement in accordance with Article 8 of Regulation No 664/2009.

4.3. MAKING UP THE BALANCE

The CJEU has adopted in the Lugano Opinion and Opinion 1/13 a wide understanding of the Union's external competences in the area of private international law. As soon as a policy area is covered by the common rules, an implied exclusive external competence will arise, even if the risk that external action by the Member States will undermine the common rules seems to be remote at best. By exercising its implied external competences, the Union has become over time an important international actor in the area of judicial cooperation in civil matters having cross-border implications. The importance of the Union has amongst others been recognised by the Member States. The European Council, for example in the Stockholm Programme, called upon the Union to define a strategy in the area of civil matters for the coming years which is coherent with overall Union external action. The European Council, moreover, urged the Commission to strive for the widest possible ratification by third countries of the most relevant Hague Conventions.

There is an apparent contradiction in the call made by the European Council to further develop the Union's international efforts in the area of judicial cooperation and the continued practice of some Member States to continue to enter into bilateral agreements with third countries. Member States appear to want to have the best of both worlds. In the area of private international law, there are

Commission to France in application of Articles 4 and 5 of Regulation (EC) No 664/2009, COM (2010) 8577.

68 Décret no. 2013-281 du 2 avril portant publication de l'accord entre le Gouvernement de la République française et le Gouvernement de la Fédération de Russie relatif à la création d'une commission pour la protection des droits de l'enfant dans le cadre des conflits familiaux (2011), *Journal officiel* No 80/2013, 5665.

certain advantages to negotiating in a block. For example, Member States have long and unsuccessfully sought the accession of Russia to the Hague Convention on Child Abduction. By joining forces, the political pressure to ratify the Hague Convention on Child Abduction becomes ever more forceful. Moreover, in particular smaller Member States may lack the political clout and resources to conclude a sufficient network of bilateral agreements with third countries.

The exclusive external competence of the Union comes inherently at the expense of the ability of Member States to shape the bilateral relations with third countries as they see fit. In private international law, a particular dimension arises because historical, cultural and political ties have often been decisive factors for the conclusion of bilateral agreements with third countries. The extent and depth of these bilateral relations differs from Member State to Member State. The regulation of cross-border civil matters, moreover, deeply impacts on the lives of the individuals affected. If action by the Union is not feasible, or a political deadlock in the Council arises, Member States should be allowed to remedy the situation themselves. The primary instruments to achieve this flexibility are Regulations No 662/2009 and No 664/2009. In the words of the Commission, Regulation No 664/2009 enables 'Member States to fill, even temporarily, a significant legislative void'.[69]

The first thing that stands out is that, five years after their entry into force, only two requests for the authorisation to open formal negotiations with a third country have been made. Both requests were, moreover, made by the same Member State (France). There may be several reasons which can explain the modest number of applications under Regulations Nos 662/2009 and 664/2009. First of all, as the practice of Member States towards the acceptance of the accession of third countries to the Hague Convention demonstrated, the exclusive external competence of the Union was still not recognised by the Member States in all areas covered by Regulation No 664/2009. Member States did not apply for authorisation under Regulation No 664/2009, because they considered the conclusion of bilateral agreements with third countries to fall within their own sphere of competences.[70] Another explanation could be that most Member States already have a network of bilateral agreements in place with those third countries with which they consider they have particular close historical, cultural and political ties. The necessity to enter into new bilateral agreements with third countries may therefore be limited. Finally, Member States may perceive

---

69 Commission Decision of 7 December 2010, n 67, Recital 13.

70 The wording of Regulation 664/2009 was not unequivocal and did leave some room to argue that the exclusive competence of the Union did not encompass the conclusion of bilateral agreements with third countries regarding the issue of recognition and enforcement. In more detail, see: J Kuipers, 'The Exclusive Competence of the Union under Article 81 TFEU. Lugano re-opened?', in M Cremona, J Monar and S Poli (eds), *The External Dimension of the Area of Freedom Security and Justice* (Peter Lang 2011), 287.

the conditions imposed by Regulations Nos 662/2009 and 664/2009 overly restrictive. For several reasons, the latter explanation does not seem very plausible, however.

The Commission has been remarkably pragmatic in testing whether the requirements of Regulations Nos 662/2009 and 664/2009 were met. For example, France requested and obtained authorisation to conclude the CERN agreements with Switzerland and CERN, even though they did not contain a replacement or denunciation clause as required by Article 8(2)(c) in conjunction with Article 5(2) of Regulation No 662/2009. Moreover, the Commission granted France the authorisation to open formal negotiations with Russia in order to conclude an agreement on the wrongful removal of children and the facilitation of cross border rights of access for the parent not having custody of the child, even though the Union itself actively encouraged the accession of Russia to two Hague Conventions in the same policy area. The argument could therefore at least be made that the envisaged agreement would undermine the object and purpose of the Union's external relations policy as decided by the Union. As is explained above, the Commission considered the risk of undermining the Union's external policy sufficiently addressed by limiting the envisaged bilateral agreement in time, but also noted that:

> the Commission is of the opinion that the best interests of the child come before strategic considerations.[71]

The Commission thus seems sensitive to the argument that the regulation of cross-border civil matters deeply affects the private life of the individuals concerned. In the recital referred to above, the Commission implies that the substantive interests underlying the need for a bilateral agreement may override the full pursuit of the Union's own external policy objectives. If this really is the case, Regulations Nos 662/2009 and 664/2009 have indeed successfully guaranteed the flexibility required by the Member States to preserve their special ties with third countries and to provide for an adequate legal framework to meet the specific needs of the parties concerned.

4.4. A REGULATION FOR MATTERS FALLING WITHIN THE SCOPE OF THE BRUSSELS Ia REGULATION?

Whereas the Commission appears to be sensitive to the flexibility required by the Member States in the substantive areas covered by Regulations Nos 662/2009 and 664/2009, the Commission's approach to the Brussels Ia Regulation is dif-

[71] Commission Decision of 7 December 2010, n 67, Recital 13.

ferent. That may be surprising as the Brussels Ia Regulation leaves exactly the same 'legislative voids' as the Brussels IIa Regulation. As the practice of Italy and Spain demonstrated, there is precisely in this area still a necessity to conclude bilateral agreements with third countries. It is therefore remarkable that the Brussels Ia Regulation is neither covered by Regulation No 662/2009 nor by Regulation No 664/2009. The rumour is that the Member States very much insisted on the adoption of a similar regulation with regard to the areas covered by Brussels Ia, but that this was refused by the Commission.[72]

The reason for the exclusion of Brussels Ia from the scope of Regulation No 664/2009 is most likely that individual action by the Member States in the area of civil and commercial matters is from the perspective of the Union more prone to undermine the Union's external policy. On the international level, the Union has been very active in the substantive areas covered by Brussels Ia. The Union has extended by means of the Lugano Convention the geographical scope of the predecessor of Brussels Ia, Brussels I, to Iceland, Norway and Switzerland. The Union has, moreover, ratified the Hague Choice of Court Convention. The other signatories are Mexico, Singapore and the United States. At the time of writing, the Hague Choice of Court Convention was only ratified by Mexico, but in December 2014 the Council, on behalf of the European Union, adopted the decision on the approval of the Convention.[73] The Union is expected to deposit its instrument of approval in the summer of 2015. The Convention will enter into force on the first day of the month following a period of three months after the deposit of the instrument of approval by the Union.

The Union (Community) became a member of the Hague Conference in 2007 and actively participated in the preparation of the Hague Choice of Court Convention.[74] The negotiations within the framework of the Hague Conference coincided with the revision of the Brussels I Regulation. The Commission strived to ensure coherence between the Union rules on choice of court in civil and commercial matters and those of the Convention.[75] The Commission regards the Hague Choice of Court Convention as an instrument to further enhance party autonomy. Under the Union rules, parties may designate the competent jurisdiction or jurisdictions by means of a choice of court clause.[76] A court or

[72] J Bischoff, 'Notwendige Flexibilisierung oder Ausverkauf von Kompetenzen? : zur Rückübertragung von Außenkompetenzen der EG für privatrechtliche Abkommem durch die Verordnungen (EG) Nr. 662/2009 und Nr. 664/2009' (2010) 18 *Zeitschrift für europäisches Privatrecht* 321.

[73] Decision 2014/887 on the approval, on behalf of the European Union, of the Hague Convention of 30 June 2005 on Choice of Court Agreements [2014] OJ L 353/5.

[74] P Beaumont, 'Hague Choice of Court Agreements Convention 2005: Background, Negotiations, Analysis and Current Status' (2009) 15 *Journal of Private International Law* 125.

[75] Proposal for a Council Decision on the approval, on behalf of the European Union, of the Hague Convention of 30 June 2005 on Choice of Court Agreements, COM (2014)46 final, Recital 5.

[76] Article 25 Brussels Ia.

the courts of a Member State will have jurisdiction to settle any disputes between the parties if it has been duly designated by the parties. The Union rules only provide for a choice of court in favour of the court of a Member State; a choice of court in favour of a court outside the European Union (or a signatory to the Lugano Convention) will not be upheld. According to the Commission:

> [t]he recent amendments to the Brussels I Regulation (the Brussels I Regulation (recast)) have strengthened party autonomy by ensuring that choice of court agreements may not be circumvented by parties seizing other courts in violation of such agreements. At the same time, these amendments ensure that the approach to choice of court agreements for intra-EU situations is consistent with the one that would apply to extra-EU situations under the Convention, once approved by the Union. The Brussels I Regulation (recast) thus prepares the ground for the EU to proceed with the approval of the Convention.

Although in the process of transforming the Brussels I Regulation into Brussels Ia Regulation, several amendments were introduced to strive for coherency with the Hague Choice of Court Convention, the rule that the derogatory effect of choice of court clauses in favour a court in a third country is not recognised was not changed.[77] If party autonomy was truly at the heart of the Commission's concerns, it would have been quite natural to introduce a rule requiring a court in a Member State to decline jurisdiction in case of an exclusive choice of court agreement in favour of the courts of a third country. Party autonomy could then still not be fully guaranteed, since the Brussels Ia Regulation cannot determine the conditions under which a court in a third country will recognise an exclusive choice of court clause in favour of, for example, the courts of England. The reason behind the hostile treatment of 'foreign' choice of court agreements in the Brussels Ia Regulation is to entice third countries to ratify the Hague Choice of Court Convention. By ratifying the Convention, a third country will ensure that an exclusive choice of court in favour of the courts of that country will be recognised by the courts of the Member States. Since the Hague Choice of Court Convention works on a reciprocal basis, this would strengthen the effectiveness of choice of court agreements in favour of the courts of the Member States.

The Hague Choice of Court Convention also lays down rules for the recognition and enforcement of judgments.[78] Article 8 provides that a judgment given by a court of a Contracting State designated in an exclusive choice of court agreement shall be recognised and enforced in other Contracting States. Recognition or enforcement may be refused only on exhaustively specified grounds. The enforceability of judgments rendered by court in a Member State which

[77] T Hartley, *Choice-of-Court Agreements under the European and International Instruments* (Oxford University Press 2013), 182.

[78] Ibid, 195-201.

based its jurisdiction on a choice of court agreement will be enhanced if the Hague Choice of Court Convention is ratified by the Union's main trading partners. According to the Commission, 'the benefits to EU business that emerge from approval by the EU of the Convention will increase with the number of ratifications of the Convention in particular by the Union's main commercial partners'. In accordance with the Stockholm Programme, the Union will strive for the widest possible ratification by third countries of the Hague Choice of Court Convention. The conclusion of bilateral agreements between Member States and third countries on the recognition and enforcement of judgments may undermine this objective since it could reduce the necessity of these third countries to accede to the Hague Choice of Court Convention.

In the light of the objectives pursued by the Union, there appears to be less scope for manoeuvring for the Member States under Brussels Ia than under Brussels IIa. This does not fully explain the absence of an instrument akin to Regulation No 664/2009 with regard to the Brussels Ia Regulation. Significant legislative voids continue to exist, in particular with regard to the recognition and enforcement of judgments not given by a court in a third country designated in a choice of court clause. Since the Commission will only provide authorisation under Regulation No 664/2009 if the bilateral agreement does not undermine the object and purpose of the Community's external relations policy, the risk that a bilateral agreement on recognition and enforcement of judgments in civil and commercial matters may undermine the Union's external policy objectives could be assessed on a case-by-case basis. In order to preserve the flexibility that may be required in the area of private international law, it is desirable that an instrument akin to Regulation No 664/2009 is adopted with regard to the area covered by Brussels Ia.

5. CONCLUSION

Regulations Nos 662/2009 and 664/2009 guarantee the flexibility required by the Member States to enter, despite the Union's exclusive competence, into agreements with third countries in the areas covered by the private international law Regulations. Despite the reluctance of the Member States to apply for authorisation under the Regulations, the Commission has been very pragmatic in testing whether the formal conditions are met. In that sense, these instruments are a successful template for guaranteeing the continuance of international cooperation in civil matters having a cross-border implication. Regulations Nos 662/2009 and 664/2009 should be complemented with an instrument establishing a procedure for the negotiation and conclusion of agreements between Member States and third states in the areas covered by the Brussels Ia Regulation.

PART IV

EU LEGISLATION ON PRIVATE INTERNATIONAL LAW AND EXTRA-EUROPEAN SITUATIONS

THE INTERPLAY OF EU LEGISLATION AND INTERNATIONAL DEVELOPMENTS IN PRIVATE INTERNATIONAL LAW

Pietro Franzina
University of Ferrara

1. THE VIRTUAL GLOBAL REACH OF EU LEGISLATION ON PRIVATE INTERNATIONAL LAW

When judicial cooperation in civil matters was still in its early stage of development within the EU legal system, some expressed the view that EU legislation in this area could address only matters featuring a strictly European character, that is matters connected solely, or essentially, with two or more Member States.[1] The view rested on the assumption that EU private international law is basically concerned with the diversity of Member States' legal systems and with the challenges posed by that diversity to the proper functioning of the internal market. According to this opinion, the regional unification of private international law was meant, as such, to improve the coordination between the legal systems of the various Member States. Situations linked with a third country

1 The topic first rose to prominence as an object of debate among scholars and within the EU political institutions in the legislative process that later resulted in Regulation (EC) No 864/2007 on the law applicable to non-contractual obligations (Rome II) [2007] OJ L 199/40. Taking the Rome Convention of 19 June 1980 on the law applicable to contractual obligations as a model, the Commission had in fact proposed to provide the conflict-of-law rules of the Regulation with an *erga omnes* effect. The solution made its way into the final text: pursuant to Article 3, '[a]ny law specified by this Regulation shall be applied whether or not it is the law of a Member State'. The issue whether the Treaties allow the institutions to adopt 'universal' conflict-of-law rules is discussed, among others, in an opinion of the Council Legal Service of 2 March 2004 (doc. No 7015/04), available through the Public Register of Council Documents at <http://register.consilium.europa.eu>. See further J Carruthers and EB Crawford, 'Variations on a Theme of Rome II. Reflections on Proposed Choice of Law Rules for Non-Contractual Obligations: Part I' (2005) 9 *Edinburgh Law Review* 65, 69 f., and, more generally, A Dickinson, 'European Private International Law: Embracing New Horizons Or Mourning The Past?' (2005) 1 *Journal of Private International Law* 197, 209 ff, and J Heymann, *Le droit international privé à l'épreuve du fédéralisme européen* (Economica 2010), 86 ff.

were regarded as lying, in principle, outside the scope of EU law, and accordingly left to the domestic rules of private international law of the Member States, or to uniform rules to be agreed upon between individual Member States, on the one hand, and the third countries concerned, on the other.[2]

This approach no longer finds support in legal literature and within the institutions. Today, it is generally accepted that EU legislation in the field of private international law can address, in principle, both intra-European and extra-European situations. The Court of Justice acknowledged in Opinion 1/03 that EU measures relating to judicial cooperation are not intended only 'for intra-Community disputes', but are concerned, more generally, with situations featuring 'an international element'.[3] The actual legislative measures enacted on the basis of Article 81 TFEU (previously, Article 65 TEC) show that the EU political institutions are in no way reluctant to regulate relationships that feature a significant connection with third countries. As a matter of fact, extra-European situations are normally dealt with under the same measures that govern purely regional matters.

Several pieces of EU legislation in the area of private international law have, at least in some respects, a 'global' reach. For example, Member States' courts must refer to Regulation (EC) No 4/2009 on maintenance obligations[4] whenever they assess their jurisdiction over claims for family maintenance involving a foreign element. This occurs no matter whether the claimant or the defendant possess the nationality of, or habitually reside in, a Member State rather than a third country, and regardless of whether a particular objective link exists between the subject matter of the dispute and one or more Member States.

1.1. A COMPLEX PICTURE

Upon closer inspection, the picture is more complex than the latter example would seem to suggest.

On the one hand, the European legislator does not invariably follow a global approach when it deals with private international law.

---

2 On this debate, see generally S Francq, *L'applicabilité du droit communautaire dérivé au regard des méthodes du droit international privé* (Bruylant 2005), 50 ff. See also S Bariatti, *Cases and Materials on EU Private International Law* (Hart Publishing 2011), 29 f.

3 Opinion 1/03, EU:C:2006:81, para. 143. The point had already been made by the Court with reference to the Brussels Convention of 27 September 1968 on jurisdiction and the recognition of judgments in civil and commercial matters in Case C-281/02, *Owusu v Jackson*, EU:C:2005:120, para. 34: the uniform rules of jurisdiction contained in the latter convention, the Court stated, 'are not intended to apply only to situations in which there is a real and sufficient link with the working of the internal market, by definition involving a number of Member States'.

4 Regulation (EC) No 4/2009 on jurisdiction, applicable law, recognition and enforcement of decisions and cooperation in matters relating to maintenance obligations [2009] OJ L 7/1.

Some legislative texts have, in fact, a strictly regional scope and their rules cannot be relied upon in situations involving a third country. Generally speaking, this occurs in areas where the legislature regards reciprocity as an essential premise to a fruitful harmonisation of law. For example, Regulation (EC) No 1206/2001 on cooperation in the taking of evidence in civil and commercial matters is only concerned with the assistance that a Member State may be requested to provide to the authorities of another Member State.[5] Under the Regulation, the requested State is required to provide the same assistance that the requesting State itself would have to ensure if it was for the former State to look for evidence abroad. Nothing is provided in the Regulation as regards requests coming from third countries. In the Member States, these requests will be handled in conformity with the international agreements in force with the third country in question, if any, or under the relevant domestic rules on international judicial assistance.

On the other hand, when the EU legislator does adopt a 'global' approach, this approach may result in different normative schemes.

The scheme referred to above with respect to maintenance obligations is the most simple. It consists in laying down a single body of rules of universal application, under which European and non-European situations are treated alike. A different scheme involves the adoption of legislation including one or more special provisions that are intended to apply to particular sets of 'remote' cases. In this way, two distinct legal regimes operate side-by-side in the same area of law: one governs purely regional cases (or cases featuring a qualified connection with the territory of the Member States or the social and economic environment of the EU), while the other is concerned with extra-European situations (or situations displaying a lower degree of integration in the European area). The articulation of the two regimes may be rather complex, as in Regulation (EC) No 2201/2003 on matrimonial matters and matters of parental responsibility.[6] The uniform rules laid down in this Regulation to deal with jurisdiction in matters of divorce, legal separation and marriage annulment are applicable to any proceedings brought before the courts of a Member State. However, pursuant to Article 6, the uniform rules in question apply to the exclusion of all others only if proceedings are initiated against a defendant who habitually resides in, or is a national of, an EU Member State. According to Article 7, if none of these conditions are met and no court of a Member State has jurisdiction in accordance with the rules of the Regulation, jurisdiction is to be determined, in each Member State, 'by the laws of that State'. Because the grounds of jurisdiction

5 Regulation (EC) No 1206/2001 on cooperation between the courts of the Member States in the taking of evidence in civil or commercial matters [2001] OJ L 174/1.

6 Regulation (EC) No 2201/2003 concerning jurisdiction and the recognition and enforcement of judgments in matrimonial matters and the matters of parental responsibility [2003] OJ L 338/1.

contemplated by the laws of the various Member States apply in this scenario *by virtue* of the Regulation, the latter appears to have a global reach.[7] Within this reach, however, the functioning of the Regulation varies depending on the intensity of the ties between the situation concerned and the European environment. Strong connections trigger the exclusive application of uniform regional provisions, whereas weaker connections allow Member States to rely on the continuing operation of local rules, albeit under the umbrella of EU law.

The purpose of this paper is to analyse the relationship between the EU legislation on judicial cooperation in civil matters and the international efforts aimed at the harmonisation of private international law. Specifically, our focus will be on the coordination and mutual influence of the body of EU rules created through secondary legislation, on the one hand, and the international legal instruments elaborated outside the EU to deal with cross-border cases, on the other, *insofar as the latter instruments are not binding upon the EU as a matter of international law.*[8] In other terms, we intend to study the ways in which the EU, where it merely acts through internal legislation, not through external action, can nevertheless exert an influence on (or receive an influence from) such rules of private international law as have been developed (or are in the process of being developed) internationally. We will examine the techniques whereby the interaction between these two 'sides' of private international law expresses itself, and the political significance of their interplay, namely as regards the development of the external relations of the Union in this area.

The need to consider these issues arises precisely because, as noticed above, EU legislation features, to some extent, a global reach. An EU rule with a global reach may in fact be seen as a rule that purports to perform a task that an 'external' rule can in principle perform just as efficiently, if not more efficiently.

The latter point deserves to be discussed further before we move on with the analysis.

---

7 The Court of Justice observed in Opinion 1/03, n 3, para. 148, that the similar reference made in Article 4(1) of Regulation (EC) No 44/2001 on jurisdiction and the recognition and enforcement of judgments in civil and commercial matters [2001] OJ L 12/1, to the domestic rules of jurisdiction of the Member State of the forum 'must be interpreted as meaning that it forms part of the system implemented by that regulation, since it resolves the situation envisaged by reference to the legislation of the Member State before whose court the matter is brought'.

8 We will consider both international instruments to which the EU is not a party (at least at the time when legislation is enacted) and international instruments that, while being internationally binding on the EU, do not prevent the EU from regulating a particular issue within their scope. The two scenarios are equivalent for our purposes, since the EU is free to follow in both situations a unilateral course of action. We wish to determine whether, based on which considerations and in which manner, the EU nevertheless takes into account, in its legislation, the rules or principles underlying those international instruments.

1.2. 'GLOBAL' LEGISLATION AND EXTERNAL ACTION AS COMPETING STRATEGIES

International negotiation can be as good as legislation, or better than legislation, for at least two reasons. Both reasons have to do with the goals of private international law: the general goal of decisional harmony, on the one hand, and the substantive policies that the individual rules of private international law may intend to advance, on the other.

A. *The General Goal of Decisional Harmony*

Decisional harmony, or the principle whereby the possibility of conflicting decisions should be minimised,[9] has been one the fundamental objectives of private international law ever since the rise of particularism.

Private international law rules vary from one legal system to another. As such, these rules can only provide 'relative' answers to the issues raised by cross-border relationships. Nothing can be said of the legal treatment of such a relationship as long as it has not been established – hypothetically, as the case may be – which country (ie, which national legal system) will serve as a standpoint for examining the relationship in question and deciding the issues that arise in connection therewith (jurisdiction, applicable law etc.). The rules of private international law in force in the chosen country will say how the above issues are to be decided *from the particular perspective of the country in question*, that is by the courts of that State, if they are in fact seised of the matter.

Generally speaking, States are considered to be free to enact their own rules of private international law without having to consider the way in which the situation concerned would be dealt with under the rules of private international law of another country. The same holds true for EU legislation on judicial cooperation in civil matters. In principle, nothing prevents the institutions from ignoring, in the elaboration of EU rules of private international law, the point of view of such third States as may have an interest in regulating, or otherwise dealing with, a particular matter.

Yet, disregarding the point of view of the countries with which the situation is connected may lead to unwelcome results. In particular, it could frustrate decisional harmony. The relative character of private international law rules poses an obvious challenge to legal certainty and to the continuity of legal relationships across borders. For example, the courts of two or more States may be instructed by the respective rules of private international law to assert their jurisdiction over the same dispute. Additionally, pursuant to the same rules, these

---

9 See, eg, on this topic, W Wengler, 'The General Principles of Private International Law' (1961) 104 *Recueil des cours de l'Académie de droit international de La Haye* 273, 365.

courts may be prevented from deferring to, or otherwise taking into account, the jurisdictional claims of each other. The litigants would be involved in duplicate proceedings, possibly leading to conflicting judgments. Legal certainty is similarly at risk in those cases where a situation is likely to be observed from the standpoint of two or more different legal orders, each having its own views as to the rights and obligations arising out of that situation. For instance, the same two persons could be considered to be husband and wife in one country, but not in another, depending on the law applicable to the validity of their marriage.

It is not infrequent for domestic and EU legal texts in the field of private international law to attempt to avert or mitigate these difficulties. One approach is to require or allow local courts, under appropriate circumstances, to consider the point of view of another country, as it results from the latter's rules of private international law or the decisions of its authorities. There are different techniques whereby the point of view of a given country may have a bearing on the operation of the private international law rules of the forum. One of these techniques is *renvoi*, as contemplated in Article 34 of Regulation (EU) No 650/2012 on successions upon death,[10] but other devices exist that make foreign rules of private international law or foreign decisions on private international law issues relevant to the treatment of transnational cases.

What matters, for our present purposes, is that the legislative efforts deployed by the EU to ensure unilateral coordination with the point of view of a foreign country aim to achieve, in practice, the same results as would be prompted – more efficiently and more securely – by an international agreement laying down uniform rules of private international law. International harmonisation appears to be more efficient than unilateral coordination in that it eliminates at the outset the discrepancies that make the point of view of each country relevant to the treatment of the matter. And it presents itself as more secure in the sense that it creates, if realised by means of binding agreements, a legal obligation for the EU and the States concerned to address the relevant issues in the manner indicated in the relevant international instrument.

It is worth noting that there are cases in which an efficient and secure treatment of cross-border situations is not only desirable, but is actually a legal obligation for the EU, namely one arising under EU and international rules on the protection of human rights.[11] Promoting the international coordination of the legal systems of the various countries with which a situation is connected can in fact be crucial to ensuring the protection of human rights in some areas. Fail-

---

10 Regulation (EU) No 650/2012 on jurisdiction, applicable law, recognition and enforcement of decisions and acceptance and enforcement of authentic instruments in matters of succession and on the creation of a European Certificate of Succession [2012] OJ L 201/107.

11 On the relationship between private international law and the law of human rights, see generally, and for further references, LR Kiestra, *The Impact of the European Convention on Human Rights on Private International Law* (Springer 2014).

ing coordination, the enjoyment of individual rights – for example, the right to have a judicial decision enforced, even if rendered abroad, or the right to have a personal status recognised, even if created by a foreign court order[12] – may ultimately lack the required degree of effectiveness.[13]

B. *The Substantive Policies of Private International Law Rules*

Private international law rules are not neutral. They reflect substantive policies. This is particularly true for EU rules, since judicial cooperation in civil matters is explicitly understood by the TFEU to serve the 'proper functioning of the internal market' and the creation of an area of freedom security and justice in Europe. Regional measures are thus instrumental to the objectives of the EU and must comply with the fundamental policies of its legal order.

When legislation is enacted that has a global reach, it is to be presumed that the institutions are pursuing a political objective that requires the measure in question to apply to both European and non-European situations. It is true that the European legislator does not always state the reasons why a certain rule should be universal in scope, ie, why the rule would fail to achieve its intended purpose if it were to apply solely to purely regional cases.[14] That said, if the institutions believe that a given policy requires a global safeguard, it is to be presumed that the policy in question would be better served (or less easily frustrated) if the authorities of the third country with which the situation may happen to be connected were requested to deal with it in a manner consistent with the approach followed in the Union.

Let us consider, for example, the special conflict-of-law rule on environmental damage which appears in Article 7 of Regulation (EC) No 864/2007 on the law applicable to non-contractual obligations. The rule has been designed in a such a way as to advance the protection of the environment. This is in fact the rationale of the provision whereby the 'person seeking compensation' for damage to the environment is allowed to choose the law of the country in which the event giving rise to the damage occurred, rather than the law of the country in which the damage itself occurred, which would normally apply under the general conflict-of-law rule on torts in Article 4(1).[15] A 'universal' provision, Article 7 can be relied upon, before the courts of a Member State, in cases relating

---

12 Cf, respectively, *Vrbica v Croatia*, ECHR:2010:0401JUD003254005, and *Negrepontis-Giannisis v Greece*, ECHR:2011:0503JUD005675908.

13 On the instrumentality of private international law to the protection of fundamental rights, see generally P Franzina, *La protezione degli adulti nel diritto internazionale privato* (Cedam 2012), 60 ff.

14 See further, in this book, the contribution of A Mills.

15 See in this respect Recital 25 of the Regulation. See also, generally, S Vrellis, 'The Law Applicable to the Environmental Damage', in J Forner Delaygua, C González Beilfuss and Viñas Farré (eds), *Entre Bruselas y La Haya - Liber amicorum Alegría Borrás* (Marcial Pons 2013), 869.

to environmental damage occurring in a third country. Businesses established in the EU (and acting on the basis of decisions taken in the EU) are thus discouraged from carrying out polluting activities in third countries where environmental laws have a low degree of development – a conduct that would not only be detrimental to the environment, but could also lead to distortions of competition in the internal market. Presumably, the policy underlying Article 7 would be better realised if there were coordination between the point of view of the EU and the point of view of the third State where the damage has been sustained. Coordination could involve the rules on the conflicts of laws, as well as the rules on jurisdiction (and *lis pendens*) and the rules on the recognition and enforcement of judgments. Otherwise stated, the effective protection of the interests that Article 7 of Regulation No 864/2007 is meant to safeguard would increase if some form of international coordination were in place, based on a common understanding of the way in which cross-border environmental damages should be dealt with in the Member States and in the third countries involved.

2. THE ARTICULATION OF EU LEGISLATION AND INTERNATIONAL DEVELOPMENTS: A MATTER OF CONVERGENCE, COMBINATION AND CONFRONTATION

The above discussion suggests that the enactment of legislation with a global reach and the development of external action represent different paths that the EU may take to ensure the effectiveness of its policies, be they general (such as the pursuit of decisional harmony) or rule-specific.

The two paths clearly differ in several respects. International negotiation, in spite of the obvious added value inherent in the uniformity that it can create, may prove extremely difficult and often requires a considerable amount of time and energy to complete. Once negotiations are over, the ratification process is in several instances slow and problematic. Furthermore, even where diplomatic efforts succeed, they almost invariably fail to bring about a truly universal unification of the relevant provisions.[16]

16 Relatively few conventions in the field of private international law have attracted a very significant number of ratifications or accessions. Some of the most widely ratified conventions in this area have been elaborated in the framework of the Hague Conference on Private International Law. These include the Convention of 5 October 1961 abolishing the requirement of legalisation for foreign public documents, with 112 contracting States, the Convention of 15 November 1965 on the service abroad of judicial and extrajudicial documents in civil or commercial matters, with 71 contracting States, the Convention of 18 March 1970 on the taking of evidence abroad in civil or commercial matters, with 59 contracting States, the Convention of 25 October 1980 on the civil aspects of international child abduction, with 95 contracting States, and the Convention

By contrast, legislative efforts deployed at the EU level mostly lead to the adoption of uniform rules in a relatively short amount of time. In addition, due to the cultural and political ties that exist between Member States, legislation is generally less exposed to the risk of watered-down compromises, and accordingly has a chance to produce texts that are technically more refined and practical if compared with international conventions that aspire to be universal. Furthermore, EU legislative measures can be easily amended as soon as the need to update or revise them arises – an occurrence that, conversely, can raise significant practical difficulties when the text to be updated or revised is an international convention, especially one in force for a high number of States.[17]

The paths of legislation and negotiation are not always mutually exclusive. There are cases in which the institutions resort both to legislation and to external action to deal with a particular issue. In these instances, the problem arises of articulating legislation and external action. The problem arises even where one option is chosen and the other is disregarded altogether. Opting for the development of EU legislation in a given sector may affect the prospect that international negotiated solutions will be reached in the same area, or turn into common global standards. Conversely, opting for the participation of the EU in a binding international instrument has the effect of limiting, in accordance with Article 216(2) TFEU, the ability of the EU institutions to address concerns that are already dealt with by the instrument in question.

The relationship between EU legislation and international developments in the field of private international law may take multiple forms, depending on considerations that are specific to the subject-matter concerned and on contingent circumstances. There are three main patterns. Legislation and international developments (either existing or contemplated) may in fact *converge*, *combine* or *confront*. We will examine these patterns in the following paragraphs, both in their normative expressions and in their political significance.

---

of 29 May 1993 on protection of children and co-operation in respect of intercountry adoption, with 97 contracting States. Of the remaining 33 conventions negotiated within the Conference, 9 have failed to attract the required number of ratifications or accessions and have accordingly never entered into force, and 10 are in force for less than 15 States. The above figures are based on information available on 20 August 2016.

17 On other respects, EU legislation and international agreements are placed on the same footing. In particular, the Court of Justice may be seised of a request for a preliminary ruling concerning the interpretation of an international convention to which the EU is a party (as first stated in Case 181/73, *Haegeman v Belgium*, EU:C:1974:41), no less than an international convention concluded by Member States in the interest of the Union (see, eg, Case C-439/01, *Libor Cipra*, EU:C:2003:31). Similarly, the European Judicial Network in civil and commercial matters is charged with facilitating discussion and exchanges of information among Member States no matter whether cooperation, in the circumstances, comes under the purview of a legislative measure, an international convention or even the domestic provisions of private international law of the States concerned: see Article 3(2) of Decision 2001/470 establishing a European Judicial Network in civil and commercial matters [2001] OJ L 174/25.

3. CONVERGENCE

Sometimes, EU legislative measures are designed to align with provisions laid down in international agreements. Where an international convention serves as a model, or a source of inspiration, for EU legislation, the chances are high that the decisions taken by the authorities of a Member State, under EU law, will not substantially differ from (or will otherwise be consistent with) the decisions that the authorities of a third country would adopt in the same circumstances (provided, of course, that the third country in question is bound by the international instrument concerned or has drawn inspiration therefrom when elaborating its domestic rules of private international law).

The enactment of 'convergent' legislation represents the nearest surrogate to the participation by the EU in an internationally binding regime laying down uniform rules of private international law. As a matter of fact, convergence enhances uniformity, without requiring the EU to undertake any international obligation to that effect.

3.1. CONVERGENCE BY REFERENCE

There may be cases in which the EU institutions seek a perfect alignment with a particular convention, and cases in which they content themselves with ensuring a certain degree of consistency between the legislative measure in question and the corresponding international regime.

The most radical way to bring legislation in line with the relevant international developments is including in the relevant legislative measure an explicit referral to the chosen convention.

Regulation No 4/2009 provides an example in this respect, though a rather peculiar one. The Regulation purports to address all kinds of private international law issues that may arise in connection with cross-border maintenance cases, including the issue of the law governing the substance of maintenance. The Regulation, however, devotes to the latter issue a single provision, which does nothing more than to refer the matter to an international convention. Pursuant to Article 15 of the Regulation, the law applicable to maintenance obligations must be determined 'in accordance' with the Hague Protocol of 23 November 2007 on the law applicable to maintenance obligations. In practice, the European legislature refrained from creating an autonomous set of conflict-of-law provisions on maintenance matters, and availed itself, instead, of the rules that already existed in the Hague Protocol.

It is important to note, for our purposes, that at the time when the Regulation was adopted, on 18 December 2008, the Protocol had not yet entered into force internationally (this only occurred on 1 August 2013). Additionally, the

EU had not yet expressed its consent to be bound by this instrument (it only did so on 8 April 2010). Actually, as contemplated in a declaration appended to the act of approval of the EU,[18] the Protocol has been applied in the Member States for more than two years, beginning on 18 June 2011 (the date of application of Regulation No 4/2009), before any third State could expect the EU and its Member States to apply the rules of the Protocol as a matter of international law. It is true that, generally speaking, under a practice reflected in Article 25 of the Vienna Convention of 21 March 1986 on the law of treaties between States and international organisations or between international organisations, a treaty, like the Hague Protocol, may be applied provisionally pending its entry into force if the treaty itself so provides or if the negotiating States and negotiating organisation 'have in some other manner so agreed'. It is also true that an agreement as to the provisional application of a treaty, such as the agreement concluded between the EU and its Member States and evidenced in the declaration mentioned above, is meant, as such, to produce legal effects at the international level.[19] However, in the circumstances, it must be considered that, up until the first ratification by a third country, namely the ratification by Serbia, whose instrument was deposited in 2013 (and did not feature any declaration regarding the provisional application of the Protocol in the relations with the EU and its Member States), the Protocol did not in fact entail any legal effect for the EU or its Member State on the international plane.

As a matter of fact, the application of the Protocol rested, until that time, on Regulation No 4/2009 (and, specifically, on the referral in Article 15 therein), and by an agreement as to the provisional application of the Protocol the effects of which where limited, in practice, to the EU itself and its Member States.

Now that the Protocol is in force internationally for the EU, Article 15 of Regulation No 4/2009 performs little more than a 'pedagogic' function. It informs those charged with applying the Regulation that, when it comes to the law applicable to maintenance obligations, the pertinent rules are to be found outside the Regulation itself, that is, in the Protocol.

There are other cases in which the EU legislator, in referring to a particular convention, similarly appears to be providing information, rather than enacting actual prescriptions. For instance, most of the legislative measures enacted by the EU to deal with adjudicatory jurisdiction, such as Regulation (EU) No 1215/2012 on jurisdiction in civil and commercial matters (Brussels Ia),[20] in-

---

18 See Article 4(2) of Decision (EC) 2009/941 on the conclusion by the European Community of the Hague Protocol of 23 November 2007 on the Law Applicable to Maintenance Obligations [2009] OJ L 331/17.

19 D Mathy, 'Article 25', in O Corten and P Klein (eds), *The Vienna Conventions on the Law of Treaties* (Oxford University Press 2011), 639, 652.

20 Regulation (EU) No 1215/2012 on jurisdiction and the recognition and enforcement of judgments in civil and commercial matters [2012] OJ L 351/1.

clude a provision – Article 28(1) of the Brussels Ia Regulation – whereby the seised court must stay the proceedings 'so long as it is not shown that the defendant has been able to receive the document instituting the proceedings or an equivalent document in sufficient time to enable him to arrange for his defence, or that all necessary steps have been taken to this end'.[21] However, this is only a fall back-rule. According to the legislative measures that follow this pattern (and specifically, as regards the Brussels Ia Regulation, according to Article 28(2) and (3)), the stay of the proceedings must rather be decided in conformity with Article 19 of Regulation (EC) No 1393/2007 on the service of judicial and extrajudicial documents in civil or commercial matters,[22] if the document 'had to be transmitted ... pursuant to that Regulation', or, where Regulation No 1393/2007 is not applicable, in conformity with Article 15 of the Hague Convention of 15 November 1965 on the service abroad of judicial and extrajudicial documents, if the document in question 'had to be transmitted abroad pursuant to that Convention'.

The reference to the Hague Convention, which typically comes into play in judicial proceedings brought against a defendant domiciled in a non-Member State (insofar as process is to be served in such a State, and that State is bound by the Hague regime), basically serves as a reminder that the situation, in the relevant aspects (including the conditions for, and the effects of, a stay of proceedings), comes with the scope of the Convention and not with the scope of the Regulation on the service of documents. The latter, in fact, pursuant to its Article 1(1), only applies where a document 'has to be transmitted from one Member State to another for service there'.

There is just one case, that seldom arises in practice, in which the above reference to the Hague Convention could perform a normative function, as opposed to a merely informative function. The referral, as we have seen, only operates where the Regulation is not applicable and the document instituting the proceedings is to be transmitted 'pursuant to' the Hague Convention. This may happen where, in respect of proceedings contemplated in a Member State, the initial document is to be transmitted in another Member State, if the subject-matter of the dispute is the alleged 'liability of the State for actions or omissions in the exercise of state authority (*acta iure imperii*)'. The Regulation

---

21 An identical provision may be found in Article 18 of Regulation No 2201/2003 on matrimonial matters and matters of parental responsibility, Article 11 of Regulation No 4/2009 on maintenance obligations, Article 16 of Regulation No 650/2012 on successions. See also Article 16 of Regulation (EU) 2016/1103 implementing enhanced cooperation in the area of jurisdiction, applicable law and the recognition and enforcement of decisions in matters of matrimonial property regimes [2016] OJ L 183/1, and Article 16 of Regulation (EU) 2016/1104 implementing enhanced cooperation in the area of jurisdiction, applicable law and the recognition and enforcement of decisions in matters of the property consequences of registered partnerships [2016] OJ L 183/30.

22 Regulation (EC) No 1393/2007 on the service in the Member States of judicial and extrajudicial documents in civil or commercial matters [2007] OJ L 324/79.

explicitly excludes these matters from its scope pursuant to Article 1(1), whereas the Convention is applicable 'in all cases, in civil or commercial matters', including matters of State liability for *acta iure imperii* (actually, in this event, the Convention merely allows the Central Authority of the requested State to refuse to effect the request for service, relying on Article 13, if it considers that doing so would interfere with the sovereignty or the security of the requested State).[23] In this peculiar scenario, the reference made by the Brussels Ia Regulation (and similar measures) to the Hague Service Convention must be understood to mean that EU law 'wants' Article 15 of the Convention to apply, instead of the fall-back rule mentioned above. The intention thus expressed by the EU legislature is particularly significant if one considers that, according to the subordination clause in Article 25 of the Hague Convention (and to the extent indicated therein), the rules adopted at the EU level by means of legislation should normally supersede the corresponding rules of the Convention.

The implications of a legislative referral to a particular convention may, in other scenarios, be definitely more meaningful. The EU legislator might wish to enact provisions that correspond to the rules of a particular convention – one that is not in force for the EU and that, differently from the Hague Protocol on maintenance obligations, the EU itself does not contemplate to conclude, or accede to. In similar circumstances, the most straightforward way to proceed would consist in adopting a piece of EU legislation that would include a reference to the chosen convention or to one or more of its provisions. This is, in principle, one of the options available to the EU if it were to adopt, based on Article 81 TFEU, a measure regarding the protection of vulnerable adults. Vulnerable adults are persons aged 18 or more who, by reason of an impairment or insufficiency of their personal faculties, are not in a position to protect their interests. Here, the obvious international reference would be the Hague Convention of 13 January 2000 on the international protection of adults. The Convention, which is already in force for seven Member States, lays down a unique set of private international law rules that are specifically intended to regulate the cross-border protection of vulnerable adults. The experience developed in the contracting States suggests that the Convention is broadly regarded as a balanced and well-conceived text, which enables State authorities to ensure the timely and efficient protection of the personal and financial interests of the adults concerned.[24] The EU cannot become a party to this Convention, as this is only open to States, not to international organisations. In these circumstances,

---

23 *Practical Handbook on the Operation of the Hague Service Convention* (Hague Conference on Private International Law 2016), 11.

24 P Franzina and J Long, *The Protection of Vulnerable Adults in EU Member States – The Added Value of EU Action in the Light of The Hague Adults Convention*, in C Salm, *Protection of Vulnerable Adults* (European Parliamentary Research Service 2016), 106, 148 ff.

if the institutions were unwilling to request Member States to ratify, or accede to, the Convention 'in the interest of the Union' – a move that would eventually make the Convention binding in its own right for all Member States, both in their mutual relations and in the relations with any contracting third country[25] – the EU could nevertheless want to incorporate in its legislation some of the solutions adopted in the Convention. Specifically, it might want to do so in a manner that would preserve the visibility of the origin of those solutions and their international character. A legislative referral to the Convention would easily meet this need. As a result, the relevant provisions would be understood and applied by Member States' authorities in the same manner as they are understood and applied, in principle, by the authorities of any other State bound by the Hague regime. This would facilitate the work of those taking care of the interests of vulnerable adults and ultimately enhance the protection of the persons concerned: the applicable rules would in fact be substantially the same, no matter whether the situation is purely regional in its scope or features a connection with a third country.

Clearly enough, incorporating into legislation a convention to which the EU is not bound internationally is not the same thing, for the EU, as becoming a party to the convention in question. On one side, international conventions that are internationally binding on the EU cannot be derogated from by legislation, pursuant to Article 216(2) TFEU. If a legislative measure were to run counter the international obligations of the EU, its validity would be affected.[26] By contrast, the mere incorporation of an international agreement into EU legislation would leave the legislator free to adjust the rules of the agreement to its needs and actually to deviate from those rules as it deems fit. On the other side, however, where the EU contents itself with incorporating an international instrument in its legislation, it waives in fact the possibility of relying on that instrument with such third countries that have joined, or may join in the future, the international regime in question. Otherwise stated, if the EU enacts rules that replicate a given convention, but does not become a party thereto, it remains unable to claim for itself the rights that the convention is intended to confer. A similar waiver would prove particularly problematic (and even make

---

25 The EU followed this approach with respect to the Hague Convention of 1996 on the protection of children (on which the Hague Convention of 2000 on the protection of adults was modelled). The time needed to achieve the entry into force of the Convention for all Member States provides an illustration of the difficulties associated with this way of proceeding: the Council first authorised Member States to sign the Convention in the interest of the Community, as it was then, in December 2002 (Decision 2003/93 [2003] OJ L 48/1), and reiterated the authorisation in June 2008 with (Decision 2008/431 [2008] OJ L 151/36). One year later, only 9 Member States had ratified or acceded to the Convention. It eventually took five more years to the remaining Member States to deposit their instruments of ratification or accession. Belgium did so only in May 2014, while Italy waited until October 2015.

26 See, among others, Case C-366/10, *Air Transport Association of America*, EU:C:2011:864, paras 50 f.

little sense, in some circumstances) if the instrument in question is one based on reciprocity.

3.2. CONVERGENCE BY IMITATION

Convergence does not have to be pursued always through referrals. The obvious alternative is imitation. Multilateral conventions for the unification of private international law, specifically those adopted in the framework of the Hague Conference on Private International Law, have largely served as a model for EU legislative measures relating to judicial cooperation in civil matters.

Most of the time, international instruments are taken as a model simply because they embody solutions that have already proved effective and expedient, or because they rest on notions that are familiar to the authorities of Member States. Sometimes, however, imitation is the strategy whereby the EU deliberately connects its legislation to normative trends that have developed outside the European boundaries, so as to achieve, albeit indirectly, some of the advantages inherent in the unification of private international law realised under those trends.[27]

The design of certain EU provisions regarding jurisdiction in family matters provides an illustration of this approach. As mentioned earlier, jurisdiction in respect of divorce and legal separation proceedings is governed, in the Member States, by Regulation No 2201/2203. The uniform heads of jurisdiction that the Regulation sets forth in Article 3 largely correspond to the criteria listed in Article 2 of the Hague Convention of 1 June 1970 on the recognition of divorces and legal separations, which is currently in force for several Member States (but not the EU as such) and some third countries. Both the Regulation and the Convention, for example, contemplate the scenario of matrimonial proceedings brought in the country where the respondent is habitually resident, the country where the petitioner habitually resides (provided that certain further conditions are fulfilled), and the country of nationality of both spouses. Contrary to the Regulation, the Convention is not concerned with the allocation of jurisdiction. It only deals with the recognition of decisions rendered in a contracting State. It is for this purpose that the Convention makes use of the criteria in Article 2: in order to qualify for recognition under the Convention, a decision must – among other things – originate from one of the countries indicated in the latter provi-

[27] One corollary of imitation consists in the possibility of relying on the particular international convention used as a model (and to its explanatory report, as the case may be), as a means to clarify the interpretation of the relevant EU legislative provisions: see, for example, Case C-283/09, *Artur Weryński v Mediatel 4B*, EU:C:2011:85, paras 65 ff, referring to the Hague Convention of 18 March 1970 on the taking of evidence abroad in civil or commercial matters in a case revolving around the interpretation of Regulation No 1206/2001.

sion. In the end, thanks to the imitation of the list drawn up in the Convention, a divorce or a legal separation obtained in a Member State – namely, the Member State whose courts possess jurisdiction pursuant to Article 3 of Regulation No 2201/2003 – has a good chance of being recognised in a third country, as long as that third country is bound by (or has itself drawn inspiration from) the Hague Convention of 1970 as regards the recognition of foreign divorces. Without undertaking the international obligations that arise from the Convention, the EU in fact increases, through its legislation, the probability of Member States' divorces and legal separations being recognised in third countries.

Similar considerations may be put forward as regards the approach of the EU to the allocation of jurisdiction in cross-border maintenance proceedings and the international recognition of judgements and court settlements relating to family maintenance.

Regulation No 4/2009, as observed above, makes provision, among other things, for the jurisdiction of Member States' courts in this area and for the circulation of judgments between Member States. An international instrument, the Hague Convention of 23 November 2007 on the international recovery of child support and other forms of family maintenance, which is in force for the EU and several third countries, is in place, instead, to govern, *inter alia*, the recognition and enforcement of judgments between one contracting State and another. The Convention does not purport to determine the country or countries before whose courts an international maintenance case can or should be brought. However, it provides in Article 20 a list of bases of jurisdiction that make a judgment eligible for recognition in accordance with the Convention's regime. These bases coincide to a large extent with the grounds of jurisdiction laid down in Regulation No 4/2009. Here, again, the EU enhances the chances of recognition of Member States' decisions beyond the European boundaries by ensuring a certain degree of convergence between its legislation on jurisdiction and the international developments relating to the recognition of judgments.

3.3. THE CONDITIONS FOR CONVERGENCE AND THE IMPACT OF CONVERGENT LEGISLATION ON THE DEVELOPMENT OF EU EXTERNAL ACTION

The situations in which the EU may be willing to bring its legislation in line with an international convention are, realistically, not very numerous. Convergence appears to be justified where the EU itself has taken part in the elaboration of the international instrument in question, or where it envisages to become a party to the agreement concerned but prefers to proceed gradually by giving effect to the rules of the agreement in the EU legal order without undertaking any engagement on the international plane. Convergence may also prove appropriate where a particular international convention has become a reference in a given area, to the point that it would be inexpedient for the EU, and possibly disadvantageous, to opt for a singular EU approach and run the risk of isolation.

As EU private international law grows more elaborated, and more distinctive in its features, the room left for convergent legislation is presumably set to further diminish. The institutions may have excellent reasons to look at convincing international experiences, but, as judicial cooperation in civil matters expands, they are under an increasing pressure to ensure the internal consistency of the body of EU law that governs this area. Against this backdrop, a sheer referral to an international convention, or to some of its provisions, may prove problematic, since the terminology, the drafting style and the underlying principles of the chosen convention may not correspond to those of the existing EU legislative measures that address neighbouring or otherwise connected matters.

It would nevertheless be wrong to treat convergence as a pure accident, or as a strategy devoid of political significance. By enacting legislation that seeks to be consistent with international developments, the institutions show that they are aware of the influence that these developments may have on the pursuit of regional goals. As stated by the European Council in the Stockholm Programme, the Union and the Member States must 'work in partnership with third countries' and 'actively develop and promote European and international standards' as regards issues within the area of freedom, security and justice, such as judicial cooperation in civil matters.[28] The quest for convergence reflects the open and outward-looking approach that these policy considerations seem to imply. That said, the fact of resorting to legislation, instead of participating in the relevant international efforts, indicates the importance that the institutions attach to the progress of legal harmonisation in this field. In Europe, where the mobility of persons and undertakings across borders is far more developed than in any other region in the world, the legal problems raised by the diversity of national experiences need to be tackled at a pace that international negotiations are simply unable to afford, especially where they aim for the adoption of binding legal instruments.

4. COMBINATION

We have already observed that, as the work of the institutions unfolds in the area of judicial cooperation, the distinctive features of EU private international law become clearer and more easily recognisable. EU legislation employs a lan-

---

[28] *The Stockholm Programme – An Open And Secure Europe Serving and Protecting Citizens* [2009] OJ C 115/1, para. 7.1.

guage of its own, serves the particular goals of regional integration and builds on values that are specific to the EU legal order.

As a means to reconcile the autonomy of regional private international law with the outward-looking attitude described above, the EU legislator may sometimes be willing to combine elements of 'pure' legislation and references to international conventions. In principle, the reasons behind the references to the relevant international developments are the same as those illustrated above with respect to the convergence pattern. The strength of these reasons, however, is more limited here, and legislation is viewed as necessary either to complement or to shape the effects of the international instrument in question.

4.1. THE TWO-TIER MODEL

Legislation and international conventions may combine in a variety of ways. One scheme consists, for EU legislation, in treating a particular international instrument as the basic regime of private international law to be applied regionally, and to complement such a regime with provisions that specifically address intra-European situations. While departing in some respects from the international regime used as a basis, these regional 'concretions' are designed in such a way as to remain consistent with the underlying universal discipline. EU provisions, in other words, are meant, here, to enhance the functioning of the global regime, not to disrupt it: they build on the same basic ideas that underpin the international regime and purport to allow the universal rules to achieve their goals more fully and more securely. Typically, the outcome of this approach is a two-tier normative structure, where universal developments – the first tier – represent the ground on which regional rules – the second tier – are erected.

This approach has been followed in Regulation No 2201/2003 in respect of proceedings concerning the return of abducted children. Article 11 of the Regulation contains a number of provisions that apply to intra-European abductions. Specifically, Article 11 contemplates the situation where 'a person, institution or other body having rights of custody' applies to the courts of a Member State to deliver a judgment 'on the basis' of the Hague Convention of 25 October 1980 on the civil aspects of international child abduction in order to obtain the return of a child that has been wrongfully removed or retained in another Member State. The purpose of Article 11 is to improve, in the relations between the Member States of the EU, the operation of specific provisions of the Hague Child Abduction Convention. The EU is not a party to the Convention (which is only open to States). However, all the Member States of the Union are internationally bound by the Convention.

Some of the improvements brought about by the Regulation amount, in reality, to little more than a clarification of the way in which the Hague regime should be interpreted and applied in the Member States of the EU. For example, the Member States' courts that apply Articles 12 and 13 of the 1980 Hague Convention are required under Article 11(2) of the Regulation to ensure that the child 'is given the opportunity to be heard during the proceedings unless this appears inappropriate having regard to his or her age or degree of maturity'. The right of the child to be heard is not explicitly enshrined in the Convention, and in some contracting States children are very rarely heard, or are not heard personally and directly by the court.[29] Yet, at least in the EU, the court's duty to hear the child is somehow implicit in the Convention, namely in light of the evolution of the surrounding legal landscape which followed the adoption of the United Nations Convention on the rights of the child of 20 November 1989, which is in force for all EU Member States and contemplates the right of the child to be heard in Article 12(2), and the European Convention of 25 January 1996 on the exercise of children's rights, which is presently in force for several Member States and recognises all children with 'sufficient understanding' the right to be informed and to express their views in judicial proceedings that may affect them. Besides, Article 24(1) of the Charter of fundamental rights of the EU provides that children 'may express their views freely' and that their views must be 'taken into consideration on matters which concern them in accordance with their age and maturity'.

In other respects, Article 11 of the Regulation brings about more meaningful consequences. According to Article 11(8), '[n]otwithstanding a judgment of non-return pursuant to Article 13 of the 1980 Hague Convention', any subsequent judgment, issued by a court of a Member State having jurisdiction under the Regulation, that requires the return of the child, 'shall be enforceable' in the other Member States in conformity with the Regulation, 'in order to secure the return of the child'. The judgment, once 'certified' in accordance with the Regulation, is entitled to recognition and enforcement in all other Member States, pursuant to Article 42(1) of the Regulation, 'without the need for a declaration of enforceability and without any possibility of opposing its recognition'. In practice, as a means to facilitate the return of wrongfully removed children, the Regulation introduced, in Article 11(8), a procedure that departs from the procedure envisaged in the Hague Child Abduction Convention in some important aspects. The policy considerations behind Article 11(8) of the Regulation do not substantially differ from those underlying the Hague regime (as both instruments are primarily concerned with the interests of the child and aim to facilitate the swift return to the child to the country where he or she used to live at the time of the abduction), but the cooperation that the Regulation requires from the Member States in their mutual relations are far more pervasive and advanced than those required under the Convention.

---

29 See further R Schuz, *The Hague Child Abduction* (Hart Publishing 2013), 376 ff.

4.2. THE ASSIMILATION MODEL

EU legislation may coordinate with international developments by differentiating the treatment of extra-European situations (specifically, situations that are not covered as such by any internationally binding legal instrument) depending on whether the situation at issue arose in, or is otherwise connected with, a country that is bound by a particular convention, or not. If this condition is fulfilled, then the situation is to be regarded as similar, for particular purposes, to an intra-European situation.

Regulation No 2201/2003 on matrimonial matters and matters of parental responsibility provides, again, an example. Article 12 of the Regulation deals with prorogation of jurisdiction in matters of parental responsibility. The purpose of the rule is to set out the conditions under which the jurisdiction of a court may rest on an agreement concluded to this effect between the persons having responsibility in relation to the child concerned. Specifically, according to Article 12(3), the courts of a Member State may assert their jurisdiction in relation to parental responsibility, in proceedings other than proceedings connected to a matrimonial matter (and in addition to the cases contemplated under other rules of the Regulation), where the following requirements are met: the child must have a 'substantial connection' with the Member State of the forum, the jurisdiction of the courts of that State must have been 'accepted expressly or otherwise in an unequivocal manner by all the parties to the proceedings', and the prorogation must be 'in the best interests of the child'.

The latter condition involves, by its nature, an assessment of the particular circumstances of the case. The Regulation, however, establishes a of presumption, which affects the seised court's appreciation of the circumstances. Article 12(4) provides that if the child habitually resides in a third State 'which is not a contracting party to the Hague Convention of 19 October 1996 on jurisdiction, applicable law, recognition, enforcement and cooperation in respect of parental responsibility and measures for the protection of children', jurisdiction under Article 12(3) 'shall be deemed to be in the child's interest, in particular if it is found impossible to hold proceedings in the third State in question'. The courts of the Member States are thus instructed to consider, when assessing the interests of the child, whether the child in question habitually resides in a third State that is under an international obligation to apply the Hague Protection of Children Convention (that is, a child who benefits from the protection afforded by the authorities of such third State pursuant to Article 5(1) of the Convention), rather than in a third country that has not joined the Hague regime. In the latter scenario it is to be assumed, albeit under a rebuttable presumption, that bringing the case before the court of a Member State is consistent with the interests of the child. This presumption, which demonstrates a form of distrust regarding the country concerned, would instead be misplaced if it were to apply either to a Member State or to a third country bound by the Hague Convention of 1996. In the view of the institutions, in fact, it is appropriate for EU legislation to discriminate in this particular respect among extra-European cases: the differentiating element lies in whether the third country with which the matter is connected agrees, in this area, on the fundamental policies to which the EU is attached, and which largely correspond with the policies that inspire the Hague Protection of Children Convention.[30]

It is worth noting that the EU is not, as such, a party to the latter instrument. Additionally, when Regulation No 2201/2003 was adopted, none of its Member States (as they were then) had ratified, or acceded to, the Convention. In these circumstances, the relevance accorded to the Convention was, for the EU, a matter of unilateral coordination, rather than a concern for the international engagements of the EU and its Member States.

4.3. THE CONDITIONS FOR COMBINING LEGISLATION WITH INTERNATIONAL DEVELOPMENTS AND THE IMPACT OF THIS APPROACH ON EU EXTERNAL ACTION

Combination, as noted above, may be seen as a milder variant of convergence. The two approaches share the assumption that, in the area concerned, international developments should represent a blueprint for EU legislation. Combination provides the institutions with the flexibility they may need. Relying on the high degree of mutual trust among Member States, the EU legislator may use this flexibility to fix, regionally, the shortcomings of the chosen international instrument, so as to enhance the latter's ability to achieve its goals (as Regulation No 2201/2003 does with child abduction). Or it may use this flexibility to accord a privileged treatment to some selected extra-European situations (as the same Regulation does in connection with agreements as to jurisdiction).

In reality, the situations where a combination of legislation and international developments could prove workable and fruitful do not seem to be numerous. The articulation of legislation and international rules may prove complicated, and ultimately result in texts that could be hard to apply in practice.

The two-tier model, in particular, presupposes the possibility of drawing a clear distinction, among the situations to which the chosen international convention intends to apply, between extra-European and intra-European cases, that is, between cases that, from the standpoint of the EU, should be governed by the convention alone and cases that should trigger the concurrent operation of EU 'supplementary' provisions. Distinguishing the two sets of situations may

[30] Concerning this rather controversial (and seldom applied) provision, see further E Pataut, 'Article 12', in U Magnus and P Manowski (eds), *Brussels II bis Regulation* (Springer 2012), 145, 158 f.

be an easy task with conventions that rest on reciprocity (like the Hague Child Abduction Convention), but could be problematic with other instruments.

In addition, where the chosen convention is one in force internationally for the EU or its Member States (provided, in the latter case, that the Member States concerned are bound by the convention vis-à-vis one or more third countries),[31] the issue arises of whether and subject to which conditions the international instrument in question actually allows (the EU itself and) the Member States to supplement the rules provided therein, or deviate from them, albeit only in their mutual relations. Everything depends, here, on the provisions laid down in the convention in question to regulate the relationship between the latter and other international or supranational instruments concerning the same subject-matter. For example, the combination will be easy to realise if the chosen convention features a disconnection clause, ie, a clause that allows two or more parties not to apply the convention in their mutual relations, in whole or in part, if a particular international or supranational regime is in force among them to govern the same matters. Similar remarks may be done if the convention referred to by the EU includes a subordination clause, according to which the convention does not intend to prevail over other instruments on the same topic, provided, as the case may be, that such other instruments require a stronger cooperation among the parties, as contemplated, for instance, in the second sentence of Article 34 of the Hague Child Abduction Convention. Absent a disconnection or a subordination clause (or any other legal device that may have a similar effect, such as a reservation, an interpretive declaration etc.), a combination of legislative and international rules following the two-tier model could prove unfeasible.

Nonetheless, in the scenarios where a combination is indeed possible, the EU institutions should assess the impact that this approach would have on the future of the international convention that serves as a basis of EU legislation. Presumably, the impact may vary depending on whether legislation is intended to alter the functioning of the convention in respect of marginal aspects, or to modify its regime extensively or in its crucial rules. In the latter case, legislation could end up frustrating the object and purpose of the chosen convention, and possibly result in a breach of the obligations arising thereunder.

5. CONFRONTATION

Where the EU legislature enacts rules with a global reach, but decides neither to refer to international developments, nor to ensure some coordination with

---

31 If the convention were in force only for two or Member States, nothing would prevent a subsequent piece of EU legislation from superseding it, according to the principle underlying Article 351 TFEU.

those developments, the relationship between legislative measures and international standards tends to take the form of a confrontation.

In this scenario, legislation and international developments are likely to be mutually exclusive. Where international standards exist, and have already been embodied into a convention, the fact, for the EU, of opting for legislation instead of becoming a party to the convention in question indicates, of course, that the EU disagrees on the principles on which the convention is based, or is otherwise unprepared to give effect to its provisions. When the EU takes this posture, its stance is likely to affect the convention's ability to attract ratifications by third States, and may even jeopardise the prospects of the convention entering into force. This occurred, for example, with the Hague Convention of 5 July 2006 on the law applicable to certain rights in respect of securities held with an intermediary. The EU had long been considering the possibility of ratifying the Convention, but eventually resolved not to join that regime.[32] It appeared that the institutions were not prepared to abandon the conflict-of-law approach followed in the EU legislative measures on financial collateral arrangements, securities settlement systems and the reorganisation and winding up of credit institutions (all based on a 'location of the account' formula), and to embrace, instead, the approach prompted by the Hague Securities Convention (which refers to the law expressed in the relevant account agreement).[33] The decision taken by the EU has apparently undermined the attractiveness of the Convention. The latter has ultimately failed to receive the required number of ratifications and accessions, and has not entered into force to this day.

By the same token, if the EU decides to join a particular international standard, and actually becomes a party to a convention based on that standard (or authorises the Member States to conclude such a convention in the interest of the Union), the obvious corollary of the entry into force of the convention for the EU is that legislation has to be amended so as to be brought in line with the rules of the convention in question. As an alternative to amendment, EU legislation can simply be disregarded to the extent to which it does not conform with the convention. The latter option is only available where the non-application of a legislative provision (resulting in the unencumbered application of the corresponding conventional rules) is enough to secure the fulfilment by the EU of its obligations under the international instrument concerned. For example, the Budapest Convention of 22 June 2001 on the contract for the carriage of

---

32 The Commission's proposal for a Council Decision concerning the signing of the Convention, adopted in 2003 (COM (2003) 783 final), was formally withdrawn in 2009. See [2009] OJ C 71/17.

33 Cf the Resolution adopted by the European Parliament on 14 December 2006 [2006] OJ C 317 E/904. See also, regarding the concerns expressed by some Member States, the note drawn up by the German Presidency of the Council on the state of play of the Convention (doc. No 11324/07), available through the Public Register of Council Documents at <http://register.consilium.europa.eu>.

goods by inland waterways (CMNI), which some Member States have ratified in the past and some others are now expected to ratify 'in the interest of the Union',[34] includes in Article 29 a conflict-of-law provision which departs in various respects from the corresponding rules of Regulation (EC) No 593/2008 on the law applicable to contractual obligations, namely Article 3 and Article 5.[35] The Regulation does not have to be amended to ensure respect for the Budapest Convention. Whenever a situation arises that comes with the scope of the Convention, the rules of the Regulation must be disregarded to the extent to which their application would amount to an infringement of the Convention.

There are different reasons why the EU institutions may adopt a confrontational attitude as regards international developments (either existing or contemplated) in the area of private international law. Of course, as in the example above regarding the law of securities, it may be that the EU legislators consider the relevant international standards to be ill-suited to advance the EU policies in the field concerned. However, there may be cases where confrontation is regarded by the EU as a means to put third States somehow under pressure to participate in international efforts aimed at the harmonisation of certain private international law rules. In its proposal for the recast of Regulation (EC) No 44/2001 on jurisdiction and the recognition and enforcement of judgments in civil and commercial matters,[36] the Commission expressed the view that the reference in that Regulation to the domestic rules of jurisdiction of the Member States should be suppressed. Actually, Regulation No 44/2001 provided for the applicability of the Member States' rules on jurisdiction, subject to certain qualifications, to proceedings against persons domiciled outside the EU. The Commission believed that the time had come to put in place a thoroughly self-sufficient jurisdictional regime in the area covered by the latter Regulation: a regime made of uniform rules that would govern jurisdiction over civil and commercial matters systematically, regardless of the domicile of the defendant. No room should have been left for domestic rules on jurisdiction, and, more specifically, for those providing for 'exorbitant' heads of jurisdiction, ie, rules whereby the seised court is entitled to hear a case based on a weak or transient connection between the case itself and the forum, such as the nationality of the plaintiff or the presence of assets belonging to the defendant.[37] The proposed

---

34 Decision (EU) 2015/1878 authorising Belgium and Poland, respectively, to ratify, and Austria to accede to the Budapest Convention on the Contract for the Carriage of Goods by Inland Waterways (CMNI) [2015] OJ L 276/1.

35 Regulation (EC) No 593/2008 on the law applicable to contractual obligations (Rome I) [2008] OJ L 177/6.

36 COM (2010) 748 final.

37 See generally on the suggested development: F Pocar, 'Faut-il remplacer le renvoi au droit national par des règles uniformes dans l'article 4 du règlement No. 44/2001?', in *Vers des nouveaux équilibres entre ordres juridiques. Liber amicorum Hélène Gaudemet-Tallon* (Dalloz 2008), 573; J Weber, 'Universal Jurisdiction and Third States in the Reform of the Brussels I Regulation' (2011)

reform would have not only simplified the legal landscape. It would have also overcome the long-standing concerns raised by the discriminatory application of rules of jurisdiction that may in fact fail to meet the requirements of fairness and reasonableness.[38]

In the end, however, this particular item of the Commission's proposal was abandoned. The text that resulted from the recast, Regulation (EU) No 1215/2012 on jurisdiction and the recognition and enforcement of judgments in civil and commercial matters,[39] keeps distinguishing, as far as jurisdiction is concerned, between EU and non-EU defendants, albeit in terms that are slightly different from those of Regulation No 44/2001.[40] One of the reasons advanced to justify the preservation of the *status quo* was that the continuing operation of domestic rules of jurisdiction for proceedings involving non-European defendants could work as an incentive for non-Member States to engage in negotiations directed at suppressing (or sterilising) the use of exorbitant heads of jurisdiction.[41] A confrontational posture on the part of the EU was believed to spur international developments in that it provides third States with a good reason to seek an agreement with the EU on the harmonisation of rules on jurisdiction, 'in exchange' of the non-application by the Member States of such 'undesired' provisions as would otherwise apply to non-European defendants.[42] This strategy was considered to increase the chances of international negotiations in this field, including the negotiations within the Hague Conference on Private International Law aimed at the adoption of a worldwide convention on (jurisdiction and) the recognition and enforcement of judgments.

For a similar strategy to be rewarding, however, some conditions must be met. To begin with, EU legislation and the envisaged international convention must be organised and drafted in such a way as to make clear that the States who decide to join the convention will, on this basis, enjoy a set of benefits that will conversely be unavailable to all other States. In practice, both instruments must be based, at least in some respects, on reciprocity. This implies that the applica-

75 *Rabels Zeitschrift für ausländisches und internationales Privatrecht* 619; and R Luzzatto, 'On the Proposed Application of Jurisdictional Criteria of Brussels I Regulation to Non-Domiciled Defendants', in F Pocar, I Viarengo and FC Villata (eds), *Recasting Brussels I* (Cedam 2012), 111.

38 See already in this connection, referring to the Brussels Convention of 27 September 1968 (the predecessor of Regulation No 44/2001), K Russell, 'Exorbitant Jurisdiction and Enforcement of Judgments: The Brussels System as an Impetus for United States Action' (1993) 19 *Syracuse Journal of International Law and Commerce* 57.

39 [2012] OJ L 351/1.

40 On the outcome of negotiations relating to this aspect of the recast, see P Vlas, 'Article 6', in U Magnus and P Mankowski (eds), *Brussels I bis Regulation* (Otto Schmidt 2016), 115.

41 Cf Resolution of the European Parliament of 7 September 2010 [2011] OJ C 308 E/36, para. 15.

42 See further P Franzina, 'L'universalisation partielle du régime européen de la compétence en matière civile et commerciale dans le règlement Bruxelles I bis: une mise en perspective', in E Guinchard (ed), *Le nouveau règlement Bruxelles I bis* (Bruylant 2014), 39, 72 ff.

bility of the undesired EU legislative provisions should specifically depend on a connection between the situation at hand and the third country in question (as it is the case with Regulation No 1215/2012, whose referral to domestic rules on jurisdiction only applies to proceedings against persons domiciled in a third country). Additionally, the envisaged international convention should rule out the possibility of resorting to any divergent 'internal' provisions in the relations between contracting parties, or should minimise the impact of their application. Furthermore, the above advantages for the interested third States must be significant enough, in their practical implications, to make the trade-off of joining the convention worthwhile.

Again, Regulation No 1215/2012 provides a good example in this respect. The Regulation is a 'double' instrument, meaning that its rules are concerned both with the allocation of jurisdiction and with the recognition and enforcement of judgments. The two functions are clearly connected to each other, but not as strongly as in other double instruments. Actually, the rules of the Regulation that deal with the recognition and enforcement of judgments apply to any judgments rendered in a Member State, regardless of whether the jurisdiction of the court of origin could be asserted, in the circumstances, pursuant to the uniform provisions laid down in the Regulation itself or pursuant to the domestic rules of jurisdiction of the forum.[43] In practice, a decision issued in a Member State against a non-EU defendant by a court relying on an exorbitant ground of jurisdiction benefits from the Regulation's liberal regime on recognition and enforcement of judgments between Member States in the same way as a decision rendered against an EU defendant, based on a uniform rule on jurisdiction.

Against this backdrop, it could prove interesting for third States to join an international regime that provides for common rules on the allocation of jurisdiction and the recognition and enforcement of judgments based on such common rules (as the Hague Convention of 30 June 2005 on choice of court agreements), or an international regime that sets forth a list of bases of jurisdiction the use of which by the courts of a contracting party makes the resulting judgment eligible for recognition in all other contracting parties (as envisaged in the preliminary draft convention on the recognition and enforcement of foreign judgments, prepared in June 2016 by a Special commission convened by Council on General Affairs and Policy of the Hague Conference on Private International Law).[44]

---

43 The approach of the Regulation does not differ from the approach that the Brussels Convention of 1968 already followed in this particular respect: P Jenard, 'Report on the Convention on Jurisdiction and the Enforcement of Judgments in Civil and Commercial Matters Signed at Brussels, 27 September 1968' [1979] OJ C 59/1, 43.

44 Available at <http://hcch.net>.

6. CONCLUDING REMARKS

The legislation enacted by the EU in the field of judicial cooperation in civil matters has been compared to a building that, while embodying some admirable achievements, 'does not seem to have enough windows and doors to the outside world'.[45]

The development of external action is crucial to ensuring a balanced and sensible treatment, in the EU, of situations connected with one or more third States. We have tried to show that, under appropriate circumstances, the EU may contribute to the elaboration and consolidation of international standards in the field of private international law without becoming a party to internationally binding legal instruments. Through legislation, the EU may unilaterally give effect to international standards, or provide third countries with an incentive for actively taking part in international efforts aimed at the harmonisation of private international law rules.

While the impact of such unilateral (but outward-looking) initiatives remains limited, their potential deserves to be taken into greater consideration. They expand the toolbox of the EU in an area that requires a distinctive ability to adapt to different situations, and provide the EU institutions with an extra amount of flexibility that may prove particularly useful.

---

[45] T Kruger, *Civil Jurisdiction Rues of the EU and their Impact on Third States* (Oxford University Press 2008), 395

JURISDICTION UNDER THE EU SUCCESSION REGULATION AND RELATIONSHIPS WITH THIRD COUNTRIES

Fabrizio Marongiu Buonaiuti
University of Macerata

1. THE LIMITED *ERGA OMNES* APPROACH UNDERLYING THE SUCCESSION REGULATION'S RULES ON JURISDICTION

1.1. THE *INTER PARTES* AND *ERGA OMNES* APPROACHES IN EU PRIVATE INTERNATIONAL LAW

A connection exists between the spatial scope of application of EU legislative measures relating to judicial cooperation in civil matters and the development of the external relations of the EU in the same field. EU measures apply, in principle, whenever an issue within their material scope of application is to be decided by a court, or other authority, of a Member State for which the relevant measure is in force. Two different scenarios, however, need to be considered in this respect, depending on whether the provision concerned is intended to apply *erga omnes* rather than *inter partes*. A provision is applicable *erga omnes*, or universally, if it is meant to cover all cases falling within its material scope of application. By contrast, a provision merely applies *inter partes* if additional requirements are set out to govern its applicability *ratione loci* or *ratione personarum*. These additional requirements have the effect of limiting the applicability of the provision in question to such situations as feature a particular connection with one or more Member States.[1]

[1] On the spatial scope of EU legislative measures relating to private international law, see, among others, B Audit and GA Bermann, 'The Application of Private International Law Norms to "Third

When EU private international law was still in its early stage of development, and EU legislative measures used to address separately either the issue of jurisdiction and the recognition and enforcement of judgments or the issue of applicable law, the coexistence of the two approaches did not give rise to particular problems. On the one side, the measures addressing solely choice-of-law issues, namely the Rome I Regulation on contractual obligations,[2] the Rome II Regulation on non-contractual obligations[3] and the Rome III Regulation on divorce and legal separation[4], all laid down rules of universal application. In this respect, they followed the example of the Rome Convention of 19 June 1980 on the law applicable to contractual obligations, which was in fact replaced by the first of the Regulations referred to above. The three Regulations are applicable universally in the sense that they also apply to those cases in which the relevant connecting factor, as set out in the Regulations themselves, would designate the law of a third country.[5] Thus, the same conflict-of-law rules – those laid down in the Regulation concerned – instruct the courts sitting in a Member State to apply, depending on the circumstances, either the law of a Member State or the law of a third country. Not only does this make the conflict-of-law process more expedient. It also facilitates the pursuit of uniformity in the treatment of cross-border situations and mitigates the difficulties inherent in distinguishing between situations falling within the personal scope of application of the relevant instrument and situations lying outside of that scope.[6]

The opposite *inter partes* approach has traditionally been followed by the EU legislator in measures concerning jurisdiction and the recognition and enforcement of judgments, as well as in the area of judicial assistance, namely as regards the service of documents and the taking of evidence. The adoption of the *inter partes* approach in these fields reflects the experience previously developed

---

Countries": The Jurisdiction and Judgments Example', in A Nuyts and N Watté (eds), *International Civil Litigation in Europe and Relations with Third States* (Bruylant 2005), 55, 56 ff; M Fallon, 'Libertés communautaires et règles de conflit de lois', in A Fuchs, H Muir Watt and E Pataut (eds), *Les conflits de lois et le système juridique communautaire* (Dalloz 2004), 31; S Francq, 'Les champs d'application (matériel et spatial) dans les textes de référence. De la cohérence terminologique à la cohérence systémique. En passant par la théorie générale…', in M Fallon, P Lagarde and S Poillot-Peruzzetto (eds), *La matière civile et commerciale, socle d'un code européen de droit international privé?* (Dalloz 2009), 35, 50 ff; M Fallon and T Kruger, 'The Spatial Scope of the EU's Rules on Jurisdiction and Enforcement of Judgments: From Bilateral Modus to Unilateral Universality?' (2012/2013) 14 *Yearbook of Private International Law* 1, 2-4.

2 Regulation (EC) No 593/2008 on the law applicable to contractual obligations (Rome I) [2008] OJ L 177/6.

3 Regulation (EC) No 864/2007 on the law applicable to non-contractual obligations (Rome II) [2007] OJ L 199/40.

4 Regulation (EU) No 1259/2010 implementing enhanced cooperation in the area of the law applicable to divorce and legal separation [2010] OJ L 343/10.

5 Article 2, Rome I Regulation; Article 3, Rome II Regulation; Article 4, Rome III Regulation.

6 Cf, among others, M Fallon, 'Les conditions d'un code européen de droit international privé', in M Fallon, P Lagarde and S Poillot-Peruzzetto (eds), n 1, 1, 13 f; S. Francq, n 1, 37 f.

by Member States by means of international conventions, most notably under the Brussels Convention of 27 September 1968, which purported to simplify the reciprocal recognition and enforcement of judgments in civil and commercial matters among the Member States of the European Economic Community, as it was then.[7] The idea of reciprocity that lies behind the Brussels Convention of 1968 equally inspired international conventions dealing with jurisdiction and/or the recognition and enforcement of judgments, negotiated and adopted outside the framework of the EU.[8] Reciprocity is also a key concept in Regulation (EC) No 44/2001 on jurisdiction and the recognition and enforcement of judgments in civil and commercial matters (Brussels I) and, with some significant variations, in Regulation (EC) No 2201/2003 on jurisdiction and the recognition and enforcement of judgments in matrimonial matters and the matters of parental responsibility (Brussels IIa).[9] The same approach, apart for some exceptions, is followed today by Regulation (EU) No 1215/2012 (Brussels Ia), adopted to replace Regulation No 44/2001. Actually, in its proposal for a recast of the Brussels I Regulation, the European Commission had taken stance in favour of an *erga omnes* application of the special rules of jurisdiction contained in the former text.[10] In this particular respect, the solution advocated by the Commission was basically the same as the one advanced by the Commission

[7] Cf Article 2 of the Brussels Convention of 1968, adopting domicile of the defendant in a Contracting State as general ground of jurisdiction, and Article 4 of the Convention, providing for jurisdiction to be governed by domestic law in cases where the defendant is not domiciled in a Contracting State: see P Jenard, 'Report on the Convention on Jurisdiction and the Enforcement of Judgments in Civil and Commercial Matters Signed at Brussels, 27 September 1968' [1979] OJ C 59/1, 8, 13 ff. See also M Fallon and T Kruger, n 1, 11 ff.

[8] Reference is made, in particular, to conventions elaborated in the framework of the Hague Conference on Private International Law, such as the Hague Convention of 5 October 1961 concerning the powers of authorities and the law applicable in respect of the protection of infants (Article 13), the Hague Convention of 1 February 1971 on the recognition and enforcement of foreign judgments in civil and commercial matters (Article 1), and, more recently, the Hague Convention of 19 October 1996 on jurisdiction, applicable law, recognition, enforcement and co-operation in respect of parental responsibility and measures for the protection of children (Articles 5 and 23), and the Hague Convention of 30 June 2005 on choice of court agreements (Article 3).

[9] Cf Articles 2 and 4, Regulation (EC) No 44/2001 [2001] OJ L 12/1, reproducing the corresponding provisions of the Brussels Convention; Articles 3 and 7, 8 and 14, Regulation (EC) No 2201/2003 [2003] OJ L 338/1. See, among others, B Audit and GA Bermann, n 1, 63-80; T Kruger, *Civil Jurisdiction Rules of the EU and Their Impact on Third States* (Oxford University Press 2008), 30 ff, 81 ff; M Fallon and T Kruger, n 1, 17 ff.

[10] Cf COM (2010) 748 final. See, among others, A Borrás, 'Application of the Brussels I Regulation to External Situations: From Studies Carried Out by the European Group for Private International Law (EGPIL/GEDIP) to the Proposal for the Revision of the Regulation' (2010) 12 *Yearbook of Private International Law* 333, 339 ff; B Hess, 'The Brussels I Regulation: Recent Case Law of the Court of Justice and the Commission's Proposed Recast' (2012) 49 *Common Market Law Review* 1075, 1105 ff; R Hausmann, 'The Scope of Application of the Brussels I Regulation', in F Pocar, I Viarengo and FC Villata (eds), *Recasting Brussels I* (Cedam 2012), 3, 21 ff; R Luzzatto, 'On the Proposed Application of Jurisdictional Criteria of Brussels I Regulation to Non-Domiciled Defendants', ibid, 111, 113 ff; F Pocar, 'Révision de Bruxelles I et ordre juridique international: quelle approche uniforme?' (2011) 47 *Rivista di diritto internazionale privato e processuale* 591, 595 ff; J

itself in a proposal for the amendment of Regulation No 2201/2003, presented in 2006,[11] and later abandoned. Actually, in the meantime, the *erga omnes* approach had been followed for Regulation (EC) No 4/2009 on maintenance obligations and Regulation (EU) No 650/2012 on successions (hereinafter, the Maintenance and the Succession Regulations), as it will be seen below in more detail.[12] Eventually, however, the universal approach was set aside during the legislative process leading to the recast of the Brussels I Regulation in favour of a definitely more conservative solution. The recast Regulation, as finally adopted, still regards the domicile of the defendant in a Member State as a requirement for the application of the special rules of jurisdiction of the Regulation, save for some exceptions. Accordingly, under the recast, jurisdiction as against non-EU domiciled defendants is still governed, to a large extent, by the domestic provisions of the Member States concerned.[13]

1.2. THE TWO APPROACHES IN MEASURES ADDRESSING BOTH JURISDICTION AND APPLICABLE LAW

The coexistence of different approaches concerning the spatial scope of conflict-of-law rules, rules on jurisdiction and rules on the recognition and enforcement of judgments has led, more recently, to some awkward situations. This concerns, in particular, those legislative measures the ambition of which is to provide a comprehensive treatment of the situations falling within their respective scope of application, by addressing, within one and the same legal framework, issues relating to jurisdiction, applicable law and the recognition and enforcement of

Weber, 'Universal Jurisdiction and Third States in the Reform of the Brussels I Regulation' (2011) 75 *Rabels Zeitschrift für ausländisches und internationales Privatrecht* 619, 626 ff.

11 Cf COM (2006) 399 final. For some general remarks, see A Bonomi, 'Sull'opportunità e le possibili modalità di una regolamentazione comunitaria della competenza giurisdizionale applicabile *erga omnes*' (2007) 43 *Rivista di diritto internazionale privato e processuale* 313, 316 ff; F Pocar, 'Faut-il remplacer le renvoi au droit national par des règles uniformes dans l'article 4 du règlement No. 44/2001?', in *Vers des nouveaux équilibres entre ordres juridiques. Liber amicorum Hélène Gaudemet-Tallon* (Dalloz 2008), 573, 575 ff.

12 See below, § 1.2.

13 Cf, in particular, Articles 6 and 7, Regulation (EU) No 1215/2012 on jurisdiction and the recognition and enforcement of judgments in civil and commercial matters (recast) [2012] OJ L 351/1. See, among others, J-P Béraudo, 'Regards sur le nouveau règlement Bruxelles I sur la compétence judiciaire, la reconnaissance et l'exécution des décisions en matière civile et commerciale' (2013) 140 *Journal du droit international* 741, 746 ff; F Cadet, 'Le nouveau règlement Bruxelles I ou l'itinéraire d'un enfant gâté', ibid, 765, 772 ff; H Gaudemet-Tallon and C Kessedjian, 'La refonte du règlement Bruxelles I' (2013) 49 *Revue trimestrielle de droit européen* 435, 439 ff; A Leandro, 'Prime osservazioni sul regolamento (UE) n. 1215/2012 ("Bruxelles I bis")' (2013) 8 *Il giusto processo civile* 583, 594 ff; PA Nielsen, 'The New Brussels I Regulation' (2013) 50 *Common Market Law Review* 503, 512 ff; A Nuyts, 'La refonte du règlement Bruxelles I' (2013) 102 *Revue critique de droit international privé* 1, 4 ff.

judgments, as well as, possibly, such further issues of judicial cooperation as may be relevant to the subject matter of the instrument concerned. So far, after a first precedent to be found in Regulation (EC) No 1346/2000 on insolvency proceedings, which has itself been the object of a recent recast,[14] this 'integral' approach has been followed by Regulation No 4/2009 on maintenance obligations[15] and Regulation No 650/2012 on successions,[16] and, more recently, by Regulation 2016/1103 on matrimonial property regimes and Regulation 2015/1104 on the property consequences of registered partnerships.[17] In all of these measures, the rules on conflicts of laws – which, in the peculiar case of Regulation No 4/2009, are to be found in an international convention, the Hague Protocol of 23 November 2007, to which the Regulation explicitly refers[18] – are applicable universally, like those contained in the EU legislative texts on conflicts of law which have been referred to earlier.[19] For their part, the rules concerning jurisdiction laid down in these acts have departed sensibly from the strictly *inter partes* approach inherited from the Brussels Convention. The legislative measures at hand provide, in fact, for grounds of jurisdiction which also operate where none of the parties is personally connected to one or more Member States. This deprives the domestic rules of jurisdiction of the Member States of any residual role as regards disputes falling within the substantive scope of

[14] Cf Regulation (EU) 2015/848 on insolvency proceedings (recast) [2015] OJ L 141/19. The regulation, as its predecessor, Regulation (EC) No 1346/2000 [2000] OJ L 160/1, establishes a coincidence between jurisdiction and applicable law by providing for insolvency proceedings to be subject to the *lex fori* of the courts before which such proceedings are opened: cf Article 7 of the recast Regulation and Article 4 of the current Insolvency Regulation. Both Regulations provide for the jurisdiction of Member States' courts to open insolvency proceedings where the debtor has the centre of his main interests (COMI) in a Member State: Article 3, Regulation No 1346/2000 and Article 3, Regulation 2015/848.

[15] Regulation (EC) No 4/2009 on jurisdiction, applicable law, recognition and enforcement of decisions and cooperation in matters relating to maintenance obligations [2009] OJ L 7/1.

[16] Regulation (EU) No 650/2012 on jurisdiction, applicable law, recognition and enforcement of decisions and acceptance and enforcement of authentic instruments in matters of succession and on the creation of a European Certificate of Succession [2012] OJ L 201/107.

[17] Regulation (EU) 2016/1103 implementing enhanced cooperation in the area of jurisdiction, applicable law and the recognition and enforcement of decisions in matters of matrimonial property regimes [2016] OJ L 183/1; Regulation (EU) 2016/1104 implementing enhanced cooperation in the area of jurisdiction, applicable law, recognition and enforcement of decisions in matters of the property consequences of registered partnerships [2016] OJ L 183/30.

[18] Cf Article 15, Regulation No 4/2009. The rule provides for the law applicable to maintenance obligations to be governed by the Protocol on the law applicable to maintenance obligations (The Hague, 23 November 2007) in the Member States subject to its application. Actually, the EU, upon ratification of the Protocol has made a declaration pursuant to Article 24 of the Protocol (available at <http://hcch.net>), whereby its Member States shall be bound by the Protocol by virtue of its conclusion by the EU (or, at that time, the EC). As specified in the declaration, Denmark and the United Kingdom are not subject to the rules in the Protocol.

[19] Cf, respectively, Article 2 of the Protocol on the law applicable to maintenance obligations and Article 20 of the Succession Regulation.

application of the relevant instruments.[20] Rather, the Regulations in question set forth some autonomous subsidiary jurisdictional rules, to be resorted to in those cases where the grounds of jurisdiction contemplated under the general rules do not apply. As a supplement to these rules, a *forum necessitatis* is provided for, to be relied upon in those exceptional cases where proceedings could not be brought, or would not be dealt with fairly, before the courts of a third country presenting a close connection with the dispute.[21] Nonetheless, the *erga omnes* approach of the system of allocation of jurisdiction embodied in both the Maintenance and the Succession Regulation, and similarly in the two more recent regulations on the property of couples, presents an inherent limitation, in that no substantial coordination is attempted, except in the extreme circumstances contemplated by the rules on *forum necessitatis*,[22] with the exercise of jurisdiction by third-country courts.[23] In particular, choice of court, insofar as it is admitted depending on the peculiarities of the matters forming the subject

---

20 As noted by A Davì and A Zanobetti, *Il nuovo diritto internazionale privato europeo delle successioni* (Giappichelli 2014), 198, the rules on jurisdiction contained in Regulation No 650/2012, in presupposing the establishment of the habitual residence of the deceased at the moment of death, are inapplicable in respect of disputes concerning a future succession which might arise during the lifetime of the *de cuius*, eg, concerning an agreement as to succession or an anticipatory waiver of succession rights. Accordingly, domestic rules of jurisdiction will continue to apply as concerns such disputes.

21 Cf, respectively, Articles 6 and 7 of Regulation No 4/2009 on maintenance obligations and Articles 10 and 11 of Regulation No 650/2012 on successions. Concerning the former, see, among others, M Castellaneta and A Leandro, 'Il regolamento CE n. 4/2009 relativo alle obbligazioni alimentari' (2009) 32 *Le nuove leggi civili commentate* 1051, 1073 ff; B Ancel and H Muir-Watt, 'Aliments sans frontières. Le règlement n° 4/2009 du 18 décembre 2008 relatif à la compétence, la loi applicable, la reconnaissance et l'exécution des décisions et la coopération en matière d'obligations alimentaires' (2010) 99 *Revue critique de droit international privé* 457, 463 ff; concerning the latter, among others, A Bonomi, 'Introduction au Chapitre II - Compétence', in A Bonomi and P Wautelet (eds), *Le droit européen des successions. Commentaire du règlement n° 650/2012 du 4 juillet 2012* (Bruylant 2013), 165, 165-166; A Davì and A Zanobetti, n 20, 195 f; H Gaudemet-Tallon, 'Les règles de compétence judiciaire dans le règlement européen sur les successions', in G Khairallah and M Revillard (eds), *Droit européen des successions internationales. Le règlement du 4 juillet 2012* (Defrénois 2013), 127, 130; M Hellner, 'El futuro reglamento de la UE sobre sucesiones. La relación con terceros estados' (2010) 10 *Anuario español de derecho internacional privado* 379, 382 ff; B Hess, 'Die internationale Zuständigkeit nach der Erbrechtsverordnung', in A Dutta and S Herrler (eds), *Die Europäische Erbrechtsverordnung* (CH Beck 2014), 131, 133 f.

22 Contained respectively in Article 7, Regulation No 4/2009 and Article 11, Regulation No 650/2012. Concerning the former, see, among others: P Franzina, 'Sul *forum necessitatis* nello spazio giudiziario europeo' (2009) 92 *Rivista di diritto internazionale* 1121; G Rossolillo, '*Forum necessitatis* e flessibilità dei criteri di giurisdizione nel diritto internazionale privato nazionale e dell'Unione europea' (2010) 2 *Cuadernos de derecho transnacional*, 403, 413-415; concerning the latter, see among others: A Bonomi, 'Article 11', in A Bonomi and P Wautelet (eds), n 21, 225 ff; A Davì and A Zanobetti, n 20, 208 ff; A Dutta, 'Art. 11 EuErbVO', in *Münchener Kommentar zum BGB* (6th ed, CH Beck 2015), Nos 1-3.

23 Except, as concerns the Succession Regulation, the peculiar form of coordination attempted through Article 12 of the Regulation, to which we shall turn below, § 3.

of the relevant instrument,[24] is contemplated only in favour of Member States' courts,[25] but for a limited exception envisaged by the Maintenance Regulation in respect of cases governed by the Lugano Convention of 2007.[26] Likewise, the rules concerning *lis alibi pendens* and related actions as laid down in the said regulations apply, strictly following the former Brussels I model, only in respect of actions pending before other Member States' courts. Consistently, the rules concerning recognition and enforcement of judgments merely address the recognition and enforcement of judgments emanating from other Member States.[27]

1.3. THE APPROACH UNDERLYING THE REGULATION'S RULES ON JURISDICTION AND THE PURSUIT OF COINCIDENCE OF JURISDICTION AND APPLICABLE LAW

The fact of adopting a limited *erga omnes* approach in the terms described above as concerns jurisdiction, in contrast to the more plainly universal attitude of the rules concerning the applicable law, is particularly critical in a legislative measure such as the Succession Regulation. The Regulation is clearly inspired by the pursuit of *Gleichlauf*, that is, a parallelism between jurisdiction and applicable law as regards disputes in matters of succession.[28] In fact, due to the

---

24 Cf, respectively, Article 4, Regulation No 4/2009, admitting a choice of court only in favour of a restricted range of alternative courts belonging to Member States presenting a qualified connection with the dispute and excluding it altogether in case of maintenance obligations towards a minor, and Article 5, Regulation No 650/2012, admitting it only in favour of the courts of the Member State whose law has been chosen by the deceased as applicable to the succession. On the latter, see below, § 2.1.

25 We will revert to this point below, § 2.1, with reference to Article 5, Regulation No 650/2012.

26 Cf Article 4(4), Regulation No 4/2009, which, except in case of maintenance obligations towards a minor, allows a choice of court in favour of the courts of a third country which is a contracting party to the Lugano Convention of 2007 on jurisdiction and the recognition and enforcement of judgments in civil and commercial matters, pursuant to the provisions of that convention, which, following the originating Brussels I scheme, continues to govern jurisdiction and the recognition and enforcement of judgments in matters of maintenance obligations.

27 See below, § 2.3.

28 Cf the Preamble to the Regulation, Recitals 23 and 27. On the role of *Gleichlauf* among the underlying objectives of the Succession Regulation, see, before the adoption of the Regulation, E-M Bajons, 'Internationale Zuständigkeit und anwendbares Recht in grenzüberschreitenden Erbrechtsfällen innerhalb des europäischen Justizraums', in *Festschrift für Andreas Heldrich zum 70. Geburtstag* (CH Beck 2005), 495, 497 ff; A Davì, 'Riflessioni sul futuro diritto internazionale privato europeo delle successioni' (2005) 88 *Rivista di diritto internazionale* 297, 307 ff; A Bonomi, 'Successions internationales: conflits de lois et de juridictions' (2010) 350 *Recueil des cours de l'Académie de droit international de la Haye* 71, 180 f. In the literature appeared subsequent to the adoption of the Regulation, see A Bonomi, n 21, 168; A Davì and A Zanobetti, n 20, 44, 199 f; P Franzina, 'Ragioni, valori e collocazione sistematica della disciplina internazionalprivatistica delle successioni *mortis causa*', in P Franzina and A Leandro (eds), *Il diritto internazionale privato europeo delle successioni mortis causa* (Giuffrè 2013), 1, 10 f; P Lagarde, 'Les principes de base du nouveau règlement européen sur les successions' (2012) 101 *Revue critique de droit international privé* 691, 694, 701 ff.

coexistence of different approaches as concerns the spatial applicability of the relevant rules within the Regulation, in cases presenting connections with third countries the establishment of a coincidence between jurisdiction and applicable law may frequently prove impossible. This is due to the mandatory allocation of jurisdiction among the courts of the Member States provided for by the Regulation. Such a mandatory allocation does not take into consideration the possibility of jurisdiction being exercised in third-country-related cases by the courts of a third country with which the succession presents a substantial connection, such as would in principle make the law of that country applicable to the succession itself.[29]

This objective of Regulation No 650/2012 is made particularly evident by the use of one and the same connecting factor – the habitual residence of the deceased at the time of death – both for the purposes of the general rule of jurisdiction in Article 4 and under the general conflict-of-law rule in Article 21.[30] The same objective is pursued through Article 5 of the Regulation, which allows the parties having an interest in the succession to reinstate parallelism between jurisdiction and applicable law through a *professio fori* in favour of the courts of the Member State of the law chosen by the deceased, provided that the latter had made a *professio iuris* in favour of the law of his nationality pursuant to Article 22.[31] As it will be seen, this possibility, however, is only available where the law of nationality of the deceased which formed the object of his choice is the law of a Member State.[32]

In fact, whereas, as noted already, the conflict-of-law rules of the Succession Regulation apply universally, the rules on jurisdiction merely apply in respect of Member States' courts. Incidentally, the Regulation does not even apply in all Member States. On the one hand, Denmark does not take part, generally, to the measures concerning the area of freedom, security and justice, due to its peculiar position under Protocol No 22 annexed to the TEU and the TFEU.[33] On the other hand, the Succession Regulation does not apply either in the United

29 In fact, Regulation No 650/2012 appears to take into account the availability of third-country courts to rule on the succession only indirectly, in that it allows a Member State court to refrain from ruling on assets belonging to the estate of the deceased which are located in a third country, whenever it can be expected that its decision won't be recognized in that country as concerns those assets: see below, § 3.

30 Cf, among others, A Bonomi, 'Article 4', in A Bonomi and P Wautelet (eds), n 21, 169, 170 f; J Carrascosa González, *El Reglamento Sucesorio Europeo 650/2012 de 4 de Julio 2012. Análisis crítico* (Comares 2014), 78 ff; A Davì and A Zanobetti, n 20, 199 f; H Gaudemet-Tallon, n 21, 129; B Hess, n 21, 134.

31 Cf, in general terms, A Bonomi, 'Article 5', in A Bonomi and P Wautelet (eds), n 21, 183 ff; A Davì and A Zanobetti, n 20, 204 ff; A Dutta, 'Art. 5 EuErbVO', in *Münchener Kommentar zum BGB*, n 22, Nos 1-3; H Gaudemet-Tallon, n 21, 131 f; B Hess, n 21, 133; R Magnus, 'Gerichtsstandsvereinbarungen im Erbrecht?' (2013) 33 *IPRax* 393, 394 ff.

32 See below, § 2.1.

33 Cf the Preamble to Regulation No 650/2012, Recital 83.

Kingdom and Ireland, as both countries decided not to avail themselves of their right of opting in, pursuant to the special regime established under Protocol No 21 annexed to the Treaties.[34] Accordingly, even absent an express provision to this effect, the references made by the Regulation to the courts of Member States must be understood as a reference to the courts of the Member States bound by the Regulation.[35] In a way, this interpretation is inevitable, since a EU Regulation could not provide for the jurisdiction of courts belonging to third countries or to such Member States as are not subject to that particular Regulation. The latter Member States, like third countries, are free to regulate the jurisdiction of their courts pursuant to their own rules.[36] At the same time, it appears questionable why Regulation No 650/2012 does not take into consideration the availability of third-country courts to exercise jurisdiction pursuant to their own domestic rules in cases more closely connected to such courts. This would have contributed on a larger scale to the achievement of the objectives of *Gleichlauf* and of unity of the succession pursued by the Regulation itself.[37] The Succession Regulation caters instead for the reverse scenario of the unavailability of the courts of a third country with which a dispute is closely connected to deal with the case. It does so by providing for the jurisdiction of the courts of a Member State possessing a sufficient connection with the case, as *fora necessitatis* pursuant to Article 11.[38]

34 Cf the Preamble to Regulation No 650/2012, Recital 82.

35 Cf, concerning in particular the impact which the adoption of the Succession Regulation is likely to have on successions presenting at the same time connections with Member States bound by the Regulation and the United Kingdom as a Member State not subject to its application, EB Crawford and JM Carruthers, 'Speculation on the Operation of Succession Regulation 650/2012: Tales of the Unexpected' (2014) 22 *European Review of Private Law* 847, 849 ff; in the same vein, concerning the impact of the Regulation on successions presenting connections with a third country located in Europe such as Switzerland, A Bonomi and A Öztürk, 'Auswirkungen der Europäischen Erbrechtsverordnung auf die Schweiz unter besonderer Berücksichtigung deutsch-schweizerischer Erbfälle' (2015) 114 *Zeitschrift für Vergleichende Rechtswissenschaft* 4, 5 ff.

36 Cf, for some considerations in this respect, CF Majer, 'Die Geltung der EU-Erbrechtsverordnung für reine Drittstaatensachverhälte' (2011) 18 *Zeitschrift für Erbrecht und Vermögensnachfolge* 445, 446 ff; more generally, M Fallon and T Kruger, n 1, 16 f.

37 As noted in respect of the Commission's Proposal by M Hellner, n 21, 386 f, this issue can be raised particularly in respect of the residual grounds of jurisdiction contemplated under Article 10, Regulation No 650/2012, which, in substance, provide for the jurisdiction of a Member State court in respect of a succession which would be more closely connected to a third country, whose law is likely to apply pursuant to the conflict-of-laws rules contained in the Regulation itself. See below, § 2.2.

38 As noted by P Lagarde, n 28, 703 f, also the provision for a *forum necessitatis* in Article 11 of the Succession Regulation entails a risk of breaching the *Gleichlauf* between jurisdiction and applicable law, since it establishes the jurisdiction of the courts of a Member State in respect of a succession which is inherently more closely connected with a third country whose law is likely to apply, as well as a risk of undermining unity of the succession, due to the possibility that the courts of the third country concerned might be unavailable to rule just as concerns part of the succession. In this case, however, the need to prevent a denial of justice justifies the drawbacks inherent in the rule.

2. RULES ADDRESSING ISSUES OF COORDINATION WITH THIRD-COUNTRY COURTS

2.1. THE EXCLUSION OF CHOICE OF FORUM IN FAVOUR OF THIRD-COUNTRY COURTS UNDER ARTICLE 5

The shortcomings described above become apparent in various instances. One of these occurs where the deceased, being a third country national or being deemed to acquire the nationality of a third country before his death, made a *professio iuris* in favour of the law of such a country, as allowed under Article 22 of the Succession Regulation. In such a case, unlike in cases where the deceased possessed the nationality of a Member State and had chosen its law as the law governing the succession, Article 5 does not allow the parties concerned to opt for the jurisdiction of the courts of the country of the chosen law. This is due to the fact that the country in question is not a Member State. Accordingly, in these cases the parties will not be able to reinstate the coincidence between *forum* and *ius* disrupted by the *professio iuris* of the deceased. In fact, one has to consider the exhaustive nature of the system of allocation of jurisdiction embodied in the Regulation, which leaves no residual room to domestic rules of jurisdiction.[39] Accordingly, it seems hardly arguable that the parties could be allowed to make a choice of forum in favour of the courts of a third country pursuant to domestic law.[40] The wording of Article 5, which expressly allows such a choice only when the deceased had chosen the law of a Member State, appears to exclude such an option. So does Article 6, which allows the courts of a Member State having jurisdiction pursuant to the Regulation to decline jurisdiction in case of choice of law only in the circumstances contemplated under the rule.[41] Furthermore, it must be mentioned that uniformity in the application of the Regulation would be jeopardised if a similar possibility were left to the domestic law of the Member States. Due account must be taken of the fact that the admissibility of choice-of-court agreements in succession matters might not be contemplated to the same extent under the different Member States' laws.[42]

---

39 Except as noted above, § 1.2, fn 20.

40 Cf, underlining the exhaustive nature of the rules of jurisdiction contained in Regulation (EU) No. 650/2012, excluding any residual scope of application for domestic rules of jurisdiction within the domain covered by the Regulation, among others, A Bonomi, n 21, 165 f; A Davì and A Zanobetti, n 20, 195 f; H Gaudemet-Tallon, n 21, 130; B Hess, n 21, 133 f.

41 Cf, among others, A Bonomi, n 31, 184 f; A Dutta, n 31, No 12.

42 Actually, differences may be found among domestic laws as to whether such a choice might be made by the heirs and other persons having an interest in the succession, as under the Successions Regulation, or whether it ought to be made by the deceased himself in a will or an agreement as to succession, as, for example, under Swiss law: cf Article 87(2) of the Swiss Federal Private International Law Act of 19 December 1987. The latter solution has been rather unpersuasively advocated in the German literature: cf R Magnus, n 31, 396 f; see also, concerning

At the same time, it must be conceded that nothing in the text of the Regulation precludes that the parties having an interest in the succession might refrain from seizing a Member State court having jurisdiction under the Regulation and revert directly to the courts of the third country of the chosen law, which might have jurisdiction pursuant to their own domestic law. Still, in case a Member State court is concurrently seised by one of the parties in disagreement with the others, the latter court would not be allowed to decline jurisdiction in favour of the courts of the third country of the chosen law. This difficulty is made more acute by the absence within the Succession Regulation of rules addressing cases of *lis pendens* and related actions pending before the courts of a third country.[43] It would have been reasonable to expressly allow, under Regulation No 650/2012, the courts of Member State, competent under the general rules, to decline their jurisdiction in favour of the courts of the third country of the chosen law, following a choice of court in favour of those courts by the parties having an interest in the succession, subject to the availability of such courts to exercise their jurisdiction, based on the parties' choice or on the objective circumstances of the dispute.[44]

2.2. SUBSIDIARY JURISDICTION OF MEMBER STATES' COURTS IN RESPECT OF SUCCESSIONS MORE CLOSELY CONNECTED TO A THIRD COUNTRY

The possibility of establishing *Gleichlauf* between jurisdiction and applicable law in respect of successions presenting close connections with a third country risks being endangered also by subsidiary jurisdiction under Article 10 of the Succession Regulation. In practice, pursuant to Article 10, the jurisdiction of the courts of a Member State may be asserted even where the habitual residence of the deceased at the moment of death would be in a third country. The law of the latter country would in principle apply to the succession pursuant to the main connecting factor adopted by the Regulation.[45]

At closer inspection, Article 10(1) appears to pose limits to the pursuit of *Gleichlauf* between jurisdiction and applicable law in the terms mentioned above, whereas the further subsidiary rule contemplated in Article 10(2) risks interfering also with the pursuit of a further goal underlying the Succession Regulation: the unity of the succession. This presupposes that one single forum

the limits to party autonomy as concerns jurisdiction deriving from the subject-matter of the dispute, D Coester-Waltjen, 'Parteiautonomie in der internationalen Zuständigkeit', in *Festschrift für Andreas Heldrich*, n 28, 549, 550 ff.

[43] Cf below, § 2.3.

[44] As suggested by R Magnus, n 31, 394 f.

[45] Cf P Lagarde, n 28, 701 f.

deals with the entire succession, applying the same law as identified pursuant to the Regulation.[46] The subsidiary grounds of jurisdiction contemplated under Article 10(1) are consistent with the objective of preserving the unity of the succession. Indeed, they provide for a general jurisdiction which is intended to extend to the succession as a whole, quite like the main ground of jurisdiction contemplated in Article 4 of the Regulation. On the contrary, Article 10(2) provides for jurisdiction which is limited to the assets located in the territory of the Member State of the court seised.[47]

One may question why the courts of a Member State should in both cases renounce to the advantages of *Gleichlauf* by exercising jurisdiction in respect of a succession which is more closely connected with a third country whose law is likely to apply to the substance of the matter. In addition, as concerns Article 10(2), it is not clear why Member States' courts should also put at risk the unity of the succession by exercising a jurisdiction limited to assets located in the Member State concerned, without being allowed to take into account the availability of the courts of the third country with which the succession is more closely connected to exercise their jurisdiction in respect of the succession as a whole. Besides, the solution adopted in the Succession Regulation in this respect is likely to result in frequent cases of concurrent proceedings between Member State courts and third-country courts. This is an occurrence which, as noted already, the Regulation omits to regulate, just as it does not address, prospectively, the handing down of conflicting decisions beyond the strict scope of the European Judicial Area.[48]

Furthermore, the subsidiary rules under consideration pose a series of practical problems in terms of their application. Some of these problems are actually inherent in any ground of jurisdiction based on the location of assets, and are therefore likely to arise in respect of both the rules of general jurisdiction contemplated in Article 10(1) and of the rule contained in Article 10(2). This is due to the fact that the location of certain categories of assets may prove controversial.[49] Further difficulties are specifically posed by Article 10(2). This presupposes that issues concerning assets located in a Member State should be isolated from those concerning the remaining assets forming the subject of the succession or, rather, the succession itself as a whole. Such an exercise is likely

46 Cf the Preamble to the Regulation, Recital 37.

47 Cf, among others, on the different nature of the subsidiary jurisdiction rules under Article 10(1) and (2), Regulation No. 650/2012, A Bonomi, 'Article 10', in A Bonomi and P Wautelet (eds), n 21, 211, 215 ff; A Davì and A Zanobetti, n 20, 201 ff; A Dutta, 'Art. 10 EuErbVO', in *Münchener Kommentar zum BGB*, n 22, Nos 10-15.

48 As noted in particular by P Lagarde, n 28, 702; A Bonomi, n 47, 213; A Davì and A Zanobetti, n 20, 203 f. See further below, § 2.3.

49 Such as moveable assets subject to registration, intellectual property rights, credits, non-registrable shares in companies: cf, in particular, A Bonomi, 'Article 10', n 47, 215 f; A Dutta, n 47, Nos 5-8.

to prove difficult. As a matter of fact, the unity of the succession, which the Regulation pursues as regards both jurisdiction and the applicable law, reflects the idea whereby the succession must substantially be regarded as a unity itself. This implies that a decision concerning the devolution of certain assets located in a given country is likely to have an impact, depending on the law governing the succession, on the devolution of the remaining assets forming part of the estate of the deceased.[50]

2.3. ABSENCE OF RULES ON *LIS ALIBI PENDENS* AND RELATED ACTIONS BEFORE THIRD-COUNTRY COURTS

The risk of fragmentation in litigation over successions connected with third countries is likely to be increased by the fact that the Succession Regulation does not include rules addressing *lis alibi pendens* and related actions involving third-country courts, as may be found, instead, in Regulation No 1215/2012.[51] This goes alongside the absence of uniform rules governing the recognition and enforcement in the Member States of decisions delivered by third-country courts in succession matters.[52] The adoption of such rules would have allowed ensuring a better, albeit unilateral, coordination[53] – with the parallel exercise of jurisdiction by the courts of a third country presenting a close connection with the succession. Furthermore, it must be noted that, differently from the situation described above in respect of the admissibility of choice-of-court agreements in favour of the courts of third countries, nothing in the Succession

---

50 On the issues raised by Article 10(2), see, among others, A Bonomi, n 47, 221; A Davì and A Zanobetti, n 20, 203 f; A Dutta, n 47, No 13.

51 Concerning *lis pendens* and related actions involving third countries under Articles 33 and 34 of Regulation No 1215/2012, see F Marongiu Buonaiuti, '*Lis alibi pendens* and Related Actions in the Relationships with the Courts of Third Countries in the Recast of the Brussels I Regulation' (2013/2014) 15 *Yearbook of Private International Law* 87, 89 ff; P Franzina, '*Lis alibi pendens* Involving a Third Country Under the "Brussels I-bis" Regulation: An Overview' (2014) 50 *Rivista di diritto internazionale privato e processuale* 23, 25 ff; F Salerno, *Giurisdizione ed efficacia delle decisioni straniere nel Regolamento (UE) n. 1215/2012 (rifusione)* (4th ed, Cedam 2015), 284 ff.

52 As noted by A Davì and A Zanobetti, n 20, 203 f, due to the absence in the Succession Regulation of rules concerning *lis pendens* and related actions pending before third-country courts, a coordination with actions pending before those courts may be achieved only ex post, that is, by means of the recognition of the decisions handed down by such courts. Clearly, the absence of common rules concerning the recognition in the Member States of decisions delivered by third-country courts in matters governed by the Regulation risks to affect uniformity in its application: for similar remarks in respect of Regulation No 1215/2012, see SM Carbone, 'What About the Recognition of Third States' Foreign Judgments?', in F Pocar, I Viarengo, FC Villata (eds), n 10, 299, 301 f; M Fallon and T Kruger, n 1, 22 ff.

53 Cf M Fallon and T Kruger, n 1, 21, underlining the unilateral attitude inspiring both the Maintenance and the Successions Regulations in adopting, as concerns direct jurisdiction, rules applicable also to situations connected with third countries, irrespective of their approach as to jurisdiction.

Regulation precludes decisions delivered by a third-country court in succession matters from being recognized and enforced in the Member States concerned, under their own domestic rules on the recognition and enforcement of foreign judgments. The same applies by implication as concerns the possibility of having recourse to domestic rules concerning *lis alibi pendens* and related actions pending before foreign courts in order to pursue a coordination with proceedings pending before a third-country court.[54] This solution had been suggested in respect of the Brussels I regime before the introduction of the specific rules addressing cases of *lis pendens* and related actions pending in front of third country-courts in the recast Regulation.[55] In fact, rules on *lis alibi pendens* and related actions are functionally linked to the rules concerning the recognition and enforcement of judgments. The former aim to prevent the adoption of conflicting decisions, which would, as such, be denied recognition.[56]

Clearly, the adoption of uniform rules on *lis pendens* and related actions pending before third-country courts, like those in the Brussels Ia Regulation, as well as the introduction of uniform rules concerning the recognition and enforcement of decisions rendered in third countries would have enhanced uniformity in the overall application of the jurisdictional system of Regulation No 650/2012. This objective runs the risk of being frustrated due to the divergences in the rules applied in the various Member States to deal with the above issues. In fact, on the one hand, most EU Member States have rules concerning international *lis pendens*. These rules, to the exclusion of the Member States belonging to the common law tradition[57] – which, as already mentioned, are not bound by Regulation No 650/2012[58] – basically follow a common pattern. They apply when the proceedings concerned appear to be identical as regards both the litigants and the subject matter of the dispute, and imply a predictive assessment

---

54 Cf A Bonomi, 'Article 17', in A Bonomi and P Wautelet (eds), n 21, 255, 259; A Davì and A Zanobetti, n 20, 214 f.

55 F Marongiu Buonaiuti, n 51, 104 ff.

56 Cf, generally, on the functional relationships between *lis alibi pendens* and the recognition of foreign judgments, among others, R Geimer, *Internationales Zivilprozessrecht* (5th ed., Otto Schmidt 2005), 831 ff; F Marongiu Buonaiuti, *Litispendenza e connessione internazionale. Strumenti di coordinamento tra giurisdizioni statali in materia civile* (Jovene 2008), 31 ff; V. Moissinac-Massénat, *Les conflits de procédures et de décisions en droit international privé* (LGDJ 2007), 25, 38 ff.

57 Where the coordination with the jurisdiction of foreign courts is traditionally based on the doctrine of *forum non conveniens*, within which the existence of a situation of *lis pendens* abroad may feature among a series of factors to be taken into account for the purposes of a discretionary evaluation of the opportunity of a stay of proceedings. The requirements to which the granting of a stay on *forum non conveniens* grounds is subject have been clearly specified, under English law, by the well-known House of Lords judgment in the case of *Spiliada Maritime Corporation v. Cansulex Ltd* [1987] A.C. 460, 475. See on this doctrine, among others, C Chalas, *L'exercice discrétionnaire de la compétence juridictionnelle en droit international privé* (PUAM 2000), 220 ff; MA Lupoi, *Conflitti transnazionali di giurisdizioni* (Giuffré 2002), 145 ff; A Nuyts, *L'exception de forum non conveniens* (Bruylant 2003), 177 ff.

58 Cf the Preamble to Regulation No 650/2012, Recital 82 (see above, § 1.3).

that the decision to be delivered by the foreign court qualifies for recognition in the forum.[59] On the other hand, domestic rules concerning related actions pending before foreign courts are less frequent.[60] Likewise, while all Member States possess rules on the recognition and enforcement of foreign judgments, these rules vary, in their content, from one country to another. These differences may well have an impact on the functioning of the rules on *lis pendens*, insofar as these rely, as noted above, on a prediction concerning the recognition of the future foreign decision.[61]

3. THE UNILATERAL COORDINATION WITH THE JURISDICTION OF THIRD-COUNTRY COURTS PURSUED BY ARTICLE 12(1) OF THE REGULATION

The Succession Regulation addresses instead the issue of coordination with the jurisdiction of third-country courts through the rule embodied in Article 12, paragraph 1. The latter rule, however, poses comparable challenges to the objective of unity of the succession from both the jurisdiction and, impliedly, the conflict-of-law perspective as are likely to arise in respect of Article 10(2) of

---

59 Such a requirement may be found, eg, in Italian law, pursuant to Article 7 of the Law No 218 of 31 May 1995 reforming the Italian system of private international law, on which, among others, see C Consolo, 'Profili della litispendenza internazionale' (1997) 80 *Rivista di diritto internazionale* 5, 38 ff; F Marongiu Buonaiuti, n 56, 34-38, 399-413. It may also be found in France, pursuant to the case law of the Supreme Court, namely as resulting from Cour de Cassation, 26 November 1974, *Soc. Miniera di Fragne*, (1975) 102 *Journal du droit international* 108. The requirement is equally known to German law (see Bundesgerichtshof, 2 October 1957 (1958) 11 *Neue Juristiche Wochenschrift* 103, on which RA Schütze, 'Die Berücksichtigung der Rechtshängigkeit eines ausländischen Verfahrens' (1963) 16 *Neue Juristiche Wochenschrift* 1486), Austrian law (see, among others, Oberster Gerichtshof, 23 February 1982 (1984) 25 *Zeitschrift für Rechtsvergleichung* 145), and Belgian law, pursuant to Article 14 of the Belgian Code of private international law, on which P Wautelet, 'Article 14. Litispendance internationale', in J Erauw et al (eds), *Het Wetboek Internationaal Privaatrecht becommentarieerd – Le Code de droit international privé commenté* (Intersentia 2006), 78, 81.

60 As an example, the Belgian Code of private international law of 2004, while providing under Article 14 for cases of foreign *lis pendens*, only contemplates, Article 9, the possibility of extending the jurisdiction of Belgian courts a regards actions related to those ordinarily included in the jurisdictional reach of such courts, without dealing with related actions pending before foreign courts. Elsewhere, only specific cases of related actions pending before foreign courts are contemplated, such as, in Italy, under Article 7(3) of Law of 31 May 1995, No 218, which grants Italian courts a discretion to stay proceedings in the case where an action concerning a preliminary issue is pending before a foreign court, provided it can be expected that the foreign court will render a judgment that is likely to be recognised in the forum: cf among others, C Consolo, n 59, 67 ff; MA Lupoi, n 57, 853 ff; F Marongiu Buonaiuti, n 56, 60 ff, 383 ff.

61 On the advantages that would be prompted by the introduction of EU rules on the recognition and enforcement of decisions of third countries see, with specific regard to the recast of the Brussels I Regulation, SM Carbone, n 52, 301 f; M Fallon and T Kruger, n 1, 22 ff.

the Regulation, which has been examined above. Article 12(1) of the Succession Regulation, in fact, provides for the power of a Member State court having jurisdiction pursuant to the Regulation to refrain, upon request by one of the parties, from deciding in respect of assets located in a third country. This on the basis of the expectation that its decision as concerns those assets will not be recognized or, in case, declared enforceable in the third country concerned.[62] The rule appears dictated by a reasonable concern to ensure that the jurisdiction of Member States' courts is not exercised in vain, and is based on corresponding provisions to be found in domestic legislation[63] as well as in a proposal by the European Group of Private International Law.[64] Nonetheless, it inevitably gives way to an undesirable fragmentation of the litigation concerning the succession. Besides, as noted in respect of the opposite rule in Article 10(2) of Regulation No 650/2012, the provision under examination gives rise to comparable problems as regards the localisation of the relevant assets. Furthermore, the solution embodied in the rule may not always be easy to apply in practice, in that it requires to distinguish, within the same action, between issues concerning assets located in the third country concerned and issues relating to the other assets of the deceased or, rather, to the succession as a whole.[65]

4. CONCLUDING REMARKS

The Succession Regulation, it is contended, could have ensured a better coordination with the jurisdiction of third-country courts, by allowing Member States' courts to decline jurisdiction where the parties have entered into a choice-of-forum agreement in favour of the courts of the third country of the law chosen by the deceased. At the same time, if the Regulation had included rules governing *lis pendens* and related actions in third countries, as well as the recognition and enforcement of decisions emanating from third countries, this would have ensured a more efficient coordination among jurisdictions beyond the strict limits of the European Judicial Area, than the limited coordination currently provided under Article 12 of the Succession Regulation.

---

62 Cf, among others, A Bonomi, 'Article 12', in A Bonomi and P Wautelet (eds), n 21, 231 ff; J Carrascosa González, n 30, 105 f; A Davì and A Zanobetti, n 20, 211; A Dutta, 'Art. 12 EuErbVO', in *Münchener Kommentar zum BGB*, n 22, Nos 1-8; H Gaudemet-Tallon, n 21, 136.

63 Cf Article 86(2) of the Swiss Federal Law on private international law, and A Bucher, 'Art. 86', in A Bucher (ed), *Loi sur le droit international privé. Convention de Lugano. Commentaire Romand* (Helbing & Lichtenhahn 2011), 791, 793 f.

64 Groupe européen de droit international privé, 'Proposition pour une convention concernant la compétence judiciaire et l'exécution des décisions en matière familiale et successorale' (1993) 82 *Revue critique de droit international privé* 841, also available at <www.gedip-egpil.eu>, Article 5(4).

65 Cf, particularly, the remarks by A Bonomi, 'Article 12', n 62, 235 f; A Davì and A Zanobetti, n 20, 211; A Dutta, n 62, No 1.

www.ingramcontent.com/pod-product-compliance
Ingram Content Group UK Ltd.
Pitfield, Milton Keynes, MK11 3LW, UK
UKHW051922100926
8556IPUK00021B/1323

9 781780 684376